W9-COS-444

Turbulence
in the
American Workplace

Turbulence
in the
American Workplace

PETER B. DOERINGER

Kathleen Christensen • Patricia M. Flynn
Douglas T. Hall • Harry C. Katz
Jeffrey H. Keefe • Christopher J. Ruhm
Andrew M. Sum • Michael Useem

New York   Oxford
OXFORD UNIVERSITY PRESS
1991

ROBERT MANNING
STROZIER LIBRARY

OCT 1 1991

Tallahassee, Florida

HD
5724
T87
1991

Oxford University Press

Oxford   New York   Toronto
Delhi   Bombay   Calcutta   Madras   Karachi
Petaling Jaya   Singapore   Hong Kong   Tokyo
Nairobi   Dar es Salaam   Cape Town
Melbourne   Auckland

and associated companies in
Berlin   Ibadan

Copyright © 1991 by Oxford University Press

Published by Oxford University Press, Inc.
200 Madison Avenue, New York, NY 10016

Oxford is a registered trademark of Oxford University Press

All rights reserved. No part of this publication may be reproduced, stored
in a retrieval system, or transmitted, in any form or by any means, electronic,
mechanical, photocopying, recording, or otherwise, without the prior
permission of Oxford University Press, Inc.

Library of Congress Cataloging-in-Publication Data
Turbulence in the American workplace / edited by Peter B. Doeringer.
   p.   cm.
   "Published for the National Planning Association."
   Includes bibliographical references and index.
   ISBN 0-19-506461-5
   1. Labor market—United States.   2. Corporate reorganizations—
United States.   3. Labor supply—United States—Effect of
technological innovations on.   4. Plant shutdowns—United States.
5. Manpower planning—United States.   I. Doeringer, Peter B.
II. National Planning Association.
HD5724.T87   1991
658.15'224—dc20   90-43299

9 8 7 6 5 4 3 2 1

Printed in the United States of America
on acid-free paper

FOREWORD

This study was sponsored by the Committee on New American Realities (NAR) of the National Planning Association, a private sector group promoting the achievement of a more competitive U.S. economy. Its members are drawn from business, labor, agriculture, and the academic professions. The NAR encourages open, nonpartisan analysis and discussion of U.S. economic performance to help define shared interests and to foster a broad-based consensus out of which effective national policies and private sector initiatives can evolve.

In 1987, the Committee identified workforce preparedness as one of the most critical issues facing business and labor in the United States. Our particular concern was that competitive pressures on the economy were making the future of work in America increasingly problematic. Within our Committee we posed the questions of who was being most affected by the turbulent economic environment; how the workforce could be better prepared to deal with turbulence in the future; and how the responsibility for preparing the future workforce should be divided between the public and private sectors.

To answer these questions, the NAR turned to a team of labor market and human resources specialists headed by Professor Peter Doeringer of Boston University. We asked Professor Doeringer and his associates to help our Committee understand how labor market turbulence is affecting the nation's human resources and to identify new policy directions that we could endorse.

The Committee designated a business-labor advisory group to work closely with Professor Doeringer to define the scope of the project, provide access to the best-available private sector thinking on workforce issues, and review the findings of the study. Over a two-year period, the full Committee met on several occasions to discuss the results of the study and consider the most appropriate policy responses. In my experience, such an extended collaboration between an academic research team and a group of business and labor leaders is exceptional.

This book is one of the fruits of this collaboration. It is a comprehensive and compelling account of how economic turbulence is changing the American labor market and of the responses that are needed to address its effects on workers and workplaces. I commend it highly to anyone seeking a serious analysis of these issues.

The policy recommendations contained in Chapter 10 reflect the research findings presented in this book. At its October 1989 meeting, the NAR reviewed the study and approved a series of recommendations to enhance workforce preparedness through new initiatives by business, labor, and government. In making these recommendations, the Committee was determined to avoid lowest common denominator solutions in order to move forward substantially the debate over how to improve the nation's human resources. It is the Committee's hope that the policy proposals will set the standard for public and private action in the coming decade to help ready the nation's workforce for the future.

I want to acknowledge the strong support of the entire Committee membership for this project as well as the assistance of the NAR Technical Steering Committee. Additional special support for the study came from a number of NAR member organizations including the AFL-CIO, AT&T, BP America Inc., General Motors Corporation, IBM Corporation, Pfizer Inc., Pioneer Hi-Bred International Inc., and Xerox Corporation.

Paul Allaire
Chair, New American Realities Committee (1987–90)
President and Chief Executive Officer,
Xerox Corporation

PREFACE

Turbulence—rapid and sometimes tumultuous change—has characterized the labor markets of the 1970s and 1980s. Turbulent competitive conditions have cut sharply into profits and have forced downsizings and wrenching readjustments in many companies. This turbulence has translated into large numbers of lost jobs and even more widespread career disruption. It has also brought a slowing in the growth of labor productivity that has affected the welfare of the American workforce and has become a problem for national competitiveness. From the perspectives of business, labor, and the national economy, labor market turbulence is the key human resources issue for the last part of the twentieth century.

This book is about how labor market turbulence has affected the American workplace and the American workforce. It is written for the key actors in the marketplace for labor—employers, workers, organized labor, and government policy-makers—to help them understand how to respond to the challenges of a turbulent economy.

The book argues that the human resources capacity of the private sector represents the first line of defense against turbulence and that the potential for private action equals that of schools and government training programs in preparing the workforce for change. It presents a policy agenda for bringing about an integrated public-private system of lifelong workforce preparedness. This agenda underscores the increased responsibilities that must be shouldered by business, labor, and government if workforce productivity and adaptability are to be enhanced and the economic hardship resulting from turbulence is to be reduced.

To address these policy issues, an interdisciplinary research team was assembled to prepare a set of background studies addressing key issues in workplace turbulence and the labor market—demographic change, plant closings and business restructuring, technological change, and the increased use of contingent labor. Starting from different vantage points and drawing upon a diverse set of research materials—labor market and organizational theories, economic data, business case studies, and other survey and empirical materials about organizational performance—the team has documented how turbulence is affecting the labor market. These materials were then supplemented with field research and discussions with business executives and union officials about recent developments in human resources strategies in large enterprises.

Day-long field interviews were held in the summer of 1988 with corporate-level human resources and industrial relations executives in five Fortune 100 companies selected by the Committee on New American Realities (NAR) of the National Planning Association (NPA). Findings from these interviews were then discussed in a series of focus group meetings in 1988 and 1989 with a group of human resources executives and trade union officials who served in an advisory capacity to the project. A synthesis of the interviews and discussions was reviewed on several occasions by the NAR. These interactions with human resources practitioners have provided the project with an up-to-date understanding of how the problems of workplace turbulence are being addressed.

This approach provided a rich empirical foundation for analyzing what economic turbulence means for workers and their employers. While no one piece of evidence is conclusive, taken together the data reveal a pattern of findings about workplace practices and business performance that demonstrates the seriousness of human resources problems caused by turbulence. The analysis points to a compelling need for private, as well as public, initiatives to prepare the nation's human resources for a more competitive economy.

Based upon these findings, a set of proposals for workforce preparedness was developed in collaboration with business and labor members of the NAR. These policy proposals point to ambitious, but nonetheless pragmatic, steps that business, labor, and government can take to prepare more effectively the nation's workforce.

A project of this scope could not have been possible without the support of a large number of contributors. Members of the research team had primary responsibility for the preparation of individual chapters. Andrew Sum and Neal Fogg examined issues of younger and older workers (Chapters 2 and 4); Christopher Ruhm prepared the materials on displaced workers (Chapter 3); Patricia Flynn covered technological change (Chapter 5); Harry Katz and Jeffrey Keefe looked at workplace adjustment in unionized settings (Chapter 6); Kathleen Christensen analyzed contingent employment (Chapter 7); Michael Useem looked at management development (Chapter 8); and Douglas T. Hall reported on strategic human resource development (Chapter 9). I provided overall direction for the project and prepared the introductory and concluding chapters. The project, however, was conceived as a unified study of workplace turbulence and was conducted as a collective effort.

Paul Allaire, now the President and Chief Executive Officer of the Xerox Corporation and chair of the NAR (1987–90), gave leadership and direction to the private sector's involvement in the project. The members of the NAR Technical Steering Committee and the NAR Subcommittee on Labor Market and Workforce Issues ensured high-level review of our work and provided helpful input at critical points in the project.

We are grateful to Edward Masters and the member organizations of the NPA for their support. While their financial resources made the study possible, the access to the business and labor community they provided was a far more important asset to the project. The NPA gave us free rein to develop our ideas, and the specific findings do not necessarily reflect the position of the NPA or its members.

A special debt is owed to Phillip Ray, who served as Vice President of the NPA and Director of the NAR during the term of this project. Phil was our liaison to business and labor; he was also among our most helpful critics, and he steered the policy discussions at critical points. Harold Tragash, Tapas Sen, Allen Kraut, Markley Roberts, Rudy Oswald, and James Booe commented on various drafts of the study and made a particular contribution to developing the policy recommendations. Charles Johnson, Jack Golodner, Jack Bowsher, and William Colucci helped to clarify our findings, and others too numerous to name gave generously of their time and ideas to our project.

Finally, we would like to thank the support group on the project for their contributions. Charlene Arzigian served as chief of staff, coordinating the work of the research team and ensuring that all the pieces of the project fell into place in a timely fashion. Daniel Sweeney and Tracie Scott provided assistance in preparing the final manuscript, and Irene Nunes did a splendid job of editing the manuscript.

Boston, Massachusetts   P.B.D.
September 1990

CONTENTS

AUTHORS

Peter Doeringer, Professor of Economics, Boston University, and Jacob Wertheim Fellow of the Center for Business and Government, John F. Kennedy School of Government, Harvard University; co-author of *Internal Labor Markets and Manpower Analysis* (1972) and *Invisible Factors in Local Economic Development* (Oxford, 1987).

Kathleen Christensen, Associate Professor of Environmental Psychology, Graduate Center, City University of New York; author of *Women and Home-Based Work* (1988).

Patricia Flynn, Professor of Economics, Bentley College; author of *Facilitating Technological Change: The Human Resource Challenge* (1988).

Douglas T. Hall, Professor of Organizational Behavior, Boston University; author of *Careers in Organizations* (1976) and *Human Resource Management* (1986).

Harry C. Katz, Professor of Collective Bargaining, New York State School of Industrial and Labor Relations, Cornell University; author of *Shifting Gears* (1985) and co-author of *The Transformation of American Industrial Relations* (1986).

Jeffrey H. Keefe, Assistant Professor, Institute of Management and Labor Relations, Rutgers University; author of articles on collective bargaining and unions.

Christopher J. Ruhm, Assistant Professor of Economics, Boston University;

author of articles in *Industrial and Labor Relations Review*, *American Economic Review*, and elsewhere on labor market issues.

Andrew M. Sum, Professor of Economics and Director of the Center for Labor Market Studies, Northeastern University; co-author of *Withered Dreams: The Declining Economic Fortunes of America's Young Adult Males* (1988) and author of numerous monographs on labor and demographic issues.

Michael Useem, Professor of Sociology and Management, University of Pennsylvania; author of *The Inner Circle: Large Corporations and the Rise of Business Political Activity in the U.S. and U.K.* (Oxford, 1984) and co-author of *Educating Managers* (1986).

Turbulence
in the
American Workplace

1

Workplace Turbulence and Workforce Preparedness

The year 1973 marked a divide in the postwar economy.[1] During the 25 years between 1948 and 1973, private sector productivity increased at an annual rate of 2.9%. Productivity improvement after 1973 fell way below this long-term trend, leveling off at about 0.6% a year until 1981 and rising to only 1.6% a year between 1981 and 1987. A similar pattern is reflected in the real wages of the workforce.[2]

The conventional interpretation of this difference in the U.S. economy before and after 1973 is that it reflects the combined influence of the OPEC oil shock and the influx into the labor market of inexperienced workers born in the postwar baby boom, possibly reinforced by growth in regulatory costs.[3] However, when the productivity data are analyzed in a growth accounting framework, these economic factors can only account for about two thirds of the productivity decline.[4]

What then explains the balance of the shortfall in productivity? Many analysts have pointed to the intangible effects on managers of increased economic uncertainty since 1973—growing business cautiousness, increased emphasis on short-term financial objectives, and inadequate entrepreneurial incentives.[5] But economic change and uncertainty can also affect productivity through their impact on jobs and workers.

Turbulence and the Disintegrating Labor Market

The OPEC oil shock and the demographic swings of the baby boom have been coupled with periodic recessions and an accelerated pace of technological change in some sectors. These changes overlay even more significant structural

1

shifts in the economy—the dramatic shakeout of U.S. industry resulting from the globalization of production and intensified competitive pressures and the continuing shift from manufacturing to service employment.

Although some workers have benefited from the employment increases in high-growth sectors, such as business services, job growth and falling unemployment over the last decade have helped to mask a substantial disintegration in employment prospects across a wide spectrum of the labor market.[6] No sector of the economy has escaped disruption, and the effects of labor market difficulties are accumulating. Increasing employment without also raising productivity will not turn around this situation.

For example, many youth and young adults are stalled in dead-end jobs as it becomes more difficult for them to move into career jobs.[7] Their real incomes have been falling as jobs with good prospects for advancement are less available and take longer to find. These diminished economic opportunities are causing the incomes of high school graduates and high school dropouts to fall farther and farther behind those of college graduates.[8]

For adults at mid-career, job attachment is becoming less secure as the risk of displacement rises. Roughly 2 million workers a year have been displaced from their jobs since the early 1970s, and the overall rate of displacement in the labor market has risen 20% to 40% since the early 1970s.[9] Virtually all workers are now subject to displacement at some time during their working lives.[10]

A common perception is that displacement is largely a blue-collar manufacturing problem. However, one in five displaced workers is in retail sales and services, and two in five are in white-collar occupations. Although some workers find replacement jobs quickly, displacement for most means being out of work for nine months to a year.[11] Between a quarter and a third of displaced workers find reemployment at wages 25% or more below their previous wages, and these losses in earnings persist. The biggest losers are high-seniority workers who have held relatively high-wage jobs and who live in economically depressed areas.[12] But a substantial group (perhaps one in five displaced workers) are hidden losers—they experience no earnings decline upon reemployment because they held such low-wage jobs to begin with.[13]

Older workers are finding that their once-secure career jobs are ending prematurely. Rather than holding a career job until retirement, one in three male workers over age 55 (and half of all those over age 60) move from career jobs to "bridge" jobs—jobs that they may hold for five or ten years until retirement.[14] Although the data are not available for determining whether these bridge jobs represent a preferred second career or employment of last resort, moving from career to bridge jobs often represents a substantial change in job duties and often results in a reduction in pay. One quarter of all bridge jobs involve a change in both the occupation and the industry of the older worker, and half of all job changes lead to a drop in earnings of 25% or more.[15]

Turbulence and the Business Community

It is easier to gauge the direct effects of turbulence on the well-being of the workforce than on the competitive performance of business. What is evident, however, is that net income after taxes of U.S. nonfinancial corporations fell during the 1970s and early 1980s by about one third from the postwar highs of the late 1960s, touching off massive business restructurings.[16]

The employment consequences of this restructuring of large firms have been well documented—one study found that one in 15 firms with 100 or more employees either closed or had a major layoff in 1983 and 1984,[17] and other studies of large firms have concluded that more than half of companies is manufacturing experienced similar problems over periods of one and a half to two years.[18] Among those jobs that remain, there is often increased use of temporary or contingent labor[19] and a greater reliance on outsourcing.[20] The general impression is of a corporate America that is deeply troubled by turbulence at the workplace and is searching for new answers.[21]

Paramount among these concerns have been issues of human resources development. Numerous studies have identified the problems of inadequate basic education and skill preparation among recent school leavers as a source of difficulty for business.[22] Other studies have highlighted potential problems arising from the changing demography of the workforce and from the quickening pace of technological change and product life cycles.[23] To these must be added an even deeper concern that various short-term responses to turbulence at the workplace will undermine the workforce productivity in ways that will affect American competitiveness in the longer term.[24]

For example, the use of contingent labor was originally seen by many employers as a cost-effective means of gaining greater staffing flexibility while reducing labor costs. Some of these same employers, however, have come to recognize that contingent labor is often not as well trained or as committed as a permanent workforce.[25] Similarly, employers who counted on downsizing as a way of becoming cost-competitive are now concerned that less secure employment may undermine employee morale, reduce labor productivity, and hamper efforts to raise product quality.

Rebuilding Our Human Resources Adjustment Capacity

Economic turbulence has strained the adjustment capacity of America's human resources development system. The deficiencies of primary and secondary education have been well documented, particularly for those groups such as minorities and the disadvantaged, who will account for a large fraction of workforce growth in the next decade.[26] Similarly, employment and training programs have led a troubled existence,[27] and apprenticeship training has reached its lowest ebb in decades.[28]

Concern with the effectiveness of such formal education and training programs, however, neglects the importance of workplace training. The resources devoted to skill development in the American workplace dwarf those of publicly supported skill development programs.[29] Moreover, many of these public programs are primarily for young labor market entrants, whereas two thirds of the workforce for the next decade has already left school and is in the labor market.[30] For these workers, the American workplace is the mainstay of the human resources development system, and improvements in schools are largely irrelevant.

Human resources development programs at the workplace, however, are also in trouble as they become stretched to their limits by economic turbulence. Downsizing of employment has created new demands for training as workers are being redeployed more widely within their companies.[31] Similarly, firms are facing pressures to provide training and job placement assistance to workers who are being permanently laid off.[32] At the same time that redeployed and redundant workers are being trained and placed in different jobs, some firms are also experiencing an acceleration in product and technology cycles that places further demands on their human resources development capacity.[33]

Enlarging the Policy Debate

For decades, the task of adapting the workforce to such changes has been defined in terms of skill development—how to prepare workers for newly emerging skills and how to retrain those whose jobs and skills have become obsolete. The disintegration of old employment patterns and the sweeping changes that are taking place in work organization, however, are giving new urgency and new meaning to the concept of workforce preparedness.

For workers, acquiring the education and compiling the work experience needed for entry into a career job that would last almost a lifetime are no longer enough. The changing structure of jobs and the increasing risks of involuntary job changing are making the traditional mechanisms for job preparation obsolete.

For those businesses whose human resources systems have been disrupted by change, workforce preparedness is also no longer solely an issue of skills development. Indeed, with the exception of technical skills associated with newly emerging technologies, most large companies find that preparation for job skills is a relatively manageable task.[34] However, preparing the employee of tomorrow to be more productive in a less certain and less secure environment requires a public and private capacity to provide workers with new skills, to encourage their acceptance of change, and to foster greater mobility without economic loss.

The public and private systems of human resources development have, however, operated largely independent of each other. The public system of workforce preparedness focused largely on the provision of basic education and generic skills for a private sector labor market that was accustomed to starting young workers in entry-level jobs and then training them in the specific skills needed for relatively stable work careers. Neither employers nor public education and training institutions had much incentive to coordinate their activities. Today, however, these incentives are changing as both educators and employers face a growing range of serious human resources problems. Yet the policy debate has continued to focus narrowly on issues of skill. Education and training are seen as the principal solutions to the problems of workplace turbulence and public sector programs have been singled out for attention while workplace programs have been neglected.

For example, the numerous studies and reports that have recently addressed the problems of workforce preparedness have almost universally highlighted improvements in primary and secondary education as being critical for workforce readiness.[35] Private sector responsibilities are mainly confined to business-education partnerships that are supposed to make instruction and curricula more responsive to business needs.[36]

With a few exceptions,[37] these studies do not assign any prominent role to the workplace. The most common recommendations for reforms in workplace human resources practices are to encourage greater labor-management cooperation and worker participation[38] and more workplace flexibility.[39] The broader behavioral dimensions of workforce preparedness—problem-solving capability, reliability, and responsiveness to change—are rarely mentioned, except in terms of what schools should do.[40] Nor is there much concern with the relationship between employment security and workplace productivity.

Although better public sector education and training programs are likely to be important steps toward improving workforce preparedness, a more comprehensive set of private sector human resources policies, predicated on improving both business performance and worker well-being, can be equally important. Such policy initiatives include involving the private sector directly in public education and training efforts; fostering lifelong learning in schools and at the workplace; developing business-to-business labor redeployment networks; devising new ways of linking workforce flexibility to economic security; and improving income maintenance programs for displaced workers. Such changes must be directed at enhancing the human resources base for the entire economy, not just targeted to meet the urgent needs of particularly vulnerable groups, as has been done in the past. These policy ideas are developed more fully in the concluding chapter.

Although such initiatives can provide medium-term solutions to the problems of workplace turbulence, they do not address critical questions of the longer-term direction of workplace human resources development. Despite its central role in developing productive human resources and in helping the workforce to adapt to change, the current system of human resources development at the workplace is very much in flux. The outcome of current change at the workplace is uncertain, but it is likely to have a profound effect on productivity, employment security, and business performance.

What Model for Human Resources Development in a Turbulent Economy?

Large enterprises in the United States have tended to follow a fairly standard and predictable strategy for human resources development. For much of the postwar period, the dominant approach was the "industrial relations" model of human resources management.[41] Under this model, workforce preparedness and adjustment to change were governed by collective bargaining agreements, or by employee handbooks that emulated such agreements. Training played a major role in improving productivity, and employment security was determined by seniority applied within well-defined job classifications and departments.

Today, however, several other models are also used to develop human resources and to manage change at the workplace. For example, there has been increasing use of the "full employment" model in large, mainly nonunion, firms. Training figures prominently in this model, but implicit employment guarantees are also an important part of the human resources package. Guaranteed employment means that adjustments to turbulence are internalized within the firm through either redeployment or voluntary attrition. Other companies are adopting "employment-at-will," or flexible employment, models in which human resources development is minimal and the relationship between the worker and the company is impermanent.

Each of these models implies a different type of commitment to human resources development. Each model also places a distinctly different imprint on the adjustment process in terms of who is affected by growth and decline, how the costs of change are distributed between companies and their employees, and how workforce productivity is enhanced.

Industrial Relations Model

The industrial relations model became broadly established in American industry during the 1940s. It was shaped by a number of factors—New Deal labor legislation, decisions of the War Labor Board of World War II, and developments in the structure and philosophy of the American trade union movement.[42] By the 1950s, it became the standard for large manufacturing enterprises and began to spread to the service sector as well.[43]

Under this model, job classifications tend to be narrow; hiring and layoffs are confined to certain job classifications; job structures and promotion ladders are well defined and relatively rigid; and seniority plays a major role in both job assignment and layoffs. Workplace turbulence is managed through formal procedures controlling who is reassigned and laid off, and employees gradually acquire employment security through accumulated seniority.

The industrial relations model is designed to regulate employment change so as to economize on training and make economic security for workers increasingly predictable. It has, however, also tended to develop bureaucratic rigidities that many employers have regarded as a serious liability when they have to compete with firms using more flexible human resources approaches.[44] Moreover, substantial downsizing of firms has undermined seniority protections and brought new pressures from workers for more reliable forms of job security.

The result has been a rethinking, by both companies and unions, of a broad range of practices affecting human resources development and employment security.[45] For example, organizational structures that sharply demarcate different types of workers—skilled workers, production workers, and exempt workers—are now being replaced by arrangements that enlarge jobs and blur distinctions among job duties.[46] In the process, there is a new emphasis on developing workforce qualities of flexibility, adaptability, and problem-solving ability, often in the context of improved employment security.[47]

Full Employment Model

During the 1960s, the full employment model of human resources development became prevalent among large, nonunion firms, such as IBM, Kodak, Procter and Gamble, Hewlett Packard, and Cummins Engine.[48] The essence of this model is that labor productivity depends on two factors—remaining free of the rigid work rules and effort norms associated with the industrial relations model and creating an employment culture that fosters effort as well as flexibility.

The full employment model incorporates some of the features of the industrial relations model in that it makes considerable investments in training and human resources development through workplace training. However, the distinguishing feature of the full employment model is that it embodies a complex package of psychological contracts, training, participatory management mechanisms, career incentives, and performance rewards in which the expectation of a long-term commitment between employees and their employers figures prominently.[49] Jobs are never guaranteed, but there is an implicit promise of lifetime employment barring unforeseen developments.

These employment guarantees have traditionally been sustained by stable or growing markets and by a level of production subcontracting that is sufficiently large to buffer employment against anticipated fluctuations in product demand. Stability of employment is seen as key to the building of loyalty and commitment to the goals of the firm, to ensuring workforce flexibility, and to securing acceptance of new work methods and increased effort norms.[50]

Downsizing pressures have been a major organizational shock to the full employment model. Downsizing threatens employment security and has the potential for undermining the psychological contracts and economic incentive systems on which individual productivity and corporate performance has depended.

To avoid or minimize the breaking of employment commitments, generous attrition incentives have been used to achieve voluntary downsizing. To increase the productivity of continuing employees, jobs have been enlarged, skills and responsibilities have been increased; and the organizational hierarchy has been thinned out. In some cases, employment options within have been broadened by extending the range of jobs within which workers can be redeployed. Enlarged jobs and broader redeployment have often required extraordinary retraining measures.

When layoffs have been necessary, many full employment companies have begun to consider substituting employability guarantees and outplacement for full employment practices as a way of preserving high levels of workforce motivation. Even when layoffs have been avoided, the enrichment of jobs and the increased redeployment have placed a premium on subtle human resources qualities such as flexibility, adaptability, and the willingness to learn new and different job skills.

Employment-at-Will Model

In employment-at-will firms, the work relationship is based more on an economic *quid pro quo* than on a mutual commitment to the well-being of the firm. These firms pay high wages for high-performance workers, but without expecting loyalty or providing a commitment to employment continuity. The expectation is that workers in such firms will be mobile, changing employers readily when business declines or when they receive competing wage offers.

Employment-at-will firms do relatively little human resources development and do not depend on human resources management to motivate labor effort, preferring instead to rely on market forces and economic incentives. Employment turbulence in such firms is handled routinely as part of the strategy of having a relatively footloose workforce.

Employment at will has been commonplace in the smaller, more marginal firms in the secondary labor market. But now it is spreading to larger primary labor market firms. For example, this type of employment relationship is characteristic of the newer and more volatile firms in the high-technology sector and in parts of the business services sector that do relatively routine data processing and computer programming.[51]

Employment Models in Small and Medium-Size Firms

The models that have been described illustrate how the human resources systems of the large establishment sector handle economic change. This sector accounts for more than half of all jobs. However, the other half of the workforce is employed in medium-size and small establishments. These firms are a diverse group, spanning mom-and-pop food stores to startup high-tech firms. Some are actively competing for top talent from large corporations; others are more passive beneficiaries of well-trained workers displaced from large firms, and some are struggling to absorb poorly educated and hard-to-employ workers rejected by better-paying large employers. On average, however, these small and medium-size firms offer lower wages and fringe benefits and are economically more marginal than their larger counterparts.

As large firms have been downsizing, employment in small and medium-size firms has been increasing.[52] Yet, with some exceptions, the adjustment processes within such firms are largely unexplored.[53] Some parts of the small-scale sector, such as the unionized construction industry, have effective workforce preparedness arrangements that are administered by unions and employer associations. In other cases, highly skilled owner-operators have been able to develop a quality labor force, usually based on the informal training of a nucleus of family members or friends.[54] However, in other parts of the small-scale sector—low-wage manufacturing, retailing, and services—workforce preparedness capabilities are generally weaker.[55]

Where the small and medium-scale enterprises fit in the larger scheme of workforce preparedness remains unclear. Such firms have been gaining slightly in their share of employment since the middle 1970s, and yet they often are the most vulnerable to economic adversity.[56] Their training capability is thought to be weak, and yet their needs are neglected by public training programs that often gravitate toward larger firms that have more jobs.[57] The wages and working conditions in the smallest firms are often poorer than those of the large-enterprise sector, and such firms are more likely to be exempt from governmental workplace regulations and less likely to be organized by unions.[58]

Human Resources Management at the Crossroads

Until recently, firms following the full employment model of human resources management ranked among the most successful corporations, and many of the features of this model—employment guarantees, quality circles, and flexible work teams—are being adopted by firms that had previously followed the industrial relations model.[59] These developments seemed to indicate that the full employment model would be replacing the industrial relations model as the dominant approach to workplace human resources development in the American economy.[60]

As leading full employment firms have matured and seen their markets affected by global competition, however, they have had increasing difficulty in maintaining their employment guarantees and career benefits.[61] Full employment firms are beginning to look for substitutes for employment guarantees in their human resources development strategies, but the concern among these firms is that the psychological effort contracts and employee commitment upon which high business performance has depended will not be sustained if employment guarantees are eliminated. Without such contracts, these firms will be burdened with high wage costs that are not offset by high labor efficiency.

Full employment firms are also examining the employment-at-will model, in which human resources investments are minimal and employment commitments are weak. They observe some of their competitors adopting this model and see it as a serious alternative for the future.

As others have noted,[62] the industrial relations model of human resources development is undergoing a transformation under the influence of domestic deregulation and more intense global competition. One prediction is that the next standard will be a model blending human resources practices of the industrial relations model with those of the full employment model. Workers will have more job security than under the industrial relations model and a larger say in the direction of work,[63] and employers will have more flexibility with respect to work assignment.

Another prediction is that both the industrial relations and full employment models will be gradually displaced by highly flexible small and medium-size firms. Human resources development practices in these firms will resemble those of journeyman and apprentice arrangements in the skilled crafts.[64]

The direction and outcome of this transformation, however, are even less certain than previous research has suggested. For example, employment guarantees seem to be central to improving employee performance under both the industrial relations and full employment models, yet increased pressures for production efficiencies are making these guarantees more and more difficult to sustain. Without greater macro-economic employment stability, both models will face difficulties in securing a high efficiency workforce.

Craft or apprenticeship models of human resources management, such as are followed by some small and medium-size firms, have demonstrated their effectiveness in situations in which skills are transferable and employment is highly volatile. Nevertheless, apprenticeship training has been declining steadily in the United States. Even though there is renewed governmental interest in apprenticeship, questions remain as to whether small and medium-scale enterprises have the resources or incentives for undertaking substantial human resources development, or whether unions will be able to organize such employers to create the kinds of job referral networks needed for training continuity in apprenticeship programs.

However, two other models of human resources management might prevail. One possibility is the widespread adoption (in both union and nonunion settings) of an improved version of the full employment model based on substantial workplace training and strong psychological effort contracts with workers, whether or not employment is stable. This would entail finding new ways of guaranteeing employability (probably by extending job rights beyond a single firm) and by devising new types of efficiency commitments by workers that could be transferred from one employer to another. Such a model would lead to growth in productivity, rising real wages, and more secure career employment.

A second possibility is that the employment-at-will model will spread. In that case, workers (rather than firms) will be mainly responsible for their training, and effort will be managed through economic incentives. This, however, will place larger stresses on the already overburdened formal system of education and training outside the workplace. It will also likely mean continued labor market insecurity and slow growth in productivity and real wages.

As the following chapters will show, none of the current models of human resources development is adequate for remedying the problems caused by current turbulence in the American workplace, and none of the potential replacements has established a commanding lead. There is, however, evidence of a clear imperative among executives of large firms and progressive union leaders to search aggressively for better approaches to workforce preparedness.

Plan of the Book

Part I of the book reviews how economic turbulence is affecting the employment, earnings, and career prospects of different segments of the labor force. In Part II, the effects of turbulence at the workplace are examined, and various human resources strategies for dealing with turbulence are evaluated. Workplace turbulence is examined in both blue-collar and white-collar jobs, and in both union and nonunion settings. The book concludes with a human resources policy agenda detailing the responsibilities of business, labor, and government for addressing the problems of turbulence at the workplace.

Notes

This chapter is primarily the responsibility of Peter B. Doeringer.

1. U.S. President, Council of Economic Advisers, *Economic Report of the President, 1989* (Washington, D.C.: Government Printing Office, 1989), Tables 1–3.
2. Frank Levy, *Dollars and Dreams* (New York: Norton, 1988); Bennett Harrison and Barry Bluestone, *The Great U-Turn* (New York: Basic Books, 1988).
3. U.S. Council of Economic Advisers, *Economic Report, 1989*, pp. 43–45.
4. Edward F. Denison, *Trends in American Economic Growth, 1929–82* (Washington, D.C.: Brookings Institution, 1985).
5. Levy, *Dollars and Dreams*; U.S. Council of Economic Advisers, *Economic Report, 1989*.
6. Harrison and Bluestone, *Great U-Turn*.
7. See Chapter 2.
8. See Chapter 2.
9. See Chapter 3.
10. See Chapter 3.
11. See Chapter 3.
12. See Chapter 3.
13. See Chapter 3.
14. Christopher J. Ruhm, "Career Employment and Job Stopping," *Industrial Relations* (forthcoming); also see Chapter 4.
15. See Chapter 4; Ruhm, "Career Employment."
16. See Chapter 8.
17. U.S. General Accounting Office, *Plant Closings: Limited Advance Notice and Assistance Provided Dislocated Workers* (Washington, D.C.: Government Printing Office, 1987).
18. American Management Association, *Responsible Reductions in Force* (New York: American Management Association, 1988); Ronald E. Berenbeim, *Company Programs to Ease the Impact of Shutdowns* (New York: Conference Board, 1986).
19. See Chapter 7.
20. Harry Katz, *Shifting Gears* (Cambridge, Mass.: MIT Press, 1985).
21. See Chapters 8 and 9.
22. National Alliance of Business *The Fourth R* (Washington, D.C.: National Alliance of Business, 1987); American Society for Training and Development and U.S.

Department of Labor, *Workplace Basics* (Alexandria, Va.: American Society for Training and Development, 1989); William B. Johnston and Arnold H. Packer, *Workforce 2000* (Indianapolis: Hudson Institute, 1987); Michael L. Dertouzos, Richard K. Lester, and Robert M. Solow, *Made in America* (Cambridge, Mass.: MIT Press, 1989).

23. Business-Higher Education Forum, *American Potential* (Washington, D.C.: Business-Higher Education Forum, 1988).

24. U.S. Department of Labor, Commission on Workforce Quality and Labor Market Efficiency, *Investing in People* (Washington, D.C.: Government Printing Office, 1989); Dertouzos, Lester, and Solow, *Made in America.*

25. See Chapter 7.

26. See Chapter 2; Ford Foundation, *The Common Good* (New York: Ford Foundation, 1989).

27. Robert A. Taggart, *A Fisherman's Guide: An Assessment of Training and Remediation Strategies* (Kalamazoo, Mich.: Upjohn Institute for Employment Research, 1981); Howard Bloom, "Estimating the Effects of Job Training Programs Using Longitudinal Data: Ashenfelter's Findings Reconsidered," *Journal of Human Resources*, Vol. XIV, No. 4 (Fall 1984); JTPA Advisory Committee, *Working Capital* (Washington, D.C.: Government Printing Office, 1989).

28. See Chapter 2; Paul Osterman, *Employment Futures* (New York: Oxford University Press, 1988).

29. Ernest Stromsdorfer, "Training in Industry," in Peter B. Doeringer (Ed.), *Workplace Perspectives on Education and Training* (Hingham, Mass.: Martinus Nijhoff Publishing, 1981); American Society for Training and Development and U.S. Department of Labor, *Workplace Basics*; U.S. Department of Labor, *Investing in People.*

30. U.S. Department of Labor, *Investing in People.*

31. See Chapters 5 and 8.

32. See Chapters 5 and 6.

33. See Chapter 5.

34. See Chapters 5 and 9.

35. Business-Higher Education Forum, *American Potential*; National Alliance of Business, *The Fourth R*; Ford Foundation, *Common Good*; Johnston and Packer, *Workforce 2000*; U.S. Department of Labor, *Investing in People*; Dertouzos, Lester, and Solow, *Made in America.*

36. National Alliance of Business, *The Fourth R*; JTPA Advisory Committee, *Working Capital.*

37. American Society for Training and Development and U.S. Department of Labor, *Workplace Basics*; U.S. Department of Labor, *Investing in People.*

38. American Society for Training and Development and U.S. Department of Labor, *Workplace Basics*; Dertouzos, Lester, and Solow, *Made in America.*

39. Ford Foundation, *Common Good*; Johnston and Packer, *Workforce 2000*; Dertouzos, Lester, and Solow, *Made in America.*

40. National Alliance of Business, *The Fourth R.*

41. Michael J. Piore and Charles Sabel, *The Second Industrial Divide* (New York: Basic Books, 1984); Thomas Kochan, Harry Katz, and Robert B. McKersie, *The Transformation of American Industrial Relations* (New York: Basic Books, 1986).

42. Sumner H. Slichter, "The American System of Industrial Relations: Some Contrasts with Foreign Systems," *Arbitration Today, Proceedings of the Eighth Annual Meeting, National Academy of Arbitrators* (Washington, D.C.: BNA, 1955); Piore and Sabel, *Second Industrial Divide*; Sanford M. Jacoby, *Employing Bureaucracy: Man-*

agers, Unions, and the Transformation of Work in American Industry (New York: Columbia University Press, 1985); Kochan, Katz, and McKersie, *Transformation of American Industrial Relations*.

43. Jacoby, *Employing Bureaucracy*; Osterman, *Employment Futures*; Paul Osterman (Ed.), *Internal Labor Markets* (Cambridge, Mass.: MIT Press, 1984).

44. Fred K. Foulkes, *Personnel Policies in Large Nonunion Companies* (Englewood Cliffs, N.J.: Prentice Hall, 1980); Jacoby, *Employing Bureaucracy*; Kochan, Katz, and McKersie, *Transformation of American Industrial Relations*.

45. Kochan, Katz, and McKersie, *Transformation of American Industrial Relations*; see Chapter 6.

46. See Chapter 6.

47. See Chapter 6.

48. Foulkes, *Personnel Policies in Large Nonunion Companies*.

49. Foulkes, *Personnel Policies in Large Nonunion Companies*; William G. Ouchi and Raymond L. Price, "Hierarchies, Clans, and Theory z: A New Perspective on Organizational Development," in J. Richard Hackman, Edward Lawler III, and Lyman W. Porter (Eds.), *Perspectives on Organizational Behavior* (New York: McGraw-Hill, 1983).

50. Warren Bennis, "Organizations of the Future," in Robert A. Sutermeister (Ed.), *People and Productivity* (3rd ed.) (New York: McGraw-Hill, 1976); Ouchi and Price, "Hierarchies, Clans, and Theory z."

51. Osterman, *Internal Labor Markets*.

52. Gary Loveman, Michael J. Piore, and Werner Sengenberger, "The Evolving Role of Small Business in Industrialized Economies and Some Implications for Employment and Training," in Katharine Abraham and Robert B. McKersie (Eds.), *New Developments in the Labor Market* (Cambridge, Mass.: MIT Press, forthcoming).

53. Peter B. Doeringer, "Internal Labor Markets and Paternalism in Rural Labor Markets," in Osterman, *Internal Labor Markets*; Peter B. Doeringer, Philip Moss, and David G. Terkla, "Capitalism and Kinship: Do Institutions Matter in the Labor Market?" *Industrial and Labor Relations Review* 40 (October 1986): 48–60; Peter B. Doeringer, Gregory C. Topakian, and David G. Terkla, *Invisible Factors in Local Economic Development* (New York: Oxford University Press, 1987).

54. Piore and Sabel, *Second Industrial Divide*; Doeringer, Moss, and Terkla, "Capitalism and Kinship."

55. Peter B. Doeringer and Michael J. Piore, *Internal Labor Markets and Manpower Analysis* (Armonk, N.Y.: M.E. Sharpe, 1985).

56. Maryellen Kelley and Bennett Harrison, "The Subcontracting Behavior of Single vs. Multi-Plant Enterprises in U.S. Manufacturing: Implications for Economic Development," *World Development* (forthcoming); Levy, *Dollars and Dreams*.

57. Doeringer, Topakian, and Terkla, *Invisible Factors in Local Development*.

58. Peter B. Doeringer and David G. Terkla, "Jobs for Older Workers: Is the Non-Bureaucratic Firm the Answer?" *Proceedings of the Forty-First Annual Meeting of the Industrial Relations Research Association*, 1989 (Madison, Wisc: Industrial Relations Research Association).

59. Thomas J. Peters and Robert H. Waterman Jr., *In Search of Excellence* (New York: Harper & Row, 1982); Kochan, Katz, and McKersie, *Transformation of American Industrial Relations*.

60. Kochan, Katz, and McKersie, *Transformation of American Industrial Relations*.

61. See Chapter 8.

62. Kochan, Katz, and McKersie, *Transformation of American Industrial Relations*; Piore and Sabel, *Second Industrial Divide*.

63. Kochan, Katz, and McKersie, *Transformation of American Industrial Relations*; Charles Hecksher, *The New Unionism* (New York: Basic Books, 1988).

64. Piore and Sabel, *Second Industrial Divide*.

I

TURBULENCE AND THE LABOR FORCE

2

Labor Market Turbulence and the Labor Market Experience of Young Adults

The 1980s has been a unique period of social, industrial, and demographic change in postwar U.S. economic history. Assessing the impacts of these changes on the overall well-being of the American worker becomes a formidable task because some groups have reaped sizable economic gains while others have lost important ground.

This chapter focuses on the labor market experiences of young adults, ages 18 to 29. It concentrates on male workers because the effects of labor market turbulence (as opposed to labor market discrimination) are more clearly revealed in the data on males. For example, male workers have faced a serious deterioration in their earnings prospects as a result of the changes taking place in U.S. labor markets, whereas female workers, for complicated reasons, have not.[1] Nevertheless, the implications of this analysis for workforce preparedness policy apply with equal force to all young adults.

There has been renewed national interest in the labor market situation of young adults in recent years. Part of this growing interest is attributable to the decrease in the size of the population of young adults. The shrinking pool of young adults, combined with a relatively strong demand for labor, has created labor shortage problems in a number of geographic areas and in a number of industries, especially those that depend on inexperienced labor force entrants to meet their employment needs.

Concern over the most recent and forthcoming cohorts of young workers, however, has not stemmed solely from the decline in the size of this pool. The demographic and socioeconomic composition of the young adult population is also changing, with growing shares of potential labor force entrants compris-

17

ing race/ethnic minorities and the children of poor or economically disadvantaged families.[2]

These demographic shifts in the young adult labor force are occurring at a time when the characteristics of new jobs and key features of existing jobs are changing. Increased concern has been expressed by public officials, national commissions, educators, and private sector employers over the potential mismatches between the educational, literacy, and behavioral attributes of young workers and the educational and skill requirements of future jobs in the new American economy.[3] Many commentators have focused on the need for a better educated, more skilled, and more adaptable workforce. For example, former Secretary of Labor William Brock recently noted that the failure to develop a strong, uniform base of reading, critical reasoning, and communication skills among the nation's current youth population would lead to a "bifurcated work force" consisting of a well-paid, employed contingent occupying "challenging, good jobs" and a large residue of unemployable adults lacking the essential skills for labor market success.[4]

The need for a new and more comprehensive approach to human resource investments in the nation's youth and young adults has been recognized by a growing number of corporate executives, economists, educators, labor representatives, and political leaders. Such investments are widely believed to be instrumental to sustained real-wage growth, increased family incomes, improved productivity, and enhanced economic competitiveness for the nation. As David Kearns and Denis Doyle recently argued, "The simple truth is that we can't have a world-class economy without a world-class work force, from senior scientists to stockroom clerks. And we cannot have a world-class work force without world-class schools."[5]

This chapter begins with an analysis of the demographic changes that already have taken place and those that are projected in the nation's young workforce. Next, the literacy abilities of our nation's young adults are briefly examined, followed by an analysis of trends in the labor market experiences of young male adults over the past 15 years. The chapter concludes with a series of recommendations on desirable directions for future workforce preparedness policies aimed at improving the use and productivity of the nation's young adult work force.

Demographic Trends

Substantial fluctuations in the absolute and relative size of the nation's 18- to 24-year-old civilian noninstitutional population have taken place over the past three decades. The number of 18- to 24-year-olds increased from 14.9 million in 1960 to 22.2 million in 1970 and reached a peak of nearly 29.0 million in 1981 (see Table 2.1). The young adult population grew far more rapidly than did the 16- to 65-year-old group during this period, thereby increasing its relative share of the working-age population (ages 16 to 65) from 14.6% in 1960 to 18.8% in 1970, eventually peaking at 20.4% in 1977.

Since 1981, the absolute number of 18- to 24-year-olds has been declining.

Table 2.1. **Trends in the Absolute and Relative Number of 18- to 24-Year-Olds in the Civilian Noninstitutional Population of the United States, Selected Years, 1960–86 (Absolute Numbers in 1000s)**

	Absolute Number			Relative Number*		
	(A)	(B)	(C)	(D)	(E)	(F)
Year	All	Men	Women	All	Men	Women
1960	14,888	6,838	8,050	14.6	14.0	15.1
1965	18,437	8,532	9,905	16.9	16.4	17.4
1970	22,199	10,160	12,040	18.8	18.1	19.5
1975	26,594	12,832	13,762	20.2	20.2	20.2
1977	27,788	13,477	14,309	20.4	20.5	20.3
1980	28,899	14,087	14,812	20.2	20.3	20.0
1981	28,965	14,121	14,845	19.9	20.1	19.8
1985	27,371	13,332	14,039	18.1	18.2	18.0
1986	26,679	13,005	13,675	17.4	17.5	17.4

*The relative number of 18- to 24-year-olds is defined as the ratio of the number of 18- to 24-year-olds to the civilian noninstitutional population of persons 16 to 65 years old.

Source: U.S. Department of Labor, Bureau of Labor Statistics, *Labor Force Statistics Derived from the Population Survey, a Databook*, Bulletin 2096; and U.S. Department of Labor, Bureau of Labor Statistics, *Employment and Earnings*, January 1986 and January 1987.

By 1986, there were 2.3 million, or 8%, fewer 18- to 24-year-olds in the civilian noninstitutional population. By 1995, the absolute number of 18 to 24-year-olds is projected to decline to 23.0 million, a figure 3.6 million, or nearly 14%, below the 1986 level (see Table 2.2). Given continued growth in the nation's working-age population, the relative number of 18- to 24-year-olds will decline even more rapidly through 1995. During that year, the 18- to 24-year-old population will shrink to 14.1% of the working-age population. The baby bust of the 1970s will thus continue to exert its influence on the size of the pool of young labor force entrants through the first half of the 1990s.

The 18- to 24-year-old cohort will resume growth in the latter half of the 1990s as a consequence of the mini baby boom that began in the late 1970s. The number of 18- to 24-year-olds is projected to rise by slightly under a million, or 4.1%, between 1995 and 2000 (See Table 2.3). The bulk of this population growth will be attributable to increasing numbers of young adults from minority backgrounds, especially Hispanics. Somewhere between 8 and 9 of every 10 net new young adults in the United States during the 1995–2000

Table 2.2. **Actual 1986 and Projected 1995 Number of 18- to 24-Year-Olds in the Civilian Noninstitutional Population of the United States, by Sex and Ethnic Group (Numbers in 1000s)**

	Actual 1986	Projected 1995	Absolute Difference	Relative Difference
Total	26,679	23,036	– 3,643	– 13.7%
Men	13,005	11,183	– 1,822	– 14.0%
Women	13,674	11,853	– 1,821	– 13.3%
Ethnic Minorities	7,026	7,496	+ 470	+ 6.7%

Source: U.S. Department of Labor, Bureau of Labor Statistics, *Projections 2000*, "Appendix Table A-2," pp. 93–95.

Table 2.3. **Projected Number of 18- to 24-Year-Olds in the Civilian Noninstitutional Population of the United States in 1995 and 2000, by Sex and Ethnic Group (Numbers in 1000s)**

	Projected 1995	Projected 2000	Absolute Difference	Relative Difference
Total	23,036	23,973	+937	+ 4.1%
Men	11,183	11,651	+468	+ 4.2%
Women	11,853	12,322	+469	+ 4.0%
Ethnic Minorities	7,496	8,315	+819	+10.9%

Source: U.S. Department of Labor, Bureau of Labor Statistics, *Projections 2000,* "Appendix Table A-2," pp. 93–95.

period will be Asian, black, or Hispanic.[6] The ability of the nation's human resource system to educate, train, and employ young minority adults will have a major influence on the future labor market success of the young adult population.

Insights into changes in the demographic composition of the pool of young workers can be gained from comparing the characteristics of the nation's 11- to 17-year-old civilian noninstitutional population in 1987—the group that will form the 18- to 24-year-old population during the mid-1990s—with similar cohorts for 1974 and 1980. Minorities clearly will represent a growing share of the young adult workforce in the mid-1990s (see Table 2.4). In March 1987, nearly 29% of all 11- to 17-year-olds were either black, Hispanic, or Asian/American Indian. This ratio is well above the 24% share of March 1980 and the 22% share prevailing in March 1974. With the exception of those completing some post-secondary education, many young minority adults, especially males, have experienced severe employment and earnings difficulties over the past 15 years.[7]

Higher fractions of America's 11- to 17-year-old population are also living in single parent families and in poor families (see Table 2.5). During March 1987, some 27% of the nation's 11- to 17-year-olds were living in a family with only one parent present in the home. This ratio was 4 percentage points above the share prevailing in 1980 and nearly 10 percentage points above the March 1974 ratio. This increase in the fraction of 11- to 17-year-olds residing in one-

Table 2.4. **Percentage Distribution of 11- to 17-Year-Olds in the Civilian Noninstitutional Population of the United States, by Ethnic Group, March 1974, March 1980, and March 1987**

Ethnic Group	March 1974	March 1980	March 1987
All	100.0	100.0	100.0
White, non-Hispanic	78.4	76.2	71.5
Black, non-Hispanic	13.5	14.4	15.2
Hispanic	6.9	7.4	9.7
Other, non-Hispanic	1.3	2.0	3.5

Source: U.S. Bureau of the Census, Current Population Survey (March), selected years, 1968–88, public use tapes.

Table 2.5. **Trends in the Share of 11- to 17-Year-Olds Living in Single-Parent Families, Poor Families, and Poor Single-Parent Families, by Ethnic Group, March 1974, March 1980, and March 1987 (Percentages)**

11- to 17-Year-Olds	March 1974	March 1980	March 1987
Living in a			
Single-Parent Family			
All	17.6	23.1	27.1
White, non-Hispanic	12.6	17.2	20.5
Black, non-Hispanic	43.9	54.5	55.8
Hispanic	22.5	24.5	33.6
Other, non-Hispanic	18.3	18.3	21.0
Living			
in a Poor Family			
All	14.2	15.3	19.1
White, non-Hispanic	8.4	9.4	11.9
Black, non-Hispanic	41.6	39.8	42.2
Hispanic	24.8	26.1	35.4
Other, non-Hispanic	24.0	21.5	21.2
Living in a			
Poor Single-Parent Family			
All	7.6	9.3	12.2
White, non-Hispanic	3.6	4.9	6.5
Black, non-Hispanic	27.9	31.1	35.7
Hispanic	12.5	12.2	19.1
Other, non-Hispanic	9.8	10.2	9.7

Source: U.S. Bureau of the Census, Current Population Survey (March), selected years, 1968–88, public use tapes.

parent families has occurred among all race/ethnic groups, although black youths (56%) remain far more likely than whites (21%) and Hispanics (34%) to be raised in a one-parent family.

Table 2.5 also shows that higher fractions of the nation's 11- to 17-year-olds are growing up in a poverty environment. In March 1987, nearly one of every five U.S. youths 11 to 17 years old was being raised in a poverty family versus only 15% in 1980. For many families, poverty is a transitory condition from which escape is likely over a fairly short period of time (1–2 years). National research on the long-term poor, however, has revealed that children raised in single-parent families, especially those headed by minority women with limited formal schooling, are at far greater risk of being poor for a major portion of their childhood years.[8] Recent research on the persistent poor revealed that children (persons ages 1 to 17) make up nearly half of the nation's persistent poor.[9] Unfortunately, the share of 11- to 17-year-olds living in poor, single-parent families has been rising over time, as Table 2.5 shows. During March 1987, approximately one of every eight U.S. youths 11 to 17 years old was a member of a poor family with only one parent present in the home. Among Hispanic and black youths, the comparable ratios were approximately one of five and one of three, respectively.

Literacy Skills

Given continued low aggregate rates of unemployment, the decline in the pool of young labor force participants is expected to create a number of recruitment and retention problems for employers, especially those that have traditionally depended heavily on new entrants. These problems will be exacerbated by the literacy and formal educational deficiencies of many new entrants.

The rising share of U.S. young people being raised in poor families has a number of serious implications for the workforce preparedness of the next cohort of young adult labor force entrants, because many teenagers living in poor families tend to have severe literacy deficits. Key findings of a 1980 national testing of 14- to 17-year-olds are presented in Table 2.6. The scores of these youths on the Armed Forces Qualification Test (AFQT) was examined to determine the rankings of teens from poor families.[10] The mean test score of all poor 14- to 15-year-olds fell at the 19th percentile, with poor black and Hispanic youths achieving mean scores that placed them at the 13th and 18th percentiles, respectively. Among poor 16- to 17-year-olds, test score performance was also quite low. The percentile ranking of the mean test score of all poor 16- to 17-year-olds was 23, indicating that nearly half of all such youth would have fallen in the bottom fifth of the basic academic skills test score distribution for all 16- to 17-year-olds in the nation.

Teenagers with low basic academic skills are more likely to perform poorly in school and to fall academically behind their peer group.[11] Youths from poor families with low basic academic skills are, thus, at greater risk of dropping out of high school. For example, of all 14- to 15-year-old students in the United States in 1979, approximately 23% of those living in poverty families and having basic skills in the bottom 20% of the AFQT test distribution dropped out of school within the following two-year period.[12] This dropout rate was 2.3 times as high as that for all 14- to 15-year-olds and seven times higher than that for 14- to 15-year-olds who had scored in the upper 40% and were living in families with an income three or more times the official poverty line.

The nation's young adult dropouts tend to be characterized by the most severe literacy deficits. Among all 18- to 23-year-olds participating in the 1980 national AFQT testing, the typical high school dropout scored at the 18th

Table 2.6. **Percentile Rankings of the Mean AFQT Test Scores of Teens in Poverty Families, by Age and Ethnic Group, United States, 1980**

Ethnic Group	14- to 15-Year-Olds	16- to 17-Year-Olds
All	19th	23rd
White, non-Hispanic	24th	36th
Black, non-Hispanic	13th	14th
Hispanic	18th	19th

Source: National Longitudinal Survey of Youth Labor Market Experience, 1979–81 interviews, public use tape.

percentile, while black and Hispanic dropouts had median AFQT test scores that placed them in the bottom 10% of the test score distribution.

To place these test scores in the context of workforce preparedness, simply consider the fact that the nation's armed forces typically will not accept for enlistment persons in the bottom 30% of the test score distribution.[13] Those in the bottom 10% are considered ineligible for enlistment, and those falling in the 10th to 30th percentile range are regarded as below average in trainability. An analysis of the AFQT scores of 18- to 23-year-old dropouts in 1980 revealed that 59% of the white, non-Hispanic dropouts and approximately 9 of every 10 black and Hispanic dropouts would have been classified by the armed services as either ineligible for enlistment or below average in trainability. With such severe basic skills deficits, these dropouts are unlikely to be viewed as "trainable" by private sector firms selecting new employees from the external labor market for career positions.

The literacy proficiencies of young adults (ages 21–25) in the United States were assessed in 1985 through a national testing effort by the Educational Testing Service.[14] Findings of this National Assessment of Educational Progress (NAEP) Young Adult Literacy Assessment clearly revealed that the literacy proficiencies of young adults were strongly associated with the years of formal schooling that they had completed (see Table 2.7). On each of four literacy scales (reading, prose, document utilization, and quantitative computation), young adults who had not completed four years of high school ranked at or near the 20th percentile, while black high school dropouts typically fell in the bottom tenth of the test score distribution. Many minority high school graduates not going on to college also have weak literacy skills, frequently falling in the bottom one-fifth to one-third of the test distribution.

Table 2.7. **Percentile Rankings of the Mean Scaled Scores of Young Adults (21–25 Years Old) by Years of Schooling Completed, Ethnic Group, and Literacy Proficiency Area**

Years of Schooling, Ethnic Group	Reading	Prose	Document Utilization	Quantitative Computation
8 or fewer	12	14	10	13
9–11				
All	24	22	20	22
Black	10	12	10	9
Hispanic	20	16	15	16
12				
All	46	42	42	42
Black	23	18	20	20
Hispanic	36	37	33	30
16				
All	80	82	83	82
Black	61	56	50	51
Hispanic	68	80	68	58

Source: 1985 NAEP Young Adult Literacy Assessment.

Table 2.8. **Percentile Rankings of the Mean Scaled Scores of Poor/Near-Poor Young Adults (21–25 Years Old) in the United States, by Sex, Ethnic Group, and Literacy Proficiency Area**

Sex, Ethnic Group	Reading	Prose	Document Utilization	Quantitative Computation
All	20	19	19	20
Men	18	16	16	16
Women	23	21	21	22
Whites	29	30	32	29
Blacks	10	9	8	10
Hispanics	6	6	5	5

Source: 1985 NAEP Young Adult Literacy Assessment.

These findings raise further concerns about the literacy skills of our forthcoming, non–college-bound workforce.[15]

Young adults from poor/near-poor families were overwhelmingly characterized by weak literacy proficiencies, typically obtaining mean scaled scores at the 20th percentile, with poor/near-poor blacks and Hispanics falling in the bottom 10% of the overall test score distribution for each of the four literacy scales (see Table 2.8). Given the growing share of race/ethnic minorities in the young adult population, especially in that segment of the population not going on to college, and the increased share of 11- to 17-year-olds being raised in poverty families, the forthcoming cohort of young labor force entrants will likely contain an above-average share of persons with weak literacy proficiencies. The declining pool of young adults will, thus, contain higher fractions who are poorly prepared for a labor market characterized by substantial turbulence, increased international competition, and rising skill requirements for the more highly paid occupations.

Earnings Deterioration

Labor market turbulence has substantially reduced real earnings opportunities for many young male adults. Young men with no post-secondary schooling, especially poorly educated black and Hispanic men, have been most adversely affected. The deterioration in earnings opportunities has not only affected the typical man's purchasing power, but research evidence also indicates that labor market success has a critical influence on their social and economic behavior, including marriage behavior, the ability to adequately support a family, and certain types of criminal behavior.[16] The labor market problems of the "forgotten half" of young adults in the United States, the half who terminate their formal schooling with a high school diploma or less, have become more widely recognized in recent years.[17] However, public policy responses have so far been minimal and ill-coordinated.

Youth employment has been one of the most comprehensively studied fields over the past two decades and has been a major focus of national employment and training policy. Most studies of youth employment problems, however, have concentrated on simple measures of labor force activity, such as unemployment rates and employment/population ratios, or on the hourly/weekly wages of employed youth.[18] Most studies have also limited their focus to the employment problems of youths under the age of 22. In contrast, this analysis focuses on the real annual earnings of young adult males (ages 18 to 29), since the labor market problems of young men persist into their late 20s.

The annual earnings of young male adults are influenced by a number of factors, including their degree of attachment to the labor force, their ability to avoid unemployment during the year, the number of hours they work per week of employment, and the hourly earnings they receive. The compound effects of these different employment variables on labor market success are best measured by their impact on real annual earnings.

The declines in real earnings experienced by many young men over the 1973–86 period represent a major departure from trends in the prior 15 years. Between 1959 and 1973, the real earnings of young men improved nearly continuously. Over this period, the mean real annual earnings of young men 20–24 and 25–29 years old increased by 24% and 35%, respectively.[19] Gains in real annual earnings occurred for young men in all major ethnic groups and for high school dropouts, high school graduates, and college graduates.[20]

In 1979, the mean real annual earnings of 18- to 29-year-old men were approximately 6% below their 1973 peak (see Table 2.9).[21] Over the next three years, a period characterized by two national economic recessions, severe inflation, and a sharp decline in employment in key goods-producing indus-

Table 2.9. **Trends in the Mean Real Annual Earnings of 18- to 29-Year-Old Civilian Males, by Age Subgroup, Ethnic Group, and Educational Attainment, United States, Selected Years 1973–86 (in 1986 Dollars)**

Group	1973	1979	1982	1986	Absolute Change 1973–86	Percentage Change 1973–86
Age						
All, 18–29	$14,541	$13,617	$10,873	$11,934	$ – 2,607	– 17.9
18–19	5,220	4,949	3,120	3,181	– 2,039	– 39.1
20–24	12,166	11,644	8,624	9,031	– 3,135	– 25.8
25–29	21,815	19,673	16,216	17,438	– 4,377	– 20.1
Ethnic Group						
White, non-Hispanic	15,270	14,498	11,847	13,069	– 2,201	– 14.4
Black, non-Hispanic	10,778	9,183	6,243	7,447	– 3,331	– 30.9
Hispanic	11,823	11,180	8,847	9,514	– 2,309	– 19.5
Educational Attainment*						
H.S. Dropouts	12,379	10,275	7,288	7,799	– 4,580	– 37.0
H.S. Graduates	17,150	15,790	12,182	13,070	– 4,080	– 23.8
Some College	16,943	16,977	14,401	15,283	– 1,660	– 9.8
College Graduates	22,798	21,305	19,741	21,961	– 837	– 3.7

*Data on educational attainment exclude those who cited school as their major activity in March of each survey year.

Source: 1985 NAEP Young Adult Literacy Assessment.

tries, the mean real annual earnings of 18- to 29-year-old males fell by 20%. Since 1982, the mean real annual earnings of young male adults have improved by nearly 10%, largely as a consequence of greater employment opportunities, including more year-round, full-time jobs. However, the 1986 mean annual earnings of these young men still remained far below their 1973 peak, falling $2,607, or nearly 18% below their 1973 level.

The relative size of these declines in the mean real annual earnings of young men varied fairly widely by age, ethnic group, and educational attainment. The youngest subgroups (18–19 and 20–24 years old) encountered the sharpest percentage declines in their real earnings, with declines of 39% and 26%, respectively, versus a decline of 20% for 25- to 29-year-old men.[22] The greater relative deterioration in the real earnings of younger men was attributable to their somewhat lower attachment to the labor market and their greater difficulties in avoiding unemployment, securing full-time jobs, and obtaining access to jobs in key goods-producing industries, especially durable manufacturing.

Although young men in each of the three major ethnic groups experienced substantial declines in their mean real annual earnings over the 1973–86 period, blacks clearly were most adversely affected by changes in labor market opportunities. The mean real earnings of young black males fell by 31% versus declines of 20% for Hispanics and 14% for white, non-Hispanic males.

For all ethnic groups, the absolute and relative size of the real earnings declines were closely associated with years of formal schooling. Those young adult men with no post-secondary schooling suffered the most severe earnings declines. The mean real annual earnings of high school dropouts fell by 37% between 1973 and 1986, while high school graduates encountered a mean earnings decline of 24%.[23] Young male college graduates came close to maintaining their 1973 mean earnings level, falling only 4% short. Over the 1979–86 period, college graduates were the only group of young male adults to improve their real earnings position.

Cumulative Earnings Losses

The findings cited on the declines in the real earnings of young male adults have focused on the mean earnings of each major subgroup of 18- to 29-year-olds, rather than on the real earnings levels of these young men over the entire 18–29 age range. As young men enter the labor force after leaving school, they historically have tended to experience fairly steep increases in their annual earnings between their late teens/early 20s and their late 20s.

The transition from school to work (regardless of years of schooling completed) typically takes place in a series of stages, with each new stage characterized by jobs in somewhat different occupations, industries, and firms within industries.[24] These improvements in the real earnings of young men result not simply from the accumulation of experience and firm specific human capital, but from access to jobs in new occupations and firms that pay higher real wages and provide more stable employment.

The estimated declines in the mean real earnings of young men are not simply the result of a more troublesome and lengthy transition from school to work in the first few years of adulthood. During 1986, young men with no post-secondary schooling experienced sharply lower real earnings than they did in 1973 at each single age over the 18–29 age range. That is, the entire age/earnings profile for such young men has shifted downward to a considerable degree. Large real earnings gaps continued to exist as they reached their late 20s. Thus the labor market problems of young men do not vanish with a few years of experience.

The pattern of earnings declines experienced by young male adults becomes even more apparent when disaggregated by age and educational attainment. As seen in Table 2.10, the average 18-year-old male high school dropout earned $4,685 in 1973 (in 1986 dollars), but only $2,762 in 1986. The difference between these two mean real earnings figures is $1,923, a measure of how much the typical 18-year-old male high school dropout (in 1986) has "lost" in real earnings relative to his identically aged counterpart in 1973. Summing the absolute values of these real earnings differences across the entire 18- to 29-year-old cohort yields earnings losses of more than $60,000. Over the 18–29 age interval, male high school dropouts would have earned on average $60,000 more in 1973 than in 1986. Similarly, young male high school graduates with no post-secondary schooling lost roughly $60,000 in real earnings over the 18–29 age interval, while young male college graduates (ages 22–29) in 1986 lost only $12,232 relative to their counterparts in 1973.

An alternative way of measuring these earnings losses would take the mean earnings difference at each age and multiply it at some compound real rate of interest (e.g., 5%) to 1986. Conceptually, this approach is equivalent to enabling a young male adult to take the mean annual earnings difference at each age and purchase a certificate of deposit earning a 5% real annual rate of interest. Summing the principal and component interest payments across the 18- to 29-year-old cohort yields earnings losses of $77,000 for high school dropouts and $76,000 for high school graduates, but only $14,000 for college graduates.

The sizeable nature of these earnings losses have had a number of adverse effects on the economic and social behavior of young adult men. The young adult years are critically formative ones, traditionally characterized by movement into stable and more remunerative career jobs frequently accompanied by marriage and growing family responsibilities.

As recently as 1974, a majority of young male dropouts and high school graduates would have been married and living with their spouses by age 22.[25] Over the past 15 years, the ability of young men with no post-secondary school to marry, raise families, and purchase homes has clearly deteriorated.[26] For example, the cumulative earnings losses noted previously can be compared to the purchase price of homes. In 1973, the median price of existing one-family

Table 2.10. **Mean Real Annual Earnings of 18- to 29-Year-Old Civilian Males, by Age and Educational Attainment, United States, 1973 and 1986 (in 1986 Dollars)**

Age	1973	1986	Absolute Change 1973–86	Compounded at 5%
High School Dropouts Only				
18	$ 4,685	$ 2,762	$ 1,923	$ 3,289
19	8,260	4,764	3,496	5,695
20	8,816	5,019	3,797	5,890
21	9,960	5,310	4,650	6,870
22	13,194	7,340	5,854	8,237
23	12,773	7,197	5,576	7,472
24	14,239	8,771	5,468	6,979
25	15,045	9,334	5,711	6,942
26	16,213	9,147	7,066	8,180
27	16,539	11,195	5,344	5,892
28	17,019	12,347	4,672	4,906
29	17,757	11,154	6,603	6,603
			60,160	76,954
High School Graduates Only				
18	$ 6,530	$ 4,463	$ 2,067	$ 3,535
19	9,352	5,984	3,368	5,486
20	12,091	8,355	3,736	5,796
21	13,517	9,755	3,762	5,558
22	15,910	11,336	4,574	6,436
23	17,936	11,950	5,986	8,022
24	17,528	13,058	4,470	5,705
25	20,908	14,580	6,328	7,692
26	21,348	15,635	5,713	6,614
27	23,076	17,227	5,849	6,449
28	24,938	17,571	7,367	7,735
29	24,651	17,495	7,156	7,156
			60,376	76,183
College Graduates Only				
22	$10,154	$ 9,569	$ 585	$ 823
23	13,809	12,920	889	1,191
24	17,778	15,712	2,066	2,637
25	20,876	20,901	− 25	− 30
26	25,183	23,903	1,280	1,482
27	25,841	25,184	657	724
28	29,530	24,714	4,816	5,057
29	31,157	29,193	1,964	1,964
			12,232	13,848

Source: 1985 NAEP Young Adult Literacy Assessment.

houses was \$28,900, or \$71,305 in 1986 dollars.[27] In 1986, the median price of existing one-family houses was \$80,200. Whereas in 1973 the mean annual earnings of young men (ages 18 to 29) represented 20.4% of the price of an existing home, by 1986 their mean earnings had dropped to 14.9% of the purchase price.

Sources of Real Earnings Declines

The real earnings declines experienced by young male adults have been caused by a number of developments, including growth in the proportion of young adult men with no reported employment during the entire calendar year and reduced availability of year-round, full-time employment. However, even among those employed year-round full-time—those working for 50–52 weeks during the year and for 35 or more hours per week—real annual earnings have fallen considerably. Table 2.11 reveals that the mean real annual earnings of young males employed at least one week fell by approximately 15% between 1973 and 1986 while the mean earnings of those employed year-round, full-time dropped by 13% over the same period. Although real earnings declines have not been solely confined to young adult men, the relative size of the real earnings declines of young men greatly exceeded those of men in every other major age subgroup as Table 2.11 shows.

Other forces contributing to the deterioration in the real earnings position of young adult men have been a relatively high incidence of unemployment, reduced access to career jobs offering stable year-round employment, and

Table 2.11. **Mean Real Annual Earnings of 18- to 29-Year-Old Males and Other Age Subgroups, by Employment Status, United States, 1973 and 1986 (in 1986 Dollars)**

Group	1973	1986	Absolute Difference, 1973–86	Relative Difference, 1973–86
18- to 29-Year-Olds				
All	\$14,541	\$11,934	\$ – 2,607	– 17.9%
Employed	15,639	13,331	– 2,308	– 14.8
Employed Year-Round, Full-Time	21,955	19,151	– 2,804	– 12.8
Other Males, Employed Year-Round, Full-Time				
30- to 44-Year-Olds	32,744	30,250	– 2,494	– 7.6
45- to 54-Year-Olds	33,397	33,455	+ 58	+ 0.2
55- to 62-Year-Olds	30,636	30,716	+ 80	+ 0.3

Source: 1985 NAEP Young Adult Literacy Assessment.

somewhat greater dependence on part-time jobs, particularly in trade and services industries. Each of these factors is cyclically sensitive, rising in importance during periods of economic recession and falling during periods of sustained economic growth.

During 1973, slightly under 49% of all 18- to 29-year-old civilian males worked year-round, full-time (see Table 2.12). This ratio fell slightly to 48% in 1979 and plummeted below 41% in 1982. After four years of recovery from the national economic recession of 1982, the share of young adult males working year-round, full-time during 1986 was nearly 48%, only slightly below the ratio of 1973. Comparing 1973 with 1986, the roughly equivalent fraction of young adult men able to secure year-round, full-time employment masks important differences among demographic subgroups. In particular, large ethnic disparities appear in the trends in year-round, full-time employment. The fraction of white, non-Hispanic and Hispanic males working year-round, full-time in 1986 was slightly above or identical to their 1973 rates. In contrast, black males were far more adversely affected, experiencing a relative decline of 20% in their full-time, year-round employment rate. During 1973, the gap between the fraction of young white and black men holding year-round, full-time jobs was only 6 percentage points. By 1986, this gap had widened considerably to nearly 16 percentage points.

Table 2.12. **Percentage of 18- to 29-Year-Old Civilian Males Who Were Employed Year-Round, Full-Time, by Age Subgroup, Ethnic Group, and Educational Attainment, United States, Selected Years 1973–86**

Group	1973	1979	1982	1986	Percentage Change 1973–86
All, 18–29	48.8%	48.1%	40.6%	47.6%	− 2.5%
Age Group					
18–19	15.8	15.7	10.2	11.3	− 28.5
20–24	43.9	43.8	34.6	40.6	− 7.5
25–29	70.7	67.3	58.6	65.9	− 6.8
Ethnic Group					
White, non-Hispanic	49.7	50.1	43.2	50.2	+ 1.0
Black, non-Hispanic	43.8	37.7	27.3	34.9	− 20.3
Hispanic	47.2	43.9	38.8	47.2	0.0
Educational Attainment*					
H.S. Dropouts	50.0	39.0	31.2	40.3	− 19.4
H.S. Graduates	62.2	59.1	48.6	57.9	− 6.9
Some College	57.4	60.5	54.3	58.9	+ 2.6
College Graduates	64.5	70.2	67.6	69.8	+ 8.2

*Data on educational attainment exclude those who cited school as their major activity in March of each survey year.

Source: 1985 NAEP Young Adult Literacy Assessment.

The trends in year-round, full-time employment rates were substantially different for men with some post-secondary schooling than they were for those who completed 12 or fewer years of school. Only 40% of those males who left school without a diploma were able to obtain year-round, full-time employment during 1986. This represented a 20% decline in the fraction of dropouts who had been able to do so during 1973. Those young men with 12 years of formal schooling faced a 7% decline in their year-round, full-time employment rate between 1973 and 1986. In sharp contrast, both those men with some college and four-year college graduates were able to boost their full-time, year-round employment rates by 3% to 8% over this time period.

The downward trend in the proportion of young adult men working year-round, full-time has been accompanied by a rising fraction of men reporting no earnings whatsoever during the year (see Table 2.13). During 1973, only 7.4% of 18- to 29-year-old civilian males reported zero earnings. By 1979, this ratio had increased slightly to 8.5%, and it rose sharply to 13.0% during the recession year of 1982. During the ensuing recovery, this ratio has declined, falling to slightly under 11% in 1986, representing one of every nine young males in the nation.

A rise in the proportion of young adult men with no reported earnings took place for each major age, ethnic, and educational attainment subgroup. The

Table 2.13. **Percentage of 18- to 29-Year-Old Civilian Males Who Reported Zero Earnings, by Age Subgroup, Ethnic Group, and Educational Attainment, United States, Selected Years 1973–86**

Group	1973	1979	1982	1986	Percentage Change 1973–86
All, 18–29	7.4%	8.5%	13.0%	10.8%	45.9%
Age Group					
18–19	14.9	18.1	25.1	25.2	69.1
20–24	7.5	8.1	12.5	10.3	37.3
25–29	3.5	4.7	8.7	6.4	82.9
Ethnic Group					
White, non-Hispanic	6.2	6.5	9.8	7.5	21.0
Black, non-Hispanic	13.2	19.7	31.1	24.9	88.6
Hispanic	10.7	10.6	14.7	13.4	25.2
Educational Attainment*					
H.S. Dropouts	7.7	12.0	18.5	16.3	111.7
H.S. Graduates	3.6	3.6	8.5	5.6	55.6
Some College	3.3	3.3	5.4	3.8	15.2
College Graduates	2.4	2.1	4.0	3.2	33.3

*Data on educational attainment exclude those who cited school as their major activity in March of each survey year.

Source: 1985 NAEP Young Adult Literacy Assessment.

absolute and relative size of these increases were, however, greater for males in their late teens, greater for blacks than for whites or Hispanics, and far greater for those with the least amount of formal schooling. Comparing 1973 to 1986, one finds a rise in the ratio of young adult white males with no reported earnings from 6.2% to 7.5%. Among young black males, the fraction with no reported earnings nearly doubled from 13% to 25%.

The growing number of young black men with only a tenuous connection to the labor market, especially those with limited formal schooling, are believed to make up a major part of the nation's urban underclass, or what William Julius Wilson has referred to as "the truly disadvantaged."[28] The deteriorating economic plight of poorly educated, young black men has become a widespread phenomenon.[29]

The rise in the proportion of young adult men with no reported earnings was also strongly associated with the years of formal schooling that they had completed. Among high school dropouts, the proportion of young adult men with zero earnings more than doubled between 1973 and 1986, rising from slightly under 8% to over 16%. Among high school graduates, the ratio increased by two percentage points, or 56%, while the estimated fraction of male college graduates with no reported earnings rose by less than one full percentage point. During 1986, young male high school dropouts were nearly three times more likely than high school graduates to report zero earnings and were five times more likely to do so than college graduates. These strong associations between formal schooling and the likelihood of reporting zero earnings held true for all ethnic groups.

Influence of Shifts in the Industrial Structure

The increasing fraction of young adult men with zero earnings, the lower fraction with year-round, full-time employment, and lower annual earnings among those employed year-round, full-time have been driven by a number of factors. During the past 30 years, the U.S. economy has continued to transform its industrial employment structure from goods-producing to service-producing industries. Although in one sense these trends simply represent a continuation of a longer historical process, a more careful review of available evidence suggests that the pace of change has accelerated in recent years.

The loss in manufacturing employment, especially during the 1980s, combined with the rapid growth in the retail trade and service industries, has had a greater relative impact on the industrial distribution of the jobs held by young men as opposed to older men. This should have been expected, given the fact that older males with a foothold in the manufacturing sector would have greater seniority protections against hiring freezes or layoffs. Older males would only be affected by these industrial transformations if major reductions in force occurred or their plant was completely shut down. Younger males seeking full-time, career-oriented employment would find fewer available openings in manufacturing and, hence, would be required to seek jobs in other industries experiencing employment growth.

The "deindustrialization" of the United States, as represented by absolute declines in the level of manufacturing employment, can thus be expected to have relatively greater impact on the industrial distribution of the jobs held by young male adults.[30]. The magnitude of these shifts in employment can be illustrated by the changing industrial distribution of jobs held by employed males 18–29 years old and 30–62 years old in 1973 and 1986 (see Table 2.14).[31] During 1973, some 28% of all employed 18- to 29-year-old males worked in manufacturing industries, with durable manufacturing (autos, steel, primary and fabricated metal, electrical equipment, etc.) alone accounting for nearly one of every five jobs held by young adult men. The proportion of young adult men holding jobs in the manufacturing sector during 1973 was nearly identical to that of men in the 30–62 age group (28% versus 30%).

Between 1973 and 1986, the share of young males employed in manufacturing fell sharply, with only 19% of young adult males working in manufacturing industries by 1986. Relative losses in durable manufacturing were most severe, with a drop from 18 of 100 employed young men to only 12 of 100. Given their reduced access to jobs in manufacturing, transportation/communications, and public administration, young men had to seek jobs elsewhere and were largely absorbed by firms in the retail trade and service industries. During 1973, the fraction of young male adults employed in manufacturing was not far below that of trade and service industries combined (28% versus 35%). By 1986, the share of young adult men working in retail trade and services had risen to nearly 44%, a ratio more than twice as high as the share in manufacturing.

The impacts of industrial change in the U.S. economy have been far from

Table 2.14. **Percentage Distribution of Civilian Males, by Major Industry of Longest Job Held During Year, by Age Subgroup, United States, 1973 and 1986**

	Age 18–29		Age 30–62	
	1973	1986	1973	1986
Farming, Forestry, Fishing, Mining	5.5%	5.7%	6.4%	5.3%
Construction	11.7	12.9	10.6	11.0
Manufacturing, All	28.0	19.2	30.2	25.0
Durable Manufacturing	18.1	11.7	19.4	16.6
Nondurable Manufacturing	9.9	7.5	10.8	8.4
Transportation, Communications, Utilities	7.0	6.5	9.4	10.6
Wholesale Trade	4.5	4.8	4.9	5.4
Retail Trade	17.6	22.2	10.6	9.9
Finance, Insurance, Real Estate	3.5	3.5	4.4	5.0
Services	17.8	21.4	16.7	21.9
Public Administration	4.3	3.7	6.8	5.9
Total	100.0	100.0	100.0	100.0

Source: 1985 NAEP Young Adult Literacy Assessment.

uniform across major subgroups of young male adults (see Table 2.15). The share of employed 18- to 29-year-old males working in manufacturing industries fell by nearly one-third between 1973 and 1986. The relative sizes of these declines were higher for younger males (18–24), for blacks, and for men with 12 or fewer years of schooling.[32] Among employed blacks, 36% held a job in a manufacturing firm in 1973. By 1986, this share had declined to 20%, representing a 43% reduction in the relative importance of manufacturing as a source of jobs for young black males. These reductions occurred at a time when the employment/population ratios of young black males were also falling; thus, the ratio of employed black males in manufacturing to the population of young black men fell even more precipitately. These industrial transformations have had particularly devastating effects on job opportunities for young black men with limited formal schooling in many of the nation's older central cities.[33]

The declines in the shares of young males employed in manufacturing were most pronounced for high school dropouts and high school graduates with no post-secondary schooling. The shares of young male dropouts and graduates employed in manufacturing jobs fell by more than one-third between 1973 and 1986. In sharp contrast, the share of young male college graduates employed in manufacturing is estimated to have increased by 1.2 percentage points, or 7%, over the same period. The employment growth of high-technology manufacturing industries that use college-educated personnel (engineers, technicians, managers, computer scientists, and systems analysts) at above average rates,

Table 2.15. **Share of 18- to 29-Year-Old Civilian Males Holding Jobs in Manufacturing Industries, by Age Subgroup, Ethnic Group, and Educational Attainment, United States, 1973 and 1986 (Numbers in 1000s)**

Group	1973	1986	Absolute Change 1973–86	Percentage Change 1973–86
All, 18–29	28.0%	19.2%	− 8.8	− 31.4%
Age Group				
18–19	22.3	11.3	− 11.0	− 49.3
20–24	28.4	18.2	− 10.2	− 35.9
25–29	29.9	22.1	− 7.8	− 26.1
Ethnic Group				
White, non-Hispanic	27.0	18.8	− 8.2	− 30.4
Black, non-Hispanic	35.9	20.4	− 15.5	− 43.2
Hispanic	30.0	19.4	− 10.6	− 35.3
Educational Attainment*				
H.S. Dropouts	35.3	23.1	− 12.2	− 34.6
H.S. Graduates	34.3	21.9	− 12.4	− 36.2
Some College	24.6	17.3	− 7.3	− 29.7
College Graduates	17.9	19.1	+ 1.2	+ 6.7

*Young men citing "school" as their major activity during the reference week are excluded from the subgroups below.

Source: 1985 NAEP Young Adult Literacy Assessment.

and technological changes in other manufacturing industries favoring the employment of more highly educated workers, have been key factors influencing this development.[34] The changing occupational mix of U.S. manufacturing industries and the far more rapid growth of service and finance industries have improved employment and real earnings prospects for young college-educated males at a rate well above that for their less educated counterparts during the 1980s.

Annual Earnings by Industrial Sector

The loss of manufacturing job opportunities for young adult men, especially for those with 12 or fewer years of schooling, has had a particularly adverse impact on their real earnings position over the past 13 years, particularly when the local economies in which they reside have failed to generate a new economic base to replace that formerly occupied by manufacturing. As Darryl Swafford, a young black man raised in the once vibrant but now economically depressed steel city of Gary, Indiana, remarked to a *Time* magazine reporter:

"I always had that goal, working in the mill. Have a home, a big car. But now there's no mill and I'm down. Just trying to make it, trying to survive."[35]

The shifts in the industrial structure of job opportunities available to young males would not have any major economic or social consequence if the annual earnings of young men did not vary systematically by industrial sector. Interindustry differences in the annual earnings of young adult men, however, have traditionally been fairly large and appear to have been widening in key areas in recent years (see Table 2.16).[36]

Table 2.16. **Absolute Mean Real and Relative Annual Earnings of Employed 20- to 29-Year-Old Civilian Males, by Industry of Longest Job Held During Year, 1973 and 1986 (in 1986 Dollars)**

	1973 Mean Earnings	1986 Mean Earnings	Percentage Change	1973 Relative Earnings	1986 Relative Earnings
All, Employed Only	$17,676	$14,643	−17.2%	1.000	1.000
Farming, Forestry, Fishing, Mining	13,490	10,806	−19.9	0.763	0.738
Construction	17,558	14,201	−19.1	0.993	0.970
Manufacturing, All	18,955	17,179	−9.4	1.072	1.173
Durable Manufacturing	19,327	17,830	−7.7	1.093	1.218
Nondurable Manufacturing	18,255	16,123	−11.7	1.033	1.101
Transportation, Communications, Utilities	20,489	18,539	−9.5	1.159	1.266
Wholesale Trade	20,101	17,290	−14.0	1.137	1.181
Retail Trade	15,177	11,991	−21.0	0.859	0.819
Finance, Insurance, Real Estate	21,036	19,060	−9.4	1.190	1.302
Services	15,395	12,861	−16.5	0.871	0.878
Public Administration	21,137	16,757	−20.7	1.196	1.144

Source: 1985 NAEP Young Adult Literacy Assessment.

During 1973, the mean real annual earnings of young male adults (20–29 years of age) employed in manufacturing industries were $19,000. In comparison, the mean real annual earnings of young male adults employed in the retail trade or service industries were slightly above $15,000. Between 1973 and 1986, the mean real annual earnings of all employed 20–29 year old males plummeted by about 17%. Those young adult males who were employed in manufacturing industries during 1986 fared better than their counterparts in other sectors, especially retail trade and service industries, in maintaining real annual earnings relative to these 1973 levels.

As a result of these differential trends, the size of the annual earnings advantages of employed males in manufacturing widened relative to those in retail trade and services. For example, during 1986, the mean earnings level of young males employed in durable manufacturing industries was $17,830. This figure exceeded the mean earnings of males in retail trade industries by 49% and the mean earnings of those in service industries by 39%. Young males employed in non-durable manufacturing industries obtained mean earnings that were 35% above those employed in retail trade industries and 25% above those working in the nation's service industries.

The relative size of the annual earnings differentials between young males employed in manufacturing and those employed in retail trade and services are quite large for men in each major ethnic and educational group, and they have widened over time. During 1986, young white, non-Hispanic males employed in durable manufacturing industries had mean annual earnings that were 48% above those earned by their counterparts in retail trade and 36% above those in service industries. Black, non-Hispanic and Hispanic males working in durable manufacturing industries outearned their peers in retail trade by 51% and 35%, respectively. Young male dropouts and those with only a high school diploma who worked in durable manufacturing industries during 1986 earned substantially more than those working in either retail trade or services. The relative difference in annual earnings between those in durable manufacturing and those in retail trade was 28% for high school dropouts and 29% for high school graduates; the corresponding differences between manufacturing and services were 52% and 36%.

The annual earnings advantages of young males working in the nation's manufacturing industries reflect a variety of factors. On the one hand, the occupational mix of jobs in durable manufacturing industries is quite different from that in retail trade or service industries. Different types of work are performed in these industries, and different behavioral, manual, technical, and intellectual skills are needed to carry out these duties.

For many semiskilled operative and craft positions within manufacturing industries, skills acquisition typically involves a substantial amount of informal on-the-job training in which skills are acquired through actual production experience and through movement among a hierarchy of jobs in an internal career ladder over the working life.[37] These on-the-job training investments, coupled with greater capital intensity and a greater likelihood of union representation, allowed workers in manufacturing to secure higher earnings and more remunerative fringe benefit packages over their working lives.

Policy Implications

The continuing decline in the number of young adults entering the labor force provides a unique demographic window of opportunity for the implementation of a set of human resource programs capable of addressing the serious labor market problems that have been experienced by young adult males over the past 15 years. Given the diverse nature and causes of the employment and real earnings problems of young adult males, especially those with no post-secondary schooling, a comprehensive workforce preparedness strategy must be capable of providing an array of services over the working lives of these young men.

Substantive workforce preparation for the non–college-bound must begin in the high school years (the academic skills for labor market success need to be built from early childhood on). These preparedness activities should involve combinations of employability skills training in high school and sustained, in-school work experience in the unsubsidized job market. Responsibilities for these activities must be shared by the schools, the private sector, local employment and training programs, and the students themselves.

The Boston Compact provides one example of such an in-school, work preparedness strategy.[38] The local business community is responsible for organizing jobs for students during the school year and the summer; schools are responsible for improving the attendance and basic academic skills of students; and career specialists funded by the local Private Industry Council with monies available under the Job Training Partnership Act provide employability skills training, job placement assistance, and follow-up support services.

Because minorities and poor youths make up an ever-increasing percentage of high school students, the establishment of in-school work preparedness programs is essential. Although a rising fraction of high school students have become employed in recent years, minority youth and poor youth tend to be employed at rates well below the average for white middle-class youths.[39] Organizing access to jobs during the high school years is thus critical to efforts to improve the employment status of minority and economically disadvantaged youth. The availability of the job development, placement, and follow-up services of school-based career/job specialists is also indispensable to the labor market success of minority and disadvantaged youths in the early school-leaving period. Such youths frequently need the labor market brokering services that are traditionally provided by family, friends, and relatives in the white middle- and upper-income community.

Facilitating the transition of the non–college-bound from high school to the world of work should be an essential element of a comprehensive workforce preparedness strategy. However, these placement efforts will need to be supplemented by a series of expanded apprenticeship and structured, employer-oriented training programs for such youths during their young adult years.

Apprenticeship training, for example, has been found to be an effective way of improving the skills, knowledge, productivity, and earnings of young adults in the United States and in many other countries.[40] It is also an effective mechanism for facilitating the work socialization process for young adults.[41] The combination of on-the-job training, close supervision, and off-site related instruction typically provided by apprenticeship is particularly well suited for improving the work behavior, skills, and knowledge of our newest labor force entrants.

However, even during its peak enrollment year (1979), the registered apprenticeship system was overwhelmingly concentrated in construction (58%) and manufacturing (22%) industries. Within the rapidly growing retail trade and private service industries, registered apprentices accounted for only 5 of every 10,000 and 12 of every 10,000 wage and salary workers, respectively, during 1979. Extending this training model to a wide range of industries, especially many trade and private service industries whose productivity performance has been quite dismal over the past decade, would be an important addition to workforce preparedness programs.

Unfortunately, the nation's formal apprenticeship system has been substantially neglected over the past decade. The number of registered apprentices in training at the end of the year declined from 320,000 in 1979 and 1980 to 223,000 in 1985.[42] Over the past two years, the number of registered apprentices (excluding the armed forces) has increased, but the total number of apprentices in 1987 still remains 80,000 below the peak 1979 level. During the past three years, the annual number of registered apprentices has been equal to only 0.23% of total employment in the nation's nonagricultural industries, the lowest fraction since the end of World War II.

As a consequence of the declining number of apprenticeship openings, the share of new high school graduates going on to apprenticeship training has been abysmally low. Findings of a national longitudinal tracking of a representative sample of high school graduates from the class of 1980 indicated that fewer than 4% of the graduates were participating in some form of apprenticeship training in the first year following graduation and only 1 to 2% were doing so in the third follow-up year.[43] Only 1% of black and Hispanic high school graduates and those from low socioeconomic backgrounds were participating in an apprenticeship training program three years after graduation. This is far less then the proportion of young high school leavers entering apprenticeships in such Western European countries as West Germany, Austria, and Switzerland.[44]

The U.S. Department of Labor has shown renewed interest in apprenticeship training with the establishment of the Apprenticeship 2000 Initiative. A recent survey undertaken by the Apprenticeship 2000 Initiative revealed a high level of support for an expansion of the existing apprenticeship system to a broader array of industries and occupations.[45]

Research on the earnings experiences of young adult males also indicates an important role for company-sponsored training (both on and off the job) and for vocational/technical training programs attuned to the specific employment needs of industry.[46] Although the track record of classroom-oriented vocational training programs is somewhat mixed, especially for secondary school graduates, research evidence during the 1980s suggests that such training can benefit workers and employers when the jobs obtained by graduates make effective use of the training received in the classroom.[47]

The nation's community colleges have begun to play a more active role in promoting cooperative education programs that tie classroom training more closely to the training needs of employers.[48] A number of innovative national education programs have been developed in this area. Among these are the Ford Access program, which links franchise car dealers with community colleges to develop more highly skilled and technically competent automotive technicians through a sequenced set of on-the-job and classroom training activities.

Expansion of such apprenticeship, cooperative education, and structured training programs can play a key role in improving the employment and earnings position of young men not going on to college. Exposing young adults in the early school-leaving period to a more diverse array of jobs and training opportunities can also promote the socialization process and possibly reduce the often socially destructive behavior (crime, drug use, fathering children out of wedlock) accompanying the recent extended period of economic adolescence for non–college-bound youth.[49]

Detailed knowledge of the specific contributions that external and internal training programs can make in increasing the productivity of workers in specific industries is not currently available, even though it is sorely needed to inform current and future public policy. Recent research on the impact of unions on labor productivity has revealed that these contributions are not uniform across industries, but instead depend on a variety of factors, including the nature of the relationships between labor and management.[50] In response to such findings, Thomas Kochan has argued that industrial relations research needs "to examine more closely the determinants of successful productivity increase."[51]

Similar remarks apply to the areas of job-related education, training, and apprenticeship for young adults. If training programs for young adults in "shortage" occupations and growth industries are to be successful and replicable on a relatively large-scale basis, then a more comprehensive information base on such programs needs to be established. Such an information base would document the nature of private sector involvement with successful programs, the role of private/public partnerships in the development of such programs, the importance of management views and policies on training, and the degree of involvement in such training efforts by unions and employee associations.[52] This kind of information is critical if business, labor, and government are to learn from ongoing experience how to design and manage a better public-private workforce preparedness system.

Notes

*This chapter is primarily the responsibility of Andrew M. Sum and W. Neal Fogg.
Partial support was provided by the Ford Foundation.*

1. An analysis of the changing labor market situation for young adult women is much more complicated as a result of continuing changes in their degree of attachment to the labor force. In contrast to the generally deteriorating fortunes of young adult males over the 1973–86 period, the mean annual real earnings of all 20- to 29-year-old women in the United States increased by 26%, mainly as a result of increased weeks and hours of employment. See Andrew Sum and Neal Fogg, "Trends in the Real Annual Earnings of Young Adult Women, 1967–1986," Research Paper submitted to the Ford Foundation, Center for Labor Market Studies, Northeastern University, Boston, 1988.

2. Andrew Sum, Paul Harrington, and William Goedicke, "One-Fifth of the Nation's Teenagers: Employment Problems of Poor Youth in America, 1981–1985," *Youth and Society* 18 (March 1987): 195–237.

3. William B. Johnston and Arnold E. Packer, *Workforce 2000: Work and Workers for the Twenty-First Century* (Indianapolis: Hudson Institute, 1987).

4. *Washington Post*, November 20, 1986; Spencer Rich, "The End of Upward Mobility," *Washington Post National Weekly Edition*, June 13–19, 1988, pp. 6–7.

5. David T. Kearns and Denis P. Doyle, *Winning the Brain Race: A Bold Plan to Make Our Schools Competitive* (San Francisco: Institute for Contemporary Studies, 1988), p. 4.

6. The estimated growth in the number of race/ethnic minorities appearing in Table 2.3 is 819,000, or 87% of the total projected growth in the population of 18- to 24-year-olds between 1995 and 2000. This figure is, however, slightly biased upward because Hispanics can also be included in the count of racial minority groups, including blacks and others. Our analysis of recent Census Bureau data for March 1987 indicated that approximately 97 of every 100 Hispanic young adults in the United States were classified as white. If a similar ratio holds true in 1995 and 2000, then only 84% of the net change in the population of 18- to 24-year-olds would be attributable to growth in race/ethnic minority groups.

7. For a more detailed analysis of the changing labor market fortunes of young men with no post-secondary education in the United States, see William T. Grant Foundation Commission on Work, Family and Citizenship, *The Forgotten Half: Non-College Youth in America* (Washington, D.C.: The Commission, 1988); and Andrew Sum, Neal Fogg, and Robert Taggart, *Withered Dreams: The Decline in the Economic Fortunes of Young Non-College Educated Male Adults and Their Families*, Report Prepared for the W.T. Grant Foundation Commission on Work, Family and Citizenship, Center for Labor Market Studies, Northeastern University, Boston, April 1988.

8. For a review of the evidence on the relationships between the family living arrangements of children and their poverty status during childhood, see David Ellwood, *Divide and Conquer: Responsible Security for America's Poor* (New York: Ford Foundation Project on Social Welfare and the American Future, Occasional Paper No. 2, 1987); and David Ellwood, *Poor Support: Poverty in the American Family* (New York: Basic Books, 1988).

9. A recent 10-year longitudinal analysis of the "persistent poor" has revealed that children are most likely to be members of America's long-term urban poverty popula-

tion, accounting for 45% of all of the persistent poor in urban areas. See Terry K. Adams and Greg J. Duncan, *The Persistence of Urban Poverty and Its Demographic and Behavioral Correlates*, Survey Research Center, University of Michigan, Ann Arbor, March 1988.

10. For a more detailed account, see Andrew Sum, Paul Harrington, and William Goedicke, *Basic Skills of America's Teens and Young Adults: Findings of the 1980 National ASVAB Testing and Their Implications for Education, Employment, and Training Policies and Programs*, Center for Labor Market Studies, Northeastern University, Boston, 1986; and Gordon Berlin and Andrew Sum, *Toward a More Perfect Union: Basic Skills, Poor Families, and Our Economic Future* (New York: Ford Foundation Project on Social Welfare and the American Future, Occasional Paper No. 3, 1988).

11. Berlin and Sum, *Toward a More Perfect Union*; Sum, Harrington, and Goedicke, "One-Fifth of the Nation's Teenagers."

12. Andrew Sum, Neal Fogg, and William Goedicke, *The Economic and Social Consequences of Poor Basic Skills Among Teens and Young Adults in the U.S.*, Paper Presented to the CCP Second Annual Conference, San Antonio, October 1987.

13. Sum, Harrington, and Goedicke, *Basic Skills of America's Teens and Young Adults*.

14. The purposes and design of the Young Adult Literacy Assessment are described in Irwin S. Kirsch and Ann Jungeblut, *Literacy: Profiles of America's Young Adults* (Princeton, N.J.: Educational Testing Service, National Assessment of Educational Progress, 1986). For a review of the implications of the findings of the NAEP young adult literacy assessment for education, employment, and training programs, see Richard L. Venezky, Carl F. Kaestle, and Andrew M. Sum, *The Subtle Danger: Reflections on the Literacy Abilities of America's Young Adults* (Princeton, N.J.: Educational Testing Service, Center for the Assessment of Educational Progress, January 1987).

15. For a more in-depth analysis of the literacy problems of poor young adults, see Andrew Sum, "Poverty/Near Poverty Problems and Literacy Proficiencies of Young Adults," Center for Labor Market Studies, Northeastern University, Boston, August 1986; and Berlin and Sum, *Toward a More Perfect Union*.

16. For an examination of the relationship between the real earnings of young adult men and their marriage behavior, see Clifford Johnson and Andrew Sum, *Declining Earnings of Young Men: Their Relation to Poverty, Teen Pregnancy, and Family Formation* (Washington, D.C.: Children's Defense Fund, May 1987); and Clifford Johnson, Andrew Sum, and James D. Weill, *Vanishing Dreams: The Growing Economic Plight of America's Young Families* (Washington, D.C.: Children's Defense Fund and Center for Labor Market Studies, 1988).

17. William T. Grant Foundation Commission on Work, Family, and Citizenship, *The Forgotten Half*. In 1985, *Business Week* devoted its cover story to the employment problems of minority youth, who were referred to as "Forgotten Americans." See "The Forgotten Americans: Minority Joblessness Is Stubbornly High—But There Are Ways to Help," *Business Week*, September 5, 1985, pp. 50–55.

18. For examples of such studies on youth employment problems, see Michael Borus, "A Description of Employed and Unemployed Youth in 1981," in *Youth and the Labor Market: Analyses of the National Longitudinal Surveys* (Kalamazoo, Mich.: Upjohn Institute for Employment Research, 1984), pp. 13–56; Andrew Hahn and Robert Lerman, *What Works in Youth Employment Policy?* (Washington, D.C.: Com-

mittee on New American Realities, 1985); Robert Meyer and David Wise, "High School Preparation and Early Labor Market Experience," in *The Youth Labor Market Problem: Its Nature, Causes, and Consequences* (Chicago: University of Chicago Press, 1982), pp. 277–347; and Albert Rees, "An Essay on Youth Joblessness," *Journal of Economic Literature* 24 (June 1986): 613–628.

19. For a more comprehensive, historical assessment of the employment and earnings experiences of young male adults over the 1960–1986 period, see Sum, Fogg, and Taggart, *Withered Dreams*.

20. In fact, the relative earnings gap between young male college graduates and high school graduates narrowed during the early to mid-1970s as a result of a combination of less favorable demand and supply developments in the college labor market. See Richard B. Freeman, *The Overeducated American* (New York: Academic Press, 1976).

21. Nominal earnings were converted into their real dollar equivalents with the use of the Consumer Price Index for All Urban Consumers (CPI-U). The CPI-U is the price index used by the Bureau of the Census to convert personal and family money incomes into their real income equivalents and to update family poverty income thresholds on an annual basis. The Bureau of Labor Statistics also uses the CPI-U index to convert nominal wages into their real wage equivalents. Two alternative price indices that have been used in other studies of trends in earnings and incomes are the CPI-X and the price deflator for Personal Consumption Expenditures in the GNP accounts. Use of the latter two price indices instead of the CPI-U would yield 1986 real earnings approximately 7% above those generated through use of the CPI-U index. For further discussions of the use of these different price indices, see Congressional Budget Office, *Trends in Family Income: 1970–1986* (Washington, D.C.: U.S. Government Printing Office, 1988); and Bennett Harrison and Barry Bluestone, *The Great U-Turn: Corporate Restructuring and the Polarizing of America* (New York: Basic Books, 1988).

22. The percentage declines for each of the three age subgroups exceeded that for all 18- to 29-year-olds combined. This result is not due to any computational errors, but instead is attributable to the fact that the average age of 18- to 29-year-old men in 1986 was higher than their average age in 1973 due to the aging of the baby-boom cohorts. Real earnings of young men rise fairly substantially with age; thus, the mean for all 18- to 29-year-old males in 1986 captures the higher earnings of these slightly older males.

23. The term high school dropout is used to represent all persons whose major activity was not school in March of each survey year, who completed fewer than 12 years of formal schooling, and who do not possess a General Educational Development (GED) certificate. A small fraction (under 15%) of the subgroup of males categorized as high school dropouts actually completed eight or fewer years of school.

24. For descriptions of these various stages in the early working life cycle, see Paul E. Barton and Bryna Shore Frazer, *Between Two Worlds—Youth Transition from School to Work* (Washington, D.C.: U.S. Government Printing Office, Youth Knowledge Development Report 2.3, April 1980); Marcia Freedman, "The Youth Labor Market," in *From School to Work: Improving the Transition* (Washington, D.C.: U.S. Government Printing Office, 1976), pp. 21–36; and Paul Osterman, *Getting Started: The Youth Labor Market* (Cambridge, Mass.: MIT Press, 1980).

25. Sum, Fogg, and Taggart, *Withered Dreams*.

26. Trends in the marriage rates of young men are described and assessed in Johnson and Sum, *Declining Earnings of Young Men*, and Sum, Fogg, and Taggart, *Withered Dreams*. An analysis of trends in family homeownership rates can be found in the following publications: William C. Apgar and James H. Brown, *State of the*

Nation's Housing 1988 (Cambridge, Mass.: Joint Center for Housing Studies of Harvard University, 1988); and Johnson, Sum, and Weill, *Vanishing Dreams*.

27. U.S. Bureau of the Census, *Statistical Abstract of the United States, 1988* (Washington, D.C.: U.S. Government Printing Office, 1987), Table 1215, p. 685.

28. William Julius Wilson, *The Truly Disadvantaged* (Chicago: University of Chicago Press, 1987).

29. Sylvester Monroe, "Blacks in Britain: Grim Lives, Grimmer Prospects," *Newsweek*, January 4, 1988, p. 32.

30. Due to higher than average productivity growth, the manufacturing sector's share of gross domestic output has not fallen to the same extent that employment has. The oft-repeated claims that the goods-producing sector or the manufacturing sector's share of gross domestic output has been relatively constant over time, however, have been shown to be clearly misplaced. See Johnston and Packer, *Workforce 2000*. For a review of the issues and positions in the deindustrialization debate, see Barry Bluestone and Bennett Harrison, *The Deindustrialization of America: Plant Closings, Community Abandonment, and the Dismantling of Basic Industry* (New York: Basic Books, 1982); Robert Z. Lawrence, *Can America Compete?* (Washington, D.C.: Brookings Institution, 1984); Richard B. McKenzie, *Competing Visions: The Political Conflict over America's Economic Future* (Washington, D.C.: Cato Institute, 1985); and Lester Thurow, *The Zero-Sum Solution: An Economic and Political Agenda for the 1980s* (New York: Simon & Schuster, 1985).

31. The data appearing in this table refer to the industries of the "longest job" held by an employed person during the calendar year. The March CPS surveys capture this information on prior year employment experiences on a retrospective basis. The CPS coding procedures for industry employment classify government workers into industries on the basis of the work their agencies perform rather than lumping them into a general "all government" category. For example, a person working in a public high school will be classified into the educational services industry rather than into government.

32. Firms in the finance/insurance and private service industries have been the dominant employers of young male college graduates in the United States in recent decades, employing nearly 50% of them in both 1973 and 1986.

33. Johnson and Sum, *Declining Earnings of Young Men*; John Kasarda, "Urban Change and Minority Opportunities," in Paul Peterson (Ed.), *The New Urban Reality* (Washington, D.C.: Brookings Institution, 1985), pp. 33–67; John Kasarda, "Contemporary U.S. Migration and Urban Demographic-Job Opportunity Mismatches," Paper Presented to the Joint Economic Committee, Subcommittee on Economic Resources, Competitiveness, and Security Economics, September 1986; William Julius Wilson and Kathryn M. Neckerman, "Poverty and Family Structure: The Widening Gap Between Evidence and Public Policy Issues," in Sheldon H. Danziger and Daniel Weinberg (Eds.), *Fighting Poverty: What Works and What Doesn't* (Cambridge, Mass.: Harvard University Press, 1987), pp. 232–259.

34. For a review of the conceptual issues involved in defining high technology industries and the occupational staffing patterns of such industries in Massachusetts and the United States, see Paul E. Harrington, Marilyn Boyle, and Andrew Sum, *High Technology Careers in Massachusetts* (Boston: Massachusetts Division of Employment Security, 1987); Andrew Sum, Paul E. Harrington, and Gustav Schachter, "High Technology Industries in Massachusetts: An Analysis of Worker Earnings Levels and Their Distribution," Paper Prepared for the New England Business and Economic Development Conference, Lowell, 1986; and Richard W. Riche, Daniel E. Hecker, and

John V. Burgan, "High Technology Today and Tomorrow: A Small Slice of the Employment Pie," *Monthly Labor Review* 106 (November 1983): 50–58.

35. "Today's Native Sons," *Time*, December 1, 1986, p. 28.

36. For a review of recent evidence on rising wage inequality among U.S. workers in recent years and alternative explanations for such increasing dispersion, see Bennett Harrison, Chris Tilly, and Barry Bluestone, "Wage Inequality Takes a Great U-Turn," *Challenge*, March–April 1986, pp. 26–32; Harrison and Bluestone, *Great U-Turn*; Linda A. Bell and Richard B. Freeman, "The Facts About Rising Industrial Wage Dispersion in the U.S.," *IRRA 39th Annual Proceedings*, Madison, Wisc., 1987, pp. 331–337; Chris Tilly, Barry Bluestone, and Bennett Harrison, "What Is Making American Wages More Unequal?" *IRRA 39th Annual Proceedings*, Madison, Wisc., pp. 338–348.

37. Peter Doeringer and Michael J. Piore, *Internal Labor Markets and Manpower Analysis* (Lexington, Mass.: D.C. Heath and Company, 1973).

38. William J. Spring, "Youth Unemployment and the Transition from School to Work," *New England Economic Review*, March–April 1987, pp. 3–16; The Boston Private Industry Council, Inc., *The Class of 1987: A Followup Survey*, Boston, January 1988; William T. Grant Foundation Commission on Work, Family, and Citizenship, *The Forgotten Half*.

39. For a review of the employment problems of young high school graduates and young dropouts in the early school-leaving period, see Sharon R. Cohany, "What Happened to the High School Class of 1985?" *Monthly Labor Review*, October 1986, pp. 28–30; Sum, Harrington, and Goedicke, "One-Fifth of the Nation's Teenagers"; and James P. Markey, "The Labor Market Problems of Today's High School Dropouts," *Monthly Labor Review*, June 1988, pp. 36–43.

40. Stephen M. Hills, "How Craftsmen Learn Their Skills: A Longitudinal Analysis," in Robert E. Taylor, Howard Rosen, and Frank C. Pratzner (Eds.), *Job Training for Youth* (Columbus, Ohio: National Center for Research in Vocational Education, Ohio State University, 1982), pp. 201–239; Robert W. Glover, "American Apprenticeship and Disadvantaged Youth," in *Job Training for Youth*, pp. 165–201; Ray Marshall and Robert Glover, *Training and Entry into Union Construction* (Washington, D.C.: U.S. Department of Labor, R & D Monograph No. 34, U.S. Government Printing Office, 1975); Ernest Green, "Apprenticeship: A Potential Weapon Against Minority Youth Unemployment," in *From School to Work: Improving the Transition* (Washington, D.C.: U.S. Government Printing Office, 1977), pp. 201–226.

41. Stephen F. Hamilton, "Work and Maturity: Occupational Socialization of Non-College Youth in the United States and West Germany," *Research in the Sociology of Education and Socialization* 7 (1987): 283–312.

42. U.S. Department of Labor, Employment and Training Administration, *Training and Employment Report of the Secretary of Labor* (Washington, D.C.: U.S. Government Printing Office, 1988); U.S. Department of Labor, Bureau of Labor Statistics, *Employment and Earnings*, January 1988.

43. Calvin C. Jones, Susan Campbell, and Penny A. Sebring, *Four Years After High School: A Capsule Description of 1980 Seniors*, Report Prepared for the Center for Statistics, U.S. Department of Education, U.S. Government Printing Office, Washington, D.C., August 1986.

44. Stephen F. Hamilton, *Adolescent Problem Behavior in the United States and the Federal Republic of Germany: Implications for Prevention* (Washington, D.C.: William T. Grant Foundation Project on Youth and the Future, 1987); Beatrice G. Reubens, *Apprenticeship in Foreign Countries* (Washington, D.C.: U.S. Department of

Labor R & D Monograph No. 77, U.S. Government Printing Office, 1980); Spring, "Youth Unemployment."

45. U.S. Department of Labor, Bureau of Apprenticeship and Training, *Apprenticeship 2000: The Public Speaks* (Washington, D.C., 1988); U.S. Department of Labor and U.S. Department of Health and Human Services, *Employment and Training Report of the President* (Washington, D.C.: U.S. Government Printing Office, 1981).

46. John L. Iacobelli and S. Ray Schultz, "Earnings Impact of Employment and Training Programs for Young Men," *Growth and Change* 10 (4) 1979: 32–37; Steven L. Mangum and Arvil V. Adams, "The Labor Market Impacts of Post-School Occupational Training for Young Men," *Growth and Change*, Fall 1987, pp. 57–73.

47. Andrew Sum, "The Labor Market Impacts of Vocational Education Programs in the United States," in Gustav Schachter (Ed.), *Brazil: Vocational Education, Aspects of Economic Policy and Planning* (Boston: Center for International Higher Education Documentation, Northeastern University, 1985), pp. 112–145; Thomas N. Daymont and Russell Rumberger, "The Impact of High School Curriculum on the Earnings and Employability of Youth," in *Job Training for Youth*, pp. 279–305; John H. Bishop, *The Social Payoff from Occupationally Specific Training: The Employer's Point of View* (Columbus, Ohio: National Center for Research in Vocational Education, Ohio State University, 1983).

48. Dale Parnell, *The Neglected Majority* (Washington, D.C.: Community College Press, 1985); Ford Motor Company, *Asset Is the Answer*, undated.

49. Hamilton, "Work and Maturity"; Arvil V. Adams, "The Stock of Human Capital and Differences in Post-School Formal Occupational Training for Middle-Aged Men," *Southern Economic Journal*, April 1978, pp. 929–936; Berlin and Sum, *Toward a More Perfect Union*; Johnson and Sum, *Declining Earnings of Young Men*.

50. Richard B. Freeman and James L. Medoff, "The Two Faces of Unionism," *The Public Interest*, Fall 1979, pp. 69–93; Richard B. Freeman and James L. Medoff, "Trade Unions and Productivity: Some New Evidence on an Old Issue," unpublished National Bureau of Economic Research Working Paper, Cambridge, Mass., October 1983.

51. Thomas A. Kochan, "Industrial Relations Research: An Agenda for the 1980's," *Monthly Labor Review*, September 1980, p. 22.

52. Robert E. Taylor, Howard Rosen, and Frank C. Pratzner (Eds.), *Responsiveness of Training Institutions to Changing Labor Market Demands* (Columbus, Ohio: National Center for Research in Vocational Education, Ohio State University, 1983); Patricia Flynn, "Production Life Cycles and Their Implications for Education and Training," Report Prepared for National Institute of Education, Washington, D.C., February 1984; Patricia Flynn, *Facilitating Technological Change* (Cambridge: Ballinger, 1987); Johnston and Packer, *Workforce 2000*.

3

Labor Displacement in the United States

Dynamic economies engage in a process Schumpeter has described as "creative destruction."[1] New enterprises are continually forming while old ones disappear. Within existing companies, production processes change, organizations evolve, and labor requirements adapt to an ever-shifting marketplace. In the last two decades, international competition has intensified pressure, and, now more than ever, long-term economic success requires that firms respond to flux and strive to achieve ever-changing goals. Substantial changes in labor force patterns and population demographics have further modified work practices and norms of corporate behavior.

Two inevitable consequences of creative destruction are that jobs disappear and, in some cases, workers are displaced from companies. Advances in manufacturing, materials, transportation, and telecommunication technologies have led to increasing rates of structural change, while international competition, mergers, and leveraged buyouts have added pressure for downsizing and increased the use of temporary and subcontracted labor. These factors, combined with the secular shift of employment from manufacturing to services, have led to a rise in the number of economically dislocated workers.

At the same time that the risk of displacement has been increasing, the ability of workers to find comparable new jobs has become more uncertain. In the early 1980s, the economy was buffeted by back-to-back recessions of a severity unparalleled since the Great Depression. The subsequent recovery, which now has lasted eight years, has been fairly strong but quite uneven. Although unemployment rates are low on both coasts, they remain near recession levels throughout much of the rest of the country. Total employment has increased and the national unemployment rate is about two percentage points below its 1980 level; however, manufacturing employment continues to be stagnant, even in many economically healthy states.

The public and private sectors attempt to assist displaced workers in ways that both complement and depend on each other. The particular approaches chosen vary with the institutional setting. For example, in Japan, large corporations guarantee "lifetime" employment to approximately a third of the workforce, with the other two-thirds acting as a buffer stock, absorbing shocks in labor demand. Thus, privately provided employment security is substantial for a minority of the population (especially males under age 55), while large within-family transfers provide some measure of support to the remainder of the labor force during periods of joblessness.[2]

The tradition of lifetime employment is much weaker in most European countries, but government protection and regulation are more pervasive. Workers are frequently entitled to unemployment assistance that replaces a substantial portion of lost earnings for several years following displacement, and firms are often required to negotiate with both government and union officials before terminating employees. One cost of these protections is that employers are less willing to hire during economic expansions because of the high costs of potential subsequent terminations.[3]

To some degree, the U.S. experience differs from that of both Japan and Europe. Although stable employment was previously provided to some U.S. workers, it has never been institutionalized as in Japan, and only a few employers offer anything resembling a lifetime guarantee. Government regulations are also relatively weak. For example, unemployment insurance in the United States replaces a smaller percentage of wages and lasts for a shorter period of time than in virtually all European countries. On the other hand, the United States has relied on job creation by small enterprises to a much larger extent than either Europe or Japan. Thus, one avenue proposed for assisting displaced workers in the United States (and recently in Great Britain) is to encourage the formation of small businesses that use the expertise gained in previous employment.

Who Are Displaced Workers?

The causes and consequences of labor displacement must be understood before we can ascertain the ability of job security provisions, training programs, and direct financial assistance to mitigate the effects of economic turbulence. Displacement is a complicated process, however, and despite the attention given to problems of worker dislocation, it remains unclear when individuals should be classified as displaced. The Bureau of Labor Statistics has recently adopted a particularly problematic standard, one that excludes part-time workers and those with less than three years seniority in the pre-displacement job.[4] This criterion is unjustified for two reasons. First, it ignores more than half of all involuntarily terminated workers (those with short job tenure) and therefore provides an incorrect summary of displacement consequences.[5] Second, the standard is arbitrary and does not arise from any understanding of post-displacement adjustment patterns. Existing research provides no rationale for choosing three years as a cut-off point.[6] In addition, persons with chronically unstable employment are excluded because they fail to obtain sufficient tenure on any job.

For the purposes of this chapter, displacement is defined to include employer-initiated separations occurring for reasons unrelated to work performance or quits occurring after notice has been received that an involuntary layoff is imminent. This definition includes persons leaving employment as the result of plant closures, slack work, materials shortages, and so forth, but excludes individuals dismissed for cause.[7] This definition is quite broad in that it includes most kinds of involuntary terminations and contrasts with narrower definitions that frequently emphasize jobs lost in specific industries or occupations or persons with particular attributes (e.g., trade displaced workers). Although assistance programs may focus on groups with severe adjustment problems, it is by no means the case that all involuntarily terminated workers have such difficulties. For example, special assistance for trade displaced workers is appropriate only if they suffer significantly greater adjustment obstacles than do other dislocated individuals.

Extent of Labor Displacement

When thinking about displaced workers, we often conjure up images of unskilled and semiskilled individuals employed in mature, high-paying industries such as autos or steel, who lose jobs during recessions or as the result of plant closings and are concentrated in depressed regions. By virtue of their advanced stage in the product lifecycle and resulting relative stagnation, these sectors employ labor forces composed of disproportionately high numbers of older, high-tenure workers who are therefore expected to be especially hard hit by structural adjustment.

There is some truth to this stylized story. For example, workers in manufacturing industries and blue-collar occupations account for a disproportionate share of the dislocated. Flaim and Sehgal estimate that, between 1979 and 1983, nearly half of the persons displaced from jobs of more than three years duration left manufacturing, an industry group that employs less than a fifth of the labor force, and Horvath finds that comparable statistics for the 1981–85 period are quite similar.[8] Similarly, using the Bureau of Labor Statistics definition of displacement, operators, fabricators, and laborers had high relative incidences of displacement, as did persons living in the heavily industrialized states of the Midwest (Illinois, Indiana, Michigan, Ohio, and Wisconsin) and the Middle Atlantic region (New Jersey, New York, and Pennsylvania).

Nonetheless, virtually all individuals now face the possibility of permanent layoffs at some point in their working lives. Between 1979 and 1986, more than 2 million persons lost jobs annually as the result of plant closure or relocation, slack work, or the position or shift being abolished. Approximately one in nine jobs is destroyed each year.[9] In addition, Hamermesh provides evidence indicating that, after controlling for cyclical fluctuations, displacement rates have increased by 20% to 40% since the early 1970s.[10]

Despite the disproportionate share of jobs lost in durable goods industries, blue-collar occupations, and economically depressed regions, labor market dislocation is distributed throughout the economy. For example, of the 5.1 million workers classified as displaced by Flaim and Sehgal, 1 million left jobs in the retail sales and service sectors; 1.9 million departed from managerial, professional, technical, administrative, or sales occupations; and 260,000 were involuntarily terminated in economically healthy New England.

Nor are displacements limited to workers whose pay is relatively high. While 38% of individuals laid off between 1981 and 1986 earned more than 130% of the average private nonagricultural wage, 12% of displaced *manufacturing* workers were employed in the low-paid textile and apparel industries, and 40% of all displacements occurred in the poorly remunerated trade and service sectors.[11]

Despite the widespread image that dislocated workers have high seniority, the widely dispersed incidence of displacement implies that average length of service in hard-hit sectors plays only a small role in determining the expected tenure of displaced individuals. The widespread use of implicit or explicit policies dictating terminations in inverse order of seniority means that most dislocated workers leave jobs of relatively short duration.[12]

Rates of displacement are also surprisingly insensitive to aggregate economic conditions. For instance, an identical 2.0% of household heads lost jobs as the result of plant closings during the 1978–79 economic expansion and subsequent 1980–81 recession.[13] Two facts explain this result. First, employment reductions in some sectors will be partially or fully offset by increases in others, whatever the condition of the aggregate economy. Second, and more important, fluctuations in labor demand are much larger *within* industries or geographic regions than across the economy as a whole. Thus, gross changes in employment are much greater than *net* changes because any broadly defined sector is actually composed of a multitude of local labor markets—some growing and some declining.[14]. Further, even when total employment remains constant within a local labor market, the compositon of jobs is likely to be altered by changes in the level of technology, relative factor costs, and demand for locally produced products.

Economic Consequences of Displacement

Just as displacement occurs throughout the economy, there is a much greater diversity of adjustment experiences than is commonly realized. Most individuals suffer extensive joblessness, but a substantial proportion are reemployed at higher wages than they were paid previously.[15] Similarly, although many workers lose health insurance coverage during the period of unemployment, most regain it once they obtain new positions.[16] Unfortunately, a substantial fraction of individuals bear disproportionate adjustment burdens. For some, the result is protracted joblessness and permanent wage reductions. For others, repeated employment in chronically unstable jobs makes it impossible to ever obtain well-paid positions. These two groups are inadequately served by current policy efforts.

Joblessness

Although a few individuals are able to move directly into new employment following displacement, the vast majority are out of work for a lengthy period of time. For example, the January 1984 and January 1986 *Displaced Worker Supplements* (DWS) to the *Current Population Survey* reveal that the median worker defined as displaced by the Bureau of Labor Statistics was jobless for 24.1 and 18.3 weeks, respectively, in the one to four years following the permanent layoff and preceding the survey.[17]

The duration of joblessness depends on local and aggregate economic conditions. The average time out of work was eight weeks (44%) longer for displaced workers surveyed in 1984 than for those questioned in 1986 (when economic conditions were more robust). Similarly, a smaller percentage (60% versus 67%) were reemployed in 1984 than in 1986. Workers in depressed regions are also unemployed for longer than those in booming local labor markets. Each 1% increase in the area unemployment rate is associated with between one and nine extra weeks of joblessness, depending on the gender and occupation of the dislocated individual.[18]

These estimates understate total joblessness because they include recently displaced persons whose unemployment continues after the survey date. Five-year employment histories of workers dislocated from jobs in the early and middle 1970s indicate an average of more than seven months of unemployment following displacement.[19] Excluding the 15% who move directly into new positions, expected duration of unemployment exceeds nine months. When time out of the labor force is added in, total joblessness surpasses one year. Using fairly conservative assumptions, the cost of this time out of work is estimated at $25 billion per year for the U.S. economy.[20]

Some groups suffer even more extended post-displacement joblessness. In particular, nonwhite, nonprofessional, less educated, and unmarried individuals are unemployed longer than their counterparts.[21] Contrary to popular belief, there is little evidence that either age or job seniority is associated with extra time out of work. Rather, older and high-tenure workers tend to be strongly attached to the labor force. Thus, where younger individuals are more likely to briefly exit the labor force following permanent layoffs (and thus not show up as unemployed), older persons remain participants, continuing to search for work until new employment is obtained.

Displaced persons are out of work longer if they leave jobs because of slack work rather than because of plant closures or relocations. Although the reasons for this difference are not known with certainty, many economists suspect that longer joblessness occurs following partial layoffs because many workers wait, unemployed, in hopes of being rehired by their former employer. In contrast, plant closures generally eliminate the possibility of recall and so "wait unemployment" is less pervasive.

Advance notice of layoffs decreases the period of joblessness by up to one month.[22] This occurs because approximately one in six notified individuals find new employment prior to the job termination. There is no evidence that joblessness is reduced for persons unable to obtain new work before the layoff.

Earnings Changes

The interaction between permanent layoffs and subsequent earnings is complicated. Although there are big losers, and these individuals deserve greater assistance, large wage reductions are far from the norm. More striking than the size of *average* earnings losses is the diversity of displacement experiences. Between a third and half of displaced persons earn *higher* wages in their new jobs, while a quarter to a third suffer 25% or larger earnings reductions.[23] Thus, at least as many individuals benefit, in monetary terms, as experience large losses.

These findings should not be taken to imply that displacement is costless to the wage gainers. In addition to the burden of substantial initial unemployment, some individuals may accept jobs that offer pay comparable to that of their previous employment but that are less desirable in other ways.

Large post-displacement earnings losses, when they do occur, would be of less concern if they were transitory. Unfortunately, this is generally not the case. For example, 55% of displaced workers suffering 10% or larger initial wage reductions continue to have equivalent earnings losses four years later.[24]

Persons losing jobs in depressed local labor markets, those earning relatively high wages, and those with more than 20 years' seniority are likely to have larger than average wage losses. Women, however, lose *less* than men on average—due primarily to the fact that they originally had less to lose because they are more likely to have worked in low-wage jobs.[25] The latter finding suggests that earnings changes may provide a poor measure of the costs of displacement for low-paid individuals. Because depressed preseparation earnings imply little room for substantial wage reductions, small wage decreases fail to indicate how continuous vulnerability to job loss prevents these workers from ever improving their employment prospects.

Fringe Benefits

Because of data limitations, much less is known about post-displacement changes in fringe benefits than about earnings or joblessness. Information that is available for health insurance, surprisingly, provides little evidence of reduced coverage rates for job losers who obtain new employment. For example, Horvath finds that 78.9% of workers displaced (using the Bureau of Labor Statistics criteria) between 1981 and 1985 were covered by group health plans on their old jobs, as compared to an almost identical 77.6% coverage rate for individuals *reemployed* in January 1986.[26] By contrast, coverage rates were much lower for workers who remained jobless as of that date—only 39.9% of unemployed workers and 44.9% of labor force nonparticipants were covered by group health plans.

Lost pension benefits are also an area of concern. There are two primary types of pension schemes in the United States. In *defined benefit plans*, the employer guarantees specified payments, at retirement, which generally depend on age, years of service, and highest earnings. In *defined contribution plans*, the firm contributes stipulated amounts into the employee's pension account, with the ultimate pension benefit unknown and depending on the return obtained on the employee and employer contributions.[27]

Displaced workers with moderate tenure are likely to suffer large pension losses when covered by defined benefit schemes. This occurs both because benefits depend on accumulated service and because maximum earnings with the firm are typically received during the last years of work. Ironically, because the actuarial value of most defined benefit plans peaks well before normal retirement ages, workers displaced from jobs in their early to middle 50s are likely to lose more than those terminated at later ages.

With defined benefit plans, pension losses are likely to be the greatest for short-tenure workers. This occurs because there is generally a vesting period, before which the individual "owns" only the employee share of contributions. Thus, persons displaced from jobs before vesting will lose some or all of the employer pension contribution.

Current Government Policy Approaches

Structural changes in the economy represent a classic example of an economic externality, where private returns to individual companies differ from social costs and benefits. For example, technological innovations frequently yield economy-wide gains that only partially accrue to the individual firm in the form of higher profits. This is one reason the government has long subsidized research and development and provided protection in the form of patents, trademarks, and copyrights. Similarly, employers do not bear the full social costs of terminating a portion of their workforce. In part, these costs are borne by the community, as the lost jobs have a ripple effect on firms dependent on the business of the displaced workers. Part of the burden is also shared by employed persons in the form of higher taxes; these lost revenues may place additional budgetary pressure on some government programs. In the absence of any intervention, however, the major expense falls directly upon the displaced individuals.

To mitigate these adjustment burdens, the government assists dislocated workers in at least two fundamental ways. First, it provides direct aid to them in the form of income support, retraining, and job search assistance. Providing this aid distributes the costs of displacement across a wider segment of the economy. Second, the government establishes standards and procedures that private employers are expected to follow when contemplating terminations. These types of interventions encourage firms to more fully consider the social costs of permanent layoffs.

Although federal efforts in the areas of unemployment insurance and training have many flaws and should be improved, their fundamental importance is seldom questioned. There is much livelier debate about whether and how the government should regulate mass layoffs. Compared to other industrialized countries, the United States has taken a relatively passive role in this regard. As reflected by the recent passage of mandatory advance notice legislation, however, this noninterventionist posture may be changing.

The remainder of this section summarizes key existing government programs or legislation focused on displaced workers.

Unemployment Insurance

Unemployment insurance is the single most important source of government assistance to displaced workers. With an annual budget of $20 billion to $25 billion, it dwarfs the Job Training Partnership Act (JTPA) Title III or Trade Adjustment Assistance (TAA) initiatives that directly focus on the dislocated. Further, unemployment insurance is the only program that automatically provides assistance to individuals without requiring administrative actions on the part of firms, industries, or regions.

In most states, workers released from jobs for reasons unrelated to performance are eligible for unemployment insurance benefits after a one-week waiting period. Individuals quitting jobs generally do not receive benefits, nor do those with insufficient earnings in the previous four quarters. Benefits usually continue for twenty-six weeks, or until a new job is found, and the payment level remains constant throughout the period of receipt. If the state unemployment rate is substantially above the national rate, workers become eligible for 13 weeks of additional benefits. These state "triggers" were raised considerably in the early 1980s (and the national trigger eliminated altogether), so that relatively few workers now receive extended benefits.

By historical standards, a low percentage of jobless workers currently receive unemployment insurance payments. For example, fewer than 50% of the unemployed received such payments during the severe 1982–83 recession, and during the ensuing recovery, the percentage has fallen even further. This low proportion is partly because many workers exhaust benefits following extended unemployment spells. More importantly, it has resulted from decreased employment stability for some groups and from changes in labor force participation patterns, such that many of the unemployed have insufficient earnings to qualify for benefits.[28]

Training and Displacement Assistance

Policies for assisting displaced workers are not new. In response to the automation scare of the 1950s, the Area Redevelopment Act (ARA) of 1961 and Manpower Development and Training Act (MDTA) of 1962 provided funds for retraining dislocated individuals. In the 1970s, these programs were replaced by the Trade Adjustment Assistance Act (TAA), which provided income support, retraining, and relocation benefits to workers displaced by import penetration, and the Comprehensive Employment and Training Act (CETA), which, although focused on economically disadvantaged individuals, included assistance for unemployed persons in depressed local labor markets.

Recent efforts to assist dislocated workers have been more modest. CETA has been replaced by the JTPA, which includes, under Title III, specific programmatic assistance for displaced individuals. The combined annual budgets of TAA and JTPA Title III, however, were only about $230 million in the late 1980s.[29] By contrast, TAA was allocated $1.6 billion in its peak year (1980), and the public sector employment budget of CETA (much of which went to displaced workers) averaged almost $3.5 billion annually during the 1975–81 period.

Momentum has been building for several years to increase aid to dislocated individuals. The recently passed Omnibus Trade Bill includes provisions for up to $1 billion per year to be devoted to the Worker Readjustment Assistance Program (WRAP). This program will coordinate TAA and JTPA Title III efforts and should provide services fairly similar to the latter.

JTPA, as currently structured, is a decentralized program. Virtually all authority for the type and scope of assistance is delegated to the states and administered by local Private Industry Councils (PICs) and Service Delivery Areas (SDAs). This decentralization has two deleterious effects. First, the scope of delivered programs is so broad that it is virtually impossible either to evaluate or to disseminate information on the success of most efforts, and little attempt has been made to do so. Second, because of the potential complexity of programs and the inexperience of local administrators, most states have been relatively passive providers of assistance and have often failed to use their allocated budgets.[30]

There are at least two adverse incentives in current training programs. First, some individuals are encouraged to participate in costly training despite receiving little benefit from it. For example, under TAA, enrollment in training programs is a prerequisite for receiving extended unemployment benefits and other assistance.[31] Some individuals enter training to obtain these benefits rather than because they have any expectation of using the newly acquired skills; as a result, few job placements result from the training.[32] A second problem is that many individuals who would benefit from training are unable to afford it.[33] This is particularly problematic for workers with family responsibilities who, unable to forego income during the training program, may be forced to enroll in less useful short-term training or to immediately accept dead-end employment.

Advance Notice and Other Employer Regulation

In 1988, Congress passed the Worker Assistance and Retraining Notification Act (P.L. 100–379), which requires some employers to provide 60 days advance notice of plant closures and mass layoffs. This law is historic in several respects. It represents the first federal legislation of its kind to receive approval and follows more than 40 earlier attempts since 1979.[34] The manner of passage was also extremely unusual. After vetoing an earlier version of the Omnibus Trade Bill because it contained a prenotification provision, President Reagan allowed an identical mandatory notice requirement to become law when presented in separate legislation. Passage of the legislation reflected widespread public sentiment in favor of such regulation (polls indicate that more than 80% of the public supports mandatory notice) and the desire to avoid a contentious campaign issue in a presidential election year. The result is that the United States has joined virtually all other industrialized countries in regulating plant shutdowns and mass terminations.

According to the current statute, employers are required to provide 60 days advance notice of layoffs or plant closings *except* in the following cases: (1) the company employs fewer than 100 persons or is releasing fewer than 50 workers; (2) the company is terminating less than a third of the workforce and the total number of layoffs is fewer than 500; (3) plant closings are due to "unforeseeable" business developments, strikes, or lockouts; (4) the faltering company is actively seeking new capital or business; (5) the plant is closing as the result of sale of the business or consolidation within the local area; (6) displaced workers are offered new positions.

Early notification appears to reduce the period of post-displacement joblessness by up to one month, mostly because some notified workers obtain new employment before termination.[25] Written prior notice received more than two months before the termination also leads to at least a 10% wage increase upon reemployment, as compared to persons without any notice.[36]

Despite predictions that customers may disappear, access to credit markets will be impaired, productivity reduced, or absenteeism increased, there is little evidence that advance notice has *any* serious negative consequences for business. In contrast, productivity often *rises* following the notice, and, in some cases, notification results in actions that save rather than destroy the plant.[37] Although some European countries provide examples showing that extremely restrictive labor legislation can inhibit employment growth, this experience indicates that advance notice and improved economic performance are not incompatible.

Beyond any economic consequences, workers favor advance notice because they feel it to be fair. The corporate sector, on the other hand, expresses concern that advance notice represents a first step toward more onerous government interference. Debate over the proper government role is likely to continue. Nonetheless, employment security appears to have joined child labor, occupational safety, and equal opportunity as an area where regulation has become an accepted fact.

There is less consensus as to what, if any, additional worker protections should be legislated. Virtually all business and labor groups agree that health insurance coverage should be continued for a period of time following layoffs.[38] Under a federal law passed in 1986 (P.L. 99–272, Title X), most employers are required to continue group health coverage following the end of employment (except when the termination occurs because of gross misconduct).[39] Ironically, while the coverage of voluntary job leavers continues for up to three years, the maximum eligibility period is limited to 18 months for displaced workers.

Private Sector Issues

Concern over issues of labor displacement has also reached the corporate sector and the labor movement. To some degree, this has resulted from the recent inability of many companies to fulfill implicit contracts guaranteeing "lifetime" employment to workers meeting minimum performance standards and of unions to provide job security for even their most senior members. In additon to assisting newly terminated employees, businesses are grappling with how to inspire corporate loyalty and simultaneously to provide workers with the flexibility needed to obtain new types of employment within or, if necessary, outside the company.[40] Similarly, unions are struggling to ensure that their members share the benefits of productivity-enhancing innovations, while joint labor/management arrangements oriented around new technologies are altering the traditional adversarial nature of collective bargaining.

As the increased pace of economic dislocation renders a wider segment of the population vulnerable to permanent job loss, employment security becomes an important issue even for companies that have previously avoided providing long-term guarantees. In addition, some responses of large firms have spillover effects that potentially increase job instability among smaller employers. For example, increased subcontracting provides some degree of protection for "core" workers in large companies but is likely to increase the risk of displacement for their counterparts on the periphery. Indeed, while temporary work arrangements, part-time positions, and contingent jobs have become increasingly important sources of employment, most labor market institutions have failed to adjust adequately to reflect this change. Technological innovation also raises concerns in many firms over their ability to find individuals possessing the skills required to perform newly created tasks.[41]

To some degree, these difficulties are exacerbated by societal changes. More households now contain two or more earners, and, as a result, workers tend to be less willing to relocate. This unwillingness has been a source of frustration for companies who are simultaneously laying off in some areas, hiring in others, and are having limited success convincing displaced individuals to move to the expanding locations.

Employers should be concerned about job obsolescence and worker displacement for at least four reasons. First, the elimination of one class of jobs is often accompanied by the creation of positions requiring alternative (but frequently related) skills. A logical place to fill these vacancies is from within the company, thereby retaining employees with a commitment to the firm and an understanding of the corporate culture.

Second, worker morale, productivity, and attachment to the enterprise are likely to be improved when employees clearly understand how the firm institutes labor-saving technologies and structures demand-induced layoffs. For example, employees may be more willing to suggest technological or organizational improvements when their jobs are secure than if they are threatened by the changes.

Third, when employees are covered by collective bargaining agreements, the structure and success of labor-management relations are likely to depend critically on the extent to which management and the unions are able to jointly respond to changes in technology, fluctuations in product demand, and the need to redeploy workers within the firm.[42] These joint responses are increasingly occurring not only through collective bargaining but also outside contractual agreements.

Fourth, community relations are enhanced if employers demonstrate a clear understanding that their actions have repercussions beyond the confines of the firm. Similarly, progressive employment practices are likely to reduce pressure for legislated worker protections, which most firms oppose.

Implications for Policy

Labor displacement is an inevitable consequence of a dynamic economy. The benefits of change are unequally distributed, however, and without some form of assistance, a disproportionate burden is borne by dislocated workers. Moreover, spillover effects can have substantial indirect impacts (both favorable and unfavorable) on a diverse set of economic agents.

There are no easy remedies to the problems associated with labor displacement. Unfortunately, simple-minded criticisms of past efforts have often resulted in hasty policy reformulations that neither incorporate learning from previous mistakes nor anticipate shortcomings of the new approaches. The remainder of this chapter summarizes a set of policy changes designed to moderate the costs associated with structural change while preserving economic efficiency. Included are suggestions for (1) modifying the unemployment insurance system; (2) improving the evaluation and delivery of displacement assistance programs; and (3) revising the current mandatory advance notice provision. Suggestions are also included for private sector initiatives.

Unemployment Insurance

The federal-state unemployment system was designed mainly to assist experienced workers in meeting transitory income losses resulting from temporary layoffs, seasonal unemployment, or short-lasting adjustment problems following permanent job terminations. Dramatic changes in the aggregate economy have jeopardized its adequacy as a safety net, as evidenced by the decline in the percentage of unemployed workers who are eligible for benefits. The unemployment insurance system, as currently structured, inadequately supports low-wage workers and the long-term unemployed. Simultaneously, it provides excessive monetary assistance to some of the short-term jobless and creates incentives for some individuals who can easily find jobs to delay intensive search for new employment. In addition, numerous inconsistencies in payment levels and eligibility criteria exist across states.

Several changes in the system are needed to eliminate these inadequacies. First, minimum income replacement standards and eligibility criteria need to be established across states and programs. Implementing such standards may involve interstate transfers of benefits and would certainly include the payment of partial benefits, on a pro-rata basis, for workers with substantial labor force attachments who are currently excluded from receiving unemployment insurance as the result of low earnings or job instability.

Second, the duration of benefit eligibility needs to be extended in recognition that elevated labor market turbulence is increasingly resulting in long-duration or repeated spells of joblessness. Along with this increased coverage, efforts need to be made to improve the effectiveness of job search and job placement assistance by implementing new approaches that could be tested in pilot projects. These projects might include intensive employee counseling, job clubs, increases in the waiting period for first payment of benefits, job-finding bonuses, relocation benefits, or employer incentives.

Finally, unemployment insurance and other forms of worker assistance need to be coordinated in a more consistent manner throughout the country. For example, in some states workers enrolled in approved training programs are precluded from receiving the same level of unemployment benefits as similar individuals who are not in training.

Training and Displacement Assistance

Broad changes are needed in the structure of training and assistance programs focused on displaced workers.[43] Primary programmatic guidance should be returned to the federal government. In such a system, local providers would choose from a *limited* set of programs that had previously been shown to be effective. Relying on a set of pre-approved programs would substantially reduce the administrative delays that have been so problematic in current efforts, and the menu of available choices would ensure that PICs and SDAs have continued flexibility to respond to local needs.

A crucial component of these assistance efforts would be incentive funding to states (or local deliverers) to develop small-scale demonstration projects. Each of these projects should be evaluated, and those that substantially reduce adjustment problems would be incorporated into the set of federally approved programs. The use of a consistent method of evaluation would allow states and local delivery organizations to more easily select programs meeting specific needs while retaining their ability to choose from among a number of alternatives.

Current program arrangements should also be altered in such a way that workers and employers become stake holders in training programs. When they are stake holders, participants will self-select into the programs with the greatest benefit to them and avoid less useful options. Similarly, firms will have increased incentives to participate in training programs which are most needed and useful. A number of potential changes of this type deserve careful study. These might include training vouchers or a system wherein program participants share a portion of program costs but are eligible for government-guaranteed loans to cover the worker contributions and replace income forgone during training.

Advance Notice

Exemptions in existing mandatory notice regulations substantially reduce the number of workers receiving advance notice. The vague nature of some of the exclusions also encourages enterprises to circumvent the spirit of the law and undermines the attempts of many business groups to increase the prevalence of advance notice. For these reasons, broader coverage and more clearly delineated exemptions would seem appropriate.

For example, the thresholds on firm size and number of layoffs at which prenotification becomes mandatory should be reduced. The exclusion for closures due to "unforeseeable" business developments is hopelessly difficult to interpret and so should be deleted. Similarly, since one of the express purposes of the law is to make business consider the social costs of worker dislocation, it makes no sense to exempt displacements occurring as the result of a business sale or consolidation. Finally, the exemption for companies seeking new business or capital should be specified in greater detail or eliminated.

To avoid raising costs to business, this more comprehensive coverage could be combined with incentives for compliance. For example, firms providing sufficient advance notice could be granted favorable unemployment insurance treatment.[44]

Employer Policies

Most companies face the prospect of large-scale retrenchments or layoffs at some time. Employers are better prepared to respond proactively to these occurrences if they have put into place guidelines establishing minimum criteria for advance notification, transfer policies, relocation assistance, severance and other termination pay, early retirement, training and outplacement assistance, continuation of benefits, and community relations. Such procedures should be distributed throughout the enterprise and represent a minimum commitment by the firm, with more generous treatment provided if market conditions permit.

Establishing such guidelines has both direct and indirect benefits. Worker morale is likely to be improved when the conditions of employment, redeployment, and termination are clearly stated. Deciding on such policies also allows management to arrive at a consensus in the absence of the pressure of specific impending layoffs. Employer interviews also indicate that many firms, especially those previously offering considerable employment security but no longer able to do so, find it difficult to even acknowledge the prospect of large-scale retrenchments. Constructing guidelines encourages this awareness and may engender other proactive measures to reduce adjustment difficulties.[45]

Firms should strive to provide the maximum possible advance notice of impending plant shutdowns or layoffs.[46] Early warning increases the ability of displaced workers to search for new positions before becoming unemployed. It also allows outplacement assistance efforts to be initiated when the employees are still coming to the firm and can be contacted frequently. Finally, the additional time is useful for employers applying for JTPA Title III assistance.

Outplacement assistance programs tend to be more successful when they are fully operational at the time of displacements and are located on-site. Early implementation is crucial because of the difficulty in establishing regular contact with employees once the job has ended. Workers are also more likely to participate in on-site assistance programs that allow them to continue the established routine of coming to work on a regular basis.[47] Even where some activities (e.g., formal classroom training at community colleges) are logically offered off-site, others (e.g., initial skills assessment and job search workshops) can be located at the plant.

Employers frequently complain that they have great difficulty convincing employees to relocate to fill vacancies. Nonetheless, despite the increasing prevalence of two-career households, relatively few companies provide relocation assistance to the spouse. Such help can potentially take several forms. Employers can sometimes provide jobs for both members of the household. Where this is not possible, a portion of the lost income could be replaced for a specified period of time or until the spouse obtains work. Similarly, health insurance, pensions, and employment agency fees could be subsidized, and some employers may be able to directly assist in the spouse's search for employment. Finally, child care subsidies may reduce mobility costs for two-earner and single-headed households with young children.

Notes

This chapter is primarily the responsibility of Christopher J. Ruhm.

1. Joseph Schumpeter, *The Theory of Economic Development* (Cambridge, Mass.: Harvard University Press, 1934).

2. Tadashi A. Hanami, "Japan," in E. Yemin (Ed.), *Workforce Reductions and Undertakings* (Geneva: International Labor Office, 1982), pp. 174–185.

3. Philip Martin, *Labor Displacement and Public Policy* (Lexington, Mass.: Lexington Books, 1983); and Gregory Hooks, "The Policy Response to Factory Closings: A Comparison of the United States, Sweden, and France," *The Annuals of the American Academy of Political and Social Science* 475 (1984): 110–124.

4. See U.S. Secretary of Labor, Task Force on Economic Adjustment and Worker Dislocation, *Economic Adjustment and Worker Dislocation in a Competitive Society*

(Washington, D.C.: U.S. Department of Labor, 1986), for a discussion of this and alternative definitions.

5. The January 1984 and January 1986 *Displaced Worker Supplements (DWS)* to the *Current Population Survey* indicate that approximately 2.2 million workers were involuntarily terminated from jobs yearly due to slack work or plant closings, between 1979 and 1986, but that only around 1 million met the Bureau of Labor Statistics displacement criteria.

6. See Christopher J. Ruhm, "Do Long Tenure Workers Have Special Problems Following Job Displacement?" *Economic Development Quarterly* 3 (1989): 320–326, for a discussion of the relationship between preseparation tenure and adjustment difficulties.

7. Individuals ending explicitly temporary jobs or those in construction or certain craft occupations, where employer attachments are transient, are also excluded.

8. See Paul O. Flaim and Ellen Sehgal, "Displaced Workers of 1979–83: How Well Have They Fared," *Monthly Labor Review* 108 (1985): 3–16; Francis W. Horvath, "The Pulse of Economic Change: Displaced Workers of 1981–5," *Monthly Labor Review* 110 (1987): 3–12.

9. Jonathan S. Leonard, "In the Right Place at the Wrong Time: The Extent of Frictional and Structural Unemployment," in Kevin Lang and Jonathan Leonard (Eds.), *Unemployment and the Structure of Labor Markets* (New York: Basil Blackwell, 1987), pp. 141–163.

10. Daniel S. Hamermesh, "What Do We Know About Worker Displacement in the U.S.?" *Industrial Relations* 28 (1989): 51–59.

11. Lori G. Kletzer, "Determinants of the Reemployment Probabilities of Displaced Workers: Do High Wage Workers Have Longer Durations of Unemployment," mimeo, Williams College, Williamstown, Mass., 1987.

12. For example, Richard B. Freeman and James L. Medoff, in *What Do Unions Do* (Basic Books: New York, 1984), estimate that 36% of non-union and 59% of union employers always release more junior workers first, *even in the absence of contractual agreements mandating the order of terminations.* Christopher J. Ruhm, "The Economic Consequences of Labor Mobility," *Industrial and Labor Relations Review* 41 (1987): 30–42, shows that annual layoff rates in the early 1970s were 13 times as high for household heads with less than a year on the job as for counterparts with more than 20 years tenure. Similarly, Douglas L. Kruse, "International Trade and the Labor Market Experience of Displaced Workers," *Industrial and Labor Relations Review* 41 (1988): 402–417, indicates that the average job tenure of workers displaced in the early 1980s was less than five years.

13. See Hamermesh, "What Do We Know About Worker Displacement in the U.S.?"

14. Between 1977 and 1982, for instance, total manufacturing employment declined 3.8%, but this small net change was composed of a 29.3% increase in new or expanding plants, which was slightly more than offset by a 33.1% decrease in shrinking or closing plants. Timothy Dunne, Mark Roberts, and Lawrence Samuelson, "Plant Turnover and Gross Employment Flow in the U.S. Manufacturing Sector 1963–82," *Journal of Labor Economics* 7 (1987): 48–71.

15. See Ruhm, "Economic Consequences of Labor Mobility," for evidence.

16. See Horvath, "Pulse of Economic Change."

17. See Flaim and Sehgal, "Displaced Workers of 1979–83," and Horvath, "Pulse of Economic Change."

18. See Michael Podgursky and Paul Swaim, "Duration of Joblessness Following Job Displacement," *Industrial Relations* 26 (1987): 213–226.

19. See Christopher J. Ruhm, "The Extent and Persistence of Unemployment Following Permanent Quits and Layoffs," mimeo, Boston University, 1987.

20. This assumes the average joblessness of the 2 million workers displaced annually is six months and that, when employed, they produce an average of $25,000 of goods and services each year.

21. See John T. Addison and Pedro Portugal, "The Effect of Advance Notification of Plant Closings on Unemployment," *Industrial and Labor Relations Review* 41 (1987): 3–16; Kletzer, "Determinants of the Reemployment Probabilities"; Podgursky and Swaim, "Duration of Joblessness"; and Ruhm, "Extent and Persistence of Unemployment."

22. See Addison and Portugal, "Effect of Advance Notification"; and Ronald G. Ehrenberg and George H. Jakubson, *Advance Notice Provisions in Plant Closing Legislation* (Kalamazoo, Mich.: Upjohn Institute for Employment Research, 1988).

23. See Michael Podgursky and Paul Swaim, "Job Displacement and Earnings Loss: Evidence from the Displaced Worker Survey," *Industrial and Labor Relations Review* 41 (1987): 17–29, and Ruhm, "Economic Consequences of Labor Mobility."

24. See Ruhm, "Economic Consequences of Labor Mobility."

25. See Ruhm, "Economic Consequences of Labor Mobility," and Christopher J. Ruhm, "Are Workers Permanently Scarred by Job Displacements?" *American Economic Review*, forthcoming.

26. See Horvath, "Pulse of Economic Change."

27. Laurence J. Kotlikoff and Daniel E. Smith, *Pensions in the American Economy* (Chicago: University of Chicago Press, 1983) investigate the U.S. pension system in considerable detail.

28. See Gary Burtless, "Why Is the Insured Unemployment Rate So Low?" *Brookings Papers on Economic Activity* 1 (1983): 225–249.

29. In addition, the Perkins Vocational Education Act of 1984 mandates $90 million per year to support "adult" education including "update" training for employed workers and basic skills education for adults.

30. For example, by June 1986, more than $142 million in allocated JTPA funds remained unspent (see U.S. General Accounting Office, *Local Programs and Outcomes Under the Job Training Partnership Act*, GAO/HRD-87-411 [Washington, D.C.: U.S. Government Printing Office, 1987]).

31. JTPA enrollees are also exempt from the unemployment insurance job search requirement; however, participants are not provided with extended benefits.

32. See Robert Z. Lawrence and Robert E. Litan, "Living with the Trade Deficit: Adjustment Strategies to Preserve Free Trade," *Brookings Review* 4 (1985): 3–13.

33. Only 6% of JTPA Title III program participants received basic skills training (for an average duration of two weeks), and 42% obtained job-related training; conversely, 66% received job search assistance and 84% job counseling (see United States General Accounting Office, *Local Programs and Outcomes*).

34. Three states (Maine, Wisconsin, and Hawaii) legislated mandatory advance notice prior to the federal government, and three others (Massachusetts, Maryland, and Michigan) implemented voluntary programs previously. Connecticut requires non-bankrupt firms to maintain health insurance and other benefits for up to 120 days.

35. See Ehrenberg and Jakubson, *Advance Notice Provisions* and Addison and Portugal, "Effect of Advance Notification"; Christopher J. Ruhm, "Advance Notice and Postdisplacement Joblessness," mimeo, Boston University, 1989.

36. Christopher J. Ruhm, "The Impact of Formal and Informal Advance Notice on Postdisplacement Wages," mimeo, Boston University, 1990.

37. See Ronald E. Berenbeim, *Company Programs to Ease Plant Shutdowns* (New York: Conference Board, 1986); and Robert I. Sutton, "The Process of Organizational Death: Disbanding and Reconnecting," *Administrative Science Quarterly* 31 (1987): 542–569.

38. These include the Secretary of Labor's Task Force on Economic Adjustment and Worker Dislocation, Business Roundtable, United Autoworkers, National Association of Manufacturers, Committee for Economic Development, AFL-CIO, National Alliance of Business, and National Commission for Employment Policy.

39. The employee may be required to pay all or part of the premium and is given the option to convert to an individual health plan at the end of the period. Eligibility ends when the employee receives coverage under another group plan (due to own or spouse's employment) or becomes eligible for Medicare.

40. See Kim Cameron, Myung Kim, and David Whetten, "Organizational Effects of Decline and Turbulence," *Administrative Science Quarterly* 32 (1987): 222–240; and Joel Brockner, Stephen Grover, Thomas Reed, Rocki DeWitt, and Michael O'Malley, "Survivors' Reactions to Layoffs: We Get by with a Little Help from Our Friends," *Administrative Science Quarterly* 32 (1987): 526–541.

41. See Chapter 9.

42. See Markley Roberts, "A Labor Perspective on Technological Change," in Eileen Collins and Lucretia Tanner (Eds.), *American Jobs and the Changing Industrial Base* (Cambridge, Mass.: Ballinger, 1984), pp. 183–205.

43. This discussion makes no attempt to summarize the vast literature evaluating *specific* assistance programs. Recent research in this area includes Robert J. Lalonde, "Evaluating the Econometric Evaluations of Training Programs with Experimental Data," *American Economic Review* 76 (1986): 604–620; Gary Burtless and Larry Orr, "Are Classical Experiments Needed for Manpower Policy?" *Journal of Human Resources* 21 (1986): 606–639; Burt S. Barnow, "The Impact of CETA Programs on Earnings," *Journal of Human Resources* 22 (1987): 157–193; and Thomas Fraker and Rebecca Maynard, "The Adequacy of Group Designs for Evaluations of Employer Related Programs," *Journal of Human Resources* 22 (1987): 194–277.

44. Such a change would require a more fully experience-rated unemployment insurance system than what presently exists. (Around half of all firms currently pay the maximum premium rate and so are charged no extra insurance premiums for additional layoffs.) Most economists believe that more complete experience rating is desirable in its own right because full experience rating would reduce current government subsidy to firms using large amounts of temporary or seasonal labor.

45. An example of comprehensive displacement guidelines is the Levi Strauss program applied to closings of 13 of its facilities between 1982 and 1985. See Berenbeim, *Company Programs to Ease Plant Shutdowns.*

46. The desirability of providing maximum advance notice has been endorsed by groups as diverse as the U.S. Chamber of Commerce, Conference Board, Business Roundtable, Committee for Economic Development, National Association of Manufacturers, and the (Reagan Administration) Taskforce on Economic Adjustment and Worker Dislocation.

47. See Berenbeim, *Company Programs to Ease Plant Shutdowns*, for further discussion.

4

Labor Market Turbulence
and the Older Worker

The employment tenure and seniority of older workers have given them somewhat better protection against the problems of labor market turbulence than
their younger counterparts.[1] Older workers, however, have not been exempt
from the effects of plant closings, plant relocations, and downsizing efforts of
corporations or from the structural changes that have occurred in the industrial
and occupational composition of employment. The problems of older workers
have also received increasing public attention because the aging of the population has created pressures on retirement benefits and health care costs and
because the slowing of aggregate labor force growth has potential consequences for labor shortages.

The retirement behavior of America's older workers was subject to increased scrutiny during the early 1980s in response to a series of short-term and
long-run financing problems faced by the nation's Social Security system.[2] A
combination of an increasing number of beneficiaries under the Old Age,
Survivors, and Disability Income (OASDI) programs of the Social Security
system, more rapidly growing payments to such beneficiaries, and real wage
growth below projections were the underlying causes of the short-term financing problems.[3] The long-run financing problems were related to the projected
explosive growth in the number of retirees who would be supported by the
Social Security system in the early decades of the next century and the declines
in the birthrate that would reduce the number of workers available to support
these retirees.[4]

To address these financing problems, a Presidential Commission on Social
Security was formed in 1981.[5] In response to commission recommendations,

Congress passed a series of amendments to the Social Security Act in 1983, including economic provisions designed to discourage early retirement, delay retirement past age 65, and gradually increase the age at which full Social Security benefits can be collected.[6]

These steps to postpone retirement have been matched by a new focus on older workers as a potential pool of labor in a labor market environment otherwise characterized by slower growth in supply.[7] Over the 1986–95 period, the nation's civilian labor force is projected to increase by only 1.2% per year, and the annual growth rate is projected to fall further to 1% between 1995 and 2000.[8] The projected 1% annual growth rate for the latter half of the decade would represent the lowest rate of labor force growth since the 1930s.[9]

As the growth of the nation's civilian labor force declines, and as the number of young labor force entrants will decline in absolute terms through 1995, older workers were expected to be in greater demand throughout the 1990s by traditional employers of young adults in the retail trade and service industries.[10] As Ehrlich and Garland have noted in a recent review of America's changing demographics and their implications for the economy and the labor market: "The good health, skills, and work histories of the 'young old' can help the nation out of its demographic fix."[11]

The economic dislocations of the 1980s have affected older workers as well as their younger counterparts. Older workers lost jobs as a result of plant closings and major downsizing efforts of firms undergoing a major restructuring.[12] The first two Bureau of Labor Statistics dislocated worker surveys revealed that older persons accounted for nearly one-fifth of all dislocated workers with three or more years of tenure on their last jobs.[13]

Although older workers holding blue-collar positions in goods-producing industries were most at risk of dislocation during the 1979–85 period, displacement problems were encountered by older workers in all major occupational groups. For example, the national media paid increased attention to the plight of displaced white-collar workers, including mid-level managers and professionals.[14] As with dislocated blue-collar workers, those white-collar workers also experienced severe social, psychological, and family adjustment problems.[15]

Finally, although poverty problems among the nation's older population have diminished over the past decade, continued concerns have been expressed about the employment problems of the nation's working poor and the continued high rates of poverty among the elderly living alone.[16] Progress in reducing problems of poverty and near poverty among the nation's 55- to 64-year-old population has come to a halt since 1973, and within this group the less educated, minorities, and those living in small towns and rural areas have been most affected by labor market turbulence.

Devising an appropriate set of national workforce preparedness strategies for older workers in the years ahead clearly requires greater understanding of the magnitude and nature of the labor market problems encountered by older workers and the underlying causes of these problems. Older workers tend to fare

relatively well compared to their younger counterparts in avoiding most major labor market problems. However, some problems remain.[17] For example, early retirement by males will be difficult to reverse because of the retirement incentives of private pensions and asset income.[18] In addition, economic dislocation and major downsizing efforts will lead to lengthy periods of joblessness and labor force withdrawal among some subgroups of older workers in the absence of a more systematic array of workforce preparedness strategies.[19]

Demographic Trends

The older population of the United States has grown substantially over the past two decades, rising from 35.3 million in 1967 to nearly 50.3 million in 1988, an increase of 42.2%.[20] Between 1988 and the end of the century, the number of older persons in the nation's civilian noninstitutional population is projected to increase to 56.8 million.[21]

Over the remainder of the century, the older population will increase its share of both the total population and the working-age population; however, all of this increase will occur after 1995. By the year 2000, the older population will represent 21.6% of the nation's civilian noninstitutional population and 28% of the working-age population (16 and over). The growth rates of key age subgroups of the older population will vary widely over this period, however, with those persons over 75 years old experiencing the fastest rate of growth (see Table 4.1.

As with the young adult population, there is a "demographic window of opportunity" for improving the labor force attachment and use of the nation's 55- to 64-year-olds during the first half of the 1990s. Labor supply conditions will be quite favorable for workers in this age group, but this may not be sufficient to reverse longstanding trends toward earlier retirement, especially among men. Continued downsizing by large corporations that encourages early retirement and the availability of a large pool of baby boomers desiring

Table 4.1. **Projected Changes in the Nation's Older Population by Selected Age Subgroup, 1988–2000**

Age Group	Population* (in 1000s)			Population Growth Rate (percentages)		
	(A) 1988	(B) 1995	(C) 2000	(D) 1988–95	(E) 1995–2000	(F) 1988–2000
55+	52,198	55,089	59,040	5.5	7.2	13.1
55–64	21,799	21,325	24,158	−2.2	13.3	10.8
65–74	17,873	18,930	18,243	5.9	−3.6	2.0
75+	12,528	14,834	16,639	18.4	12.2	32.8

*The population estimates include those older persons serving in the armed forces and residing in institutions, such as nursing homes.

Source: U.S. Bureau of the Census, *Projections of the Population of the United States, by Age, Sex, and Race: 1988 to 2080.*

Table 4.2. **Projected Changes in the Ethnic Composition of the 55- to 64-Year-Old Civilian Noninstitutional Population of the United States, 1986–2000**

Ethnic Group	Population (in 1000s)			Change (in 1000s)	
	(A) 1986	(B) 1995	(C) 2000	(D) 1986–95	(E) 1995–2000
Total	22,010	21,155	23,966	− 855	+ 2,811
White	19,476	18,190	20,515	− 1,286	+ 2,325
Black	2,079	2,261	2,549	+ 182	+ 288
Asian and Other	455	704	902	+ 249	+ 198
Hispanic*	1,023	1,383	1,689	+ 360	+ 306
All Minority	3,557	4,348	5,140	+ 791	+ 792
Minority as Percentage of Total	16.2%	20.6%	21.4%		

*Hispanics can be members of any racial group. In calculating the "all minority" totals appearing in Tables 4.2 and 4.3, we assumed that all Hispanics were whites. This assumption is a fairly reasonable one, given the fact that 97% of 55- to 64-year-old Hispanics in the United States at the time of the March 1988 CPS survey were classified as white.

Source: U.S. Bureau of Labor Statistics, *Projections 2000.*

career advancement may offset some of the demographic and economic forces favoring more effective use of the older worker in the years ahead.[22]

The ethnic composition of the nation's 55- to 64-year-old population will be shifting over the remainder of the century (see Table 4.2). Although the number of white, non-Hispanic persons in this age group will fall by more than 1.6 million between 1986 and 1995, the minority population is projected to rise by nearly 800,000. The bulk of the growth in the minority population in this age group will come from Asians and Hispanics, two groups whose retirement

Table 4.3. **Projected Changes in the 55- to 64-Year-Old Civilian Labor Force Between 1986 and 2000, by Sex and Ethnic Group (Numbers in 1000s)**

Group	(A) 1986	(B) 1995	(C) 2000	(D) Percentage Change 1986–95	(E) Percentage Change 1995–2000
All	11,894	11,353	12,970	− 4.5	14.2
Sex					
Men	6.954	6,438	7,238	− 7.4	12.4
Women	4,940	4,915	5,732	− .5	16.6
Ethnic Group					
White (Less Hispanic)	10,071	9,135	10,367	− 9.3	13.5
Black	1,050	1,111	1,214	5.8	9.3
Hispanic	511	704	872	37.8	23.9
Asian and Other	262	403	517	53.8	28.3
All Minority	1,823	2,218	2,603	21.7	17.4

Source: U.S. Bureau of Labor Statistics, *Projections 2000.*

experiences have not been carefully examined. Accompanying these changes in the ethnic composition of the 55- to 64-year-old population will be shifts in the ethnic characteristics of the older labor force (see Table 4.3). The number of older white, non-Hispanic labor force participants will decline while an increase is projected for minorities.

Trends in the Labor Force

Although concerns over the declining labor force attachment of older persons were renewed in the 1980s, the phenomenon is clearly not a new one. The aggregate labor force participation rate of older persons has been declining over the past 40 years; however, the rate of decline has accelerated over the past 20 years (see Table 4.4).

During the first half of this 40-year period, all the decline in the participation rate of older persons was attributable to those 65 and older. Among those 55–64 years old, the 1968 participation rate was more than five percentage points above the 1948 rate. This increase was due to a sharp rise in the participation rate of 55- to 64-year-old women, especially married women, that more than offset the declines in labor force attachment among men.[23] Since 1968, however, the participation rates of both 55- to 64-year-olds and those 65 and older have declined markedly. Combined with more rapid growth in the elderly population relative to those 55–64 years old, these developments pushed the participation rate of older persons down to 30% by 1988.

A few key differences exist between the recent labor force behavior of older men and women under the age of 65 (see Table 4.5). The participation rates of men in all age subgroups have continued to fall since 1978. In contrast, labor force attachment among women ages 55–59 has increased over the past decade,

Table 4.4. **Trends in Civilian Labor Force Participation Rates of Persons 55 + , by Age Group, United States: Selected Years, 1948–88 (Annual Averages, Percentages)**

Year	(A) All Older Persons	(B) Persons 55–64	(C) Persons 65 +
1948	43.3	56.9	27.0
1960	40.9	60.9	20.8
1968	39.3	62.2	17.2
1973	36.0	58.4	14.6
1979	33.5	56.3	13.1
1988	30.0	54.6	11.5

Sources: U.S. Bureau of Labor Statistics, *Labor Force Statistics Derived from the Current Population Survey;* U.S. Bureau of Labor Statistics, *Employment and Earnings,* January 1989.

Table 4.5. **Civilian Labor Force Participation Rates of Older Persons by Age Subgroup and Sex, United States: Annual Averages, 1978, 1982, and 1988**

Sex/Age Subgroup	(A) 1978	(B) 1982	(C) 1988
Males	47.4	43.8	39.9
55–59	82.9	81.9	79.3
60–64	62.0	57.2	54.4
65–69	30.1	26.9	25.8
70+	14.2	12.2	10.9
Females	23.2	22.8	22.3
55–59	48.6	49.6	53.3
60–64	33.1	33.4	33.8
65–69	14.9	14.9	15.4
70+	4.8	4.5	4.4
All 55+	33.8	31.9	30.0

Sources: U.S. Bureau of Labor Statistics, *Employment and Earnings,* January 1979, January 1983, and January 1989.

and women 60–69 years old have been characterized by fairly stable participation rates. These latter developments are likely to continue throughout the remainder of the century. The forthcoming cohorts of 55- to 64-year-old women have had even more work experience and completed more years of formal schooling than their current counterparts and thus should be even more strongly attached to the labor force.

Much of the growing concern over the changing labor force behavior of older persons has been focused on the increasing tendency of older workers to

Table 4.6. **Estimated Declines in the Annual Average Labor Force Participation Rates of Key Age/Sex Cohorts of Older Persons Between 1978 and 1988**

Age Cohort/Sex	(A) 1978 Participation Rate	(B) 1988 Participation Rate	(C) Percentage Withdrawing from Labor Force over These 10 Years
45–49 Years Old in 1978			
Men	93.0	79.3	14.7
Women	59.8	53.3	10.9
50–54 Years Old in 1978			
Men	89.7	54.4	39.4
Women	54.5	33.8	38.0

Sources: U.S. Bureau of Labor Statistics, *Employment and Earnings,* January 1979 and January 1989.

Table 4.7. **Percentage Distribution of Nonemployed Males 55–62 Years Old, by Major Reason for Not Working During the Previous Calendar Year, Selected Years, March 1968–March 1988**

Age Subgroup/ Reason	(A) March 1968	(B) March 1974	(C) March 1979	(D) March 1988
55–59, All Males				
Illness/Disability	74.7	67.5	62.7	52.3
Cannot Find Work	5.3	3.2	3.2	4.9
Retired	16.9	27.1	29.4	39.0
60–62, All Males				
Illness/Disability	63.7	67.7	61.5	36.1
Cannot Find Work	1.9	1.1	1.1	3.1
Retired	30.9	30.4	34.1	57.8

Source: U.S. Bureau of the Census, Current Population Survey (March), selected years, 1968–88, public use tapes.

retire at earlier ages. Table 4.6 clearly shows that high fractions of older U.S. workers in the 1980s withdrew from active labor force participation well before the normal retirement age of 65.[24] Of those 45- to 49-year-olds active in the labor force during 1978, approximately 15% of the men and 11% of the women retired before age 60. Among 50- to 54-year-olds active in the labor force during 1978, nearly 40% of both men and women retired before reaching the age of 65. The estimated declines in the labor force attachment of 55- to 62-year-old males over the past two decades have been accompanied by changes in reported reasons for not working, with "retired" gaining steadily (see Table 4.7).[25]

The substantial growth in employment opportunities in the U.S. economy over the 1982–88 period has not had any substantive impact on the employment of persons 65 and older. During this period, total employment of persons 16 and older increased by 15.4 million; however, the number of employed persons 65 and older expanded by only 274,000, accounting for only 1.8% of the net change in total employment.[26] The growth in employment among the elderly was not attributable to any rise in their degree of labor force attachment. In fact, their participation rate fell slightly over this period. Instead, all the increase was due to a rise in the population of persons 65 and over and to a small decline in their unemployment rate.

Retirement Behavior

An extensive body of literature on the retirement behavior of older workers has been built up over the past decade. This literature is primarily focused on white males and emphasizes the influences of personal health factors, Social Security benefits, and private pensions.[27]

Although its precise role in influencing retirement behavior is still debated, the health status of U.S. workers has frequently been found to be a significant factor in the decision to retire.[28] The early literature on retirement behavior in the 1950s and the early 1960s frequently cited health problems as the most important or one of the two most important reasons for early voluntary retirement among men.[29] These findings held true for wage and salary workers as well as the self-employed. Data from national longitudinal surveys and the Social Security Administration's Retirement History Survey further confirms that the health status of older men does play a key role in influencing early retirement.[30]

The role of Social Security retirement benefits and private pensions in influencing the retirement behavior of older workers received considerable attention from researchers in the 1980s. Studies of how the Social Security system influences retirement behavior have generated a diverse array of findings. The timing of retirement by older workers clearly appears to be affected by the eligibility provisions of the Social Security Act, with sharp jumps in retirement taking place at ages 62 and 65.[31] Although some researchers have argued that particular Social Security changes, such as increases in the real level of benefits, do raise early retirement rates, others have claimed that the Social Security system in the aggregate may operate to delay retirement.[32]

Although the level of real Social Security retirement benefits may affect retirement decisions, the estimated impact of even fairly large changes in monthly benefits does not seem to be substantial. For example, Fields and Mitchell estimated that even a 13% reduction in the size of a monthly Social Security payment would postpone the optimal retirement age only by a little more than one month.[33]

Growth in private pensions also has an effect on retirement behavior.[34] Pension coverage in the private sector expanded rapidly between the mid-1940s and 1975, increasing from 15% to 25% at the beginning of this period to nearly 50% at the end.[35] Growth in private-sector pension coverage has slowed since then, influenced in part by the changing industrial structure of the U.S. economy. Today, workers in many private service and trade industries have below-average pension coverage rates.[36] Comparisons of the private pension coverage of new Social Security beneficiaries over the 1969–82 period reveal rising fractions of new beneficiaries with private pension income.[37] These gains in coverage occurred across the board for men, women, whites, and blacks, although large sex and race differences in coverage rates continue to exist.[38]

Generalizations about trends in the terms of these private pension plans are difficult, given that there are an estimated 500,000 plans.[39] However, a recent study of 187 private pension plans in medium-size and large establishments revealed that provisions encouraging early retirement had been built into a growing number of plans.[40] This trend in private pension provisions favoring early retirement reflects the values and goals of both employers and workers.[41]

Human resource management consultants and specialists have also advocated early retirement schemes as an economic policy for corporations involved in downsizing and restructuring.[42] A growing number of firms have offered early retirees supplemental pension benefits that cover, if not exceed, the Social Security benefits to which they will later be entitled.[43] In times of recession and restructuring, firms have also increasingly resorted to "open windows," encouraging employees in the 50–55 age group to opt for early retirement.[44] The greater use of such early retirement schemes, however, has increasingly been questioned by observers here and abroad as being of little economic value to workers and society.[45]

Satisfaction with one's job before retirement and with the retirement experience also influence the labor supply decisions of older men. Those older men who expressed dissatisfaction with their jobs before retirement were more likely to withdraw from active labor force participation before age 65.[46] Those who held jobs in lower-status occupations and with less desirable working conditions are also more likely to retire earlier.[47]

Findings of national longitudinal research on older men consistently have revealed that a substantial majority of retired men enjoy being retired and are therefore unlikely to return to work. Life satisfaction for most of these men is quite high under retirement, and they typically do not miss work.[48] Crowley has in fact noted that a substantial majority of retired men find retirement to be as enjoyable as they had anticipated or better than expected.[49] Men who had retired for health reasons or because of an inability to find work were more likely than those retiring voluntarily to express dissatisfaction with their retirement situation.

Efforts to attract greater numbers of retirees back into the labor force are likely to be of limited success in the absence of fundamental changes in the work environments for older workers. Findings of a recent Gallup survey for the American Association of Retired Persons revealed that the three most frequently cited reasons for working by persons 63 and over were that they enjoyed the job and work, that work made them feel useful, and that work enabled them to contribute to society and help others.[50] Future jobs will have to be viewed by retired workers or potential retirees as a source of high satisfaction that can compete with the perceived value of leisure pursuits. The additional income provided by work may not be a sufficiently strong lure to induce any substantive substitution of work for leisure.

The Changing Job Market for Older Workers

Sectoral Shifts

The labor market in which older workers hold and seek jobs has changed in a number of fundamental respects over the past two decades.[51] Among the more important changes have been those related to the industrial sectors in which older persons are employed and the occupational characteristics of the jobs they hold. The continued shift in national employment away from the goods-producing sector toward the services-producing sector has affected older workers as well as those under age 55 (see Table 4.8).[52]

The construction industry was the only segment of the goods-producing

Table 4.8. **Distribution of Employed Persons (55 +) by Sector and Major Industry Group, United States: March 1968, March 1980, and March 1988 (Percentages)**

| | All Persons 55 + | | |
| | (A) March 1968 | (B) March 1980 | (C) March 1988 |
Industry Group			
Goods-Producing Sector	36.5	32.8	28.5
Agriculture, Forestry, Fishing, Mining	9.1	6.0	5.3
Construction	5.1	4.9	5.7
Nondurable Manufacturing	9.9	8.7	7.3
Durable Manufacturing	12.4	13.2	10.2
Service-Producing Sector	63.5	67.2	71.5
Transportation, Communications, Utilities	5.5	5.6	6.8
Wholesale Trade	3.3	4.2	4.2
Retail Trade	14.9	14.3	13.8
Finance, Insurance, Real Estate	4.7	5.9	7.1
Services*	29.8	31.3	34.5
Public Administration	5.4	6.0	5.2

*The services industries are a subset of the services-producing sector. Service industries include a diverse array of activities, including business, education, entertainment, health, legal, professional, and social services.

Source: U.S. Bureau of the Census, Current Population Survey (March), selected years, 1968–88, public use tapes.

sector in which older workers increased their share of employment over this period. Older workers in construction are almost exclusively (95%) male.

The shift in older worker employment away from manufacturing industries, especially durable manufacturing, accelerated in the 1980s as the forces of economic dislocation became more intense. Plant closings and major downsizings were concentrated in the nation's largest manufacturing firms.[53] Sharp differentials between the pace of retirements and new hires were characteristic of many large corporations. A recent Arthur Andersen and Company study estimates that the ratio of workers to living retirees at a typical Fortune 500 company fell from 12 to 1 in 1974 to 3 to 1 in 1988.[54]

There have been particularly large increases in the share of older workers employed by finance, insurance, and real estate industries and in services industries over the past 20 years as shown in Table 4.8. The shift in employment toward the services-producing sector has taken place among both older men and older women. However, the growth in women's share of older worker employment over this period has also been a contributing factor, given their greater concentration in the services-producing sector (84% of women versus 62% of men).[55]

Firms in the service industries provides a relatively high share (40%) of the employment opportunities for workers 65 and over. A variety of factors influence this particular outcome, including the greater representation within these industries of professional, management, and service occupations that are associated with later retirement; more frequent opportunities for part-time and part-year work; and lower rates of pension coverage that increase the need for earnings by older workers who become eligible for Social Security retirement benefits.[56]

The observed shifts in the industrial employment patterns of older workers over the past two decades are likely to continue throughout the remainder of the century. Under the moderate employment growth scenario of the U.S. Bureau of Labor Statistics, all the projected net growth in nonfarm wage and salary employment (20.1 million) between 1986 and 2000 will take place in the services-producing sector.[57] The wholesale and retail trade industries (27%) and private service industries (44%) are projected to be the fastest growing sources of net new employment opportunities for the U.S. workforce over the remainder of the century.

Occupational Employment Patterns

The changing industrial distribution of employed older workers has been accompanied by a shift in their occupational employment patterns (see Table 4.9).[58] The increase in the share of older workers holding white-collar occupations (professional, managerial, technical, sales, and administrative support) has been influenced by the shift in employment toward the services-producing sector, changes in the mix of industries within both the goods- and service-

Table 4.9. **Distribution of Employed Persons (55 +) by Major Occupational Group, United States: March 1968 and March 1988, All Persons, and March 1988, by Sex**

Occupational Group	(A) March 1968	(B) March 1988	(C) March 1988, Men	(D) March 1988, Women
White-Collar	44.1	56.0	50.3	63.9
Professional, Technical, Managerial	25.9	28.6	32.3	23.3
Sales*	6.4	12.6	12.4	12.9
Administrative Support, Including Clerical	11.8	14.8	5.6	27.7
Service Workers	16.7	14.6	8.9	22.7
Blue-Collar	31.1	24.9	33.8	12.1
Construction Crafts, Mechanics, Repairers, Precision Production	12.9	11.3	17.5	2.5
Operatives, Fabricators, Material Moving Operators, and Laborers	18.2	13.5	16.3	9.6
Farming, Forestry, Fishing	8.1	4.7	7.0	1.4

*A portion of the near doubling in the share of older workers employed in sales occupations is attributable to a shift in the classification of cashiers and real estate appraisers from clerical to sales occupations between the 1968 and 1988 survey.

Source: U.S. Bureau of the Census, Current Population Survey (March), selected years, 1968–88, public use tapes.

producing sectors, and the impacts of technological change on the occupational composition of employment within given industries.

The more rapidly expanding industries (finance/insurance, services) more intensively employ workers in white-collar occupations, especially professionals and managers.[59] Within manufacturing and high-level service industries, a growing share of employment has been accounted for by high technology industries that employ above-average shares of high-level, white-collar workers.[60] Also, the outsourcing of production by manufacturing firms to plants outside the United States has reduced the need for semiskilled and unskilled blue-collar workers.[61] Although the impacts of technological change on the skill requirements of jobs remain mixed, automation in factories and offices is more likely to lead to the displacement of blue-collar workers. White-collar workers are more frequently provided opportunities for lateral transfer.[62]

Although both older men and older women were more likely to be employed in white-collar occupations in 1988 than they were in 1968, the types of jobs occupied by older men still tend to be quite different from those occupied by older women.[63] Older women hold white-collar jobs at a higher rate than men (64% versus 50%); however, women are underrepresented in the ranks of professional, managerial, and technical employees and substantially overrepresented among administrative support workers (28% of women versus 6% of men). Older males are three times more likely than women to hold blue-collar occupations, and they clearly dominate employment in the construction, mechanics, and precision production craft occupations. Both older men and women in semiskilled and unskilled blue-collar occupations have been at greatest risk of economic dislocation in the 1980s.

Projections of occupational employment to the year 2000 suggest that recent trends in the employment patterns of older workers will continue.[64] Approximately two-thirds of the projected 21.4 million gain in national employment between 1986 and 2000 will be in white-collar occupations. The numbers of employed persons in professional, managerial, technical, and sales occupations are projected to grow at rates 50% to 100% above those for all occupations combined.

Part-Time, Full-Time, and Self-Employment

The nature of the jobs held by older workers has changed in other key respects over the past two decades. The role of self-employment has diminished somewhat in importance, largely as a consequence of the decline in family farms, and an increasing share of older workers now hold part-time jobs (fewer than 35 hours per week).[65] The employment patterns of 55- to 65-year-olds, however, differ in a number of substantive ways from those of the elderly (see Table 4.10). Among 55- to 65-year-olds, full-time employment (75%) is the norm while part-time jobs account for a majority (55%) of the employment positions held by those age 66 and over. The increased share of elderly employment accounted for by the self-employed reflects the greater labor

Table 4.10. **Distribution of Employed Older Workers (55 +) by Type of Employment, by Age Subgroup, United States: March 1988 (Percentages)**

Employment Category	(A) All 55 +	(B) 55–65	(C) 66 +
Self-Employed	15.4	13.6	23.6
Part-time	6.5	4.8	14.0
Full-time	8.9	8.8	9.6
Private Sector Wage and Salary	66.3	67.5	60.8
Part-time	18.7	15.5	33.2
Full-time	47.6	52.0	27.6
Public Sector Wage and Salary	17.4	18.2	13.7
Part-time	4.8	4.1	7.8
Full-time	12.6	14.1	5.9
Unpaid Family Worker	.6	.5	1.3
Paid Full-time, All	69.1	74.9	43.1
Paid Part-time, All	30.0	24.4	55.0
Part-time or Self-Employed or Unpaid Family Worker	38.9	33.7	65.8

Source: U.S. Bureau of the Census, Current Population Survey (March), selected years, 1968–88, public use tapes.

market attachment of the self-employed as they age, particularly those in agriculture.[66] Farmers still account for nearly 30% of the self-employed age 66 and older.

The shifts in the labor force participation and employment patterns of older workers as they move from the 55–65 to the 66 and over group tend to be accompanied by a substantial rise in the concentration of earnings among older workers (Table 4.11). The degree of inequality in the annual earnings distribution is fairly high among all older workers, but increases sharply for those 66 and over. The greater availability and higher levels of retirement income made

Table 4.11. **Shares of Total Earnings Received by Quintiles of the Earnings Distribution for Employed Older Persons (55 +) and for Selected Age Subgroups, United States: 1987 (Percentages)**

Quintile of Earnings Distribution	(A) All Older Workers 55 +	(B) Workers 55–65	(C) Elderly 66 +
Bottom 20%	1.8	2.5	0.9
Second Lowest 20%	7.6	8.8	4.4
Middle 20%	14.1	15.9	9.5
Second Highest 20%	26.5	24.9	18.9
Top 20%	49.8	48.0	66.4
Totals	100.0	100.0	100.0

Source: U.S. Bureau of the Census, Current Population Survey (March), selected years, 1968–88, public use tapes.

possible by the expansion of the Social Security and private pension systems, however, have reduced the need for employment among the elderly to avoid severe income inadequacy problems.[67]

Labor Market Problems of Older Workers: An Overview

A diverse array of labor market problems affect U.S. workers and their families. Among the more important are (1) unemployment, (2) part-time employment for economic reasons (as opposed to voluntary part-time employment), (3) the labor force "overhang" (persons wanting to be employed but not actively seeking work),[68] and (4) being employed but not earning enough to raise one's family income above some minimum adequacy threshold (such as the poverty line of the federal government).[69]

A review of the incidence of these four labor market problems among key age subgroups of the nation's adult population (20 and older) in March 1988 reveals that older persons were the least likely to experience any of these four problems (see Table 4.12).[70] Nearly one of every six adults over the age of 20 in the United States experienced one of these four labor market problems in early 1988, over twice the rate of older workers. Table 4.12 shows clearly that older persons in the aggregate were the most immune from the labor market problems affecting the U.S. workforce in 1988, and the findings for 1988 are not atypical. Similar patterns prevailed for 1979 and 1982, with the incidence of such labor market problems for all age groups being highest in the 1982 recession year.

Although older persons as a group are characterized by the lowest incidence of labor market and income inadequacy problems, the frequency of such problems among the older population does vary widely by age and by

Table 4.12. **Incidence of Selected Labor Market Problems Among Age Subgroups of the Adult Population (20 +), United States: March 1988 (Percentages, N = 169.1 Million)**

Age Subgroup	(A) Unemployed	(B) Employed Part-time for Economic Reasons	(C) Labor Force Overhang	(D) Worked, but Poor or Near Poor	(E) All Problems (A to D)
All 20 +	3.5	2.8	2.5	6.6	15.4
20–24	7.4	5.0	3.7	13.8	29.9
25–34	4.9	3.5	2.8	9.2	20.5
35–44	3.8	2.9	3.1	7.2	17.0
45–54	2.7	2.9	2.2	4.9	12.7
55 +	1.0	1.3	1.6	2.2	6.0

Source: U.S. Bureau of the Census, Current Population Survey (March), selected years, 1968–88, public use tapes.

demographic/socioeconomic subgroup (see Table 4.13).[71] The younger members of the older population would be expected to account for an above-average share of most labor market problems because they are more strongly attached to the labor market and are more likely to express an interest in employment when they are not actively participating in the labor force.[72] The youngest members of the older population (55–59 and 60–62) experience the highest incidence of all such problems, as Table 4.13 shows. To have a substantial impact, therefore, future human resource strategies aimed at combating labor market problems of older persons must focus on the age 55–65 cohort.

As expected, the incidence of labor market problems among those 55–65 years old varies considerably by ethnic origin, education, and family income (see Table 4.14). Older persons lacking a high school diploma (14%) were most at risk of experiencing one of these labor market problems. Both Hispanics and blacks were considerably more likely than whites to be members of the working poor or near poor. This finding deserves the attention of the nation's employment and training policymakers because racial minorities and Hispanics will become a larger share of the nation's population in this age group over the remainder of the century.

The incidence of labor market problems among the nation's 55- to 65-year-olds also varies considerably by geographic region, reflecting the diversity in regional labor market conditions and earnings structures. The coastal regions (New England, Middle Atlantic, and Pacific) were characterized by stronger economic conditions and lower unemployment rates through 1988, and older persons in these regions were considerably less likely to encounter any one of our four labor market problems.[73] In the full employment environment (3.1% aggregate unemployment rate) characterizing most of New England, only 5% of the region's 55- to 65-year-olds were affected by one of these four labor market problems. The ratios for the other eight geographic regions varied

Table 4.13. **Incidence of Selected Labor Market Problems Among Age Subgroups of the Older Population, United States: March 1988 (Percentages, $N = 50.0$ Million)**

Age Subgroup	(A) Unemployed	(B) Employed Part-time for Economic Reasons	(C) Labor Force Overhang	(D) Worked, but Poor or Near Poor	(E) All Problems (A to D)
All 55+	1.0	1.3	1.6	2.2	6.0
55–59	2.4	2.6	2.8	4.4	12.2
60–62	1.8	2.3	2.0	3.2	9.3
63–65	1.1	1.1	2.5	2.1	6.8
66–70	0.3	1.0	1.4	1.2	4.0
71+	0.1	0.3	0.4	0.9	1.7

Source: U.S. Bureau of the Census, Current Population Survey (March), selected years, 1968–88, public use tapes.

Table 4.14. **Incidence of Selected Labor Market Problems Among Subgroups of the 55- to 65-Year-Old Population, United States: March 1988 (Percentages, *N* = 23.7 Million)**

Subgroup	(A) Unemployed	(B) Employed Part-time for Economic Reasons	(C) Labor Force Overhang	(D) Worked, but Poor or Near Poor	(E) All Problems (A to D)
All	1.9	2.1	2.5	3.4	9.9
Sex					
Female	1.0	2.0	2.7	3.1	8.8
Male	2.9	2.2	2.3	3.8	11.2
Ethnic Group					
Black, non-Hispanic	2.5	2.5	3.7	6.5	15.2
Hispanic	3.6	3.7	3.6	8.7	19.6
White, non-Hispanic	1.6	2.0	2.3	2.8	8.7
Education					
Less than 12 years	2.7	3.2	2.6	5.5	14.0
12 years	1.6	1.7	2.7	2.9	8.9
13–15 years	1.3	1.5	1.6	2.0	6.4
16 or more years	1.4	1.2	2.7	1.6	6.9
Family Income Relative to Poverty Line					
Less than 1.00	3.2	3.2	5.9	22.4	34.7
1.00–1.99	2.1	2.8	3.3	6.8	15.1
2.00–2.99	2.2	2.6	2.7	.0	7.4
3.00–3.99	1.5	1.6	1.6	.0	4.6

Source: U.S. Bureau of the Census, Current Population Survey (March), selected years, 1968–88, public use tapes.

from a low of 7% for the Midatlantic region to a high of 18% in the economically depressed West South Central region (Arkansas, Louisiana, Texas, Oklahoma).

Spells of Unemployment

Although the aggregate unemployment rates of older workers in the 1980s have been low in both absolute and relative terms, the unemployment problems of key subgroups of the nation's older labor force appear to have contributed to a decline in their labor force attachment. Spells of unemployment for a relatively high fraction of unemployed older workers end by withdrawal from the labor force, rather than by returning to work.[74] For example, among workers who experienced a spell of unemployment in 1984 and who terminated that spell by early 1986, 34% of the male 55- to 64-year-olds did not find work and withdrew from the labor force instead.[75] This labor force withdrawal rate was

50% higher than that for all unemployed men age 16 and older and more than twice as high as that for prime-aged males (ages 25 to 54). The comparable withdrawal rate for unemployed women in the 55–64 age group was 41%, roughly identical to that for all women (16 and older).

Similarly, the dislocated worker surveys conducted by the U.S. Bureau of Labor Statistics in 1984, 1986, and 1988 revealed that older dislocated workers were least likely to become reemployed.[76] Of those dislocated workers 55–64 years of age who had three or more years of tenure on the jobs from which they were displaced, only 41% to 50% were employed at the time of the three surveys, a ratio well below the 65% to 77% reemployment rates for prime-aged workers.[77]

Economic Dislocation and the Older Worker

During the 1980s, the problems of economic dislocation became widely publicized.[78] The Bureau of Labor Statistics conducted three household surveys in the 1980s to estimate the numbers and characteristics of dislocated workers and to identify their labor market experiences since displacement. The size and nature of dislocation problems among older workers, as revealed in the 1986 dislocated worker survey, are examined in the next section.

How Many Dislocated Older Workers?

The annual number of dislocated workers (age 20 and over) averaged 2.3 million during the first half of the 1980s, a period marked by two economic recessions, and approximately 1.94 million over the 1983–87 period. Slightly under half of these dislocated workers had been working with their former employer for three or more years.

The labor market turbulence associated with plant closings, relocations, downsizings, and other major reductions in force strongly impacted older workers, especially those with three or more years of tenure, as Table 4.15 shows. Older workers accounted for over 11% of all dislocated workers and almost one-fifth of those with three or more years of tenure.

Dislocation Among Subgroups of Older Workers

Although all major demographic subgroups of older workers were affected by economic dislocation, the rates of dislocation over the five-year period covered by the 1986 survey varied by sex, ethnic group, and educational attainment (see Table 4.16).[79] The greatest differences in dislocation rates prevailed among educational attainment subgroups, with those older workers lacking any postsecondary schooling being most affected.

Older workers in each major industry and occupational group were affected to some degree by labor market turbulence during the 1980s (see Tables 4.17 and 4.18). However, those employed in mining and manufacturing indus-

Table 4.15. **Estimated Number and Percentage Distribution of Dislocated Workers and Dislocated Workers as Percent of the Adjusted Civilian Labor Force by Age Group, January 1986 (Numbers in 1000s)**

Age	(A) Number	(B) Percentage of Total	(C) Annual Average Number	(D) Annual Average Number as Percentage of Adjusted Civilian Labor Force*
All				
Dislocated				
Total	10,837	100.0	2,167	2.0
20–24	1,549	14.3	310	2.0
25–34	4,062	37.5	812	2.4
35–44	2,507	23.1	501	1.6
45–54	1,484	13.7	297	1.6
55–64	1,014	9.4	203	1.7
65 +	222	2.0	44	1.5
Dislocated with				
Three or More				
Years of Tenure				
Total	5,130	100.0	1,026	1.0
20–24	222	4.3	44	0.3
25–34	1,641	32.0	328	1.0
35–44	1,326	25.8	265	1.0
45–54	983	19.2	197	1.1
55–64	789	15.4	158	1.3
65 +	169	3.3	34	1.1

*The adjusted civilian labor force is defined as the number of individuals classified as employed or unemployed at the time of the January 1986 survey plus the number of dislocated workers who had withdrawn from active labor force participation during that month.

Source: U.S. Bureau of the Census, Current Population Survey (January), 1986, public use tape.

tries were the most adversely affected, with rates of dislocation two or three times the average for all 55- to 64-year-olds.

Given substantial differences in the occupational staffing patterns of major industries, one would anticipate that the large interindustry differences in dislocation rates would be accompanied by fairly large differences in dislocation rates by major occupational group. Semiskilled and unskilled blue-collar workers were far more heavily impacted by the forces of dislocation than were white-collar workers, farm/forestry workers, and those holding jobs in service occupations, as shown in Table 4.18.

These findings on substantial variability during the 1980s in the displacement rates of older workers by major occupational group stand in sharp contrast to those for the late 1960s and early 1970s.[80] There were no major differences in reported dislocation rates by occupation or educational attainment among older workers over the 1966–76 period.[81] The labor market

Table 4.16. **Estimates of the Numbers and Rates of Dislocation Among Older Workers, by Sex, Ethnic Group, and Educational Attainment, January 1981–January 1986 (Numbers in 1000s)**

Group	(A) Number	(B) Dislocation Rate* (percentage)
All	1,014	8.5
Sex		
Female	409	8.3
Male	604	8.6
Race/Ethnic Origin		
Black, non-Hispanic	83	7.9
Hispanic	39	7.5
White, non-Hispanic	870	8.5
Years of Schooling		
Fewer than 12	400	11.7
12	395	8.4
13–15	110	6.7
16 or More	109	4.9

*The dislocation rate is defined as the number of dislocated workers over the 1981–86 period divided by the adjusted civilian labor force in January 1986.

Source: U.S. Bureau of the Census, Current Population Survey (January), 1986, public use tape.

turbulence of the 1980s appears therefore to have affected the incidence of dislocation among educational and occupational subgroups, as well as the overall rate of dislocation among older workers.

Post-Displacement Labor Market Experiences of Older Dislocated Workers

Among age subgroups, older dislocated workers have experienced the most severe difficulties in obtaining reemployment. Typically, only half of the dislocated workers 55–64 years of age were employed at the time of the three Bureau of Labor Statistics dislocated worker surveys. The below-average employment/population ratios for older dislocated workers were the consequence of both lower labor force participation rates and higher rates of unemployment than their younger counterparts. Only half of all older dislocated workers were employed at the time of the January 1986 survey versus 65% to 73% of those of the younger age subgroups.

The employment rates of older dislocated workers varied somewhat by sex and ethnic origin, and they were positively associated with the number of years of schooling completed (see Table 4.19).[82] The below-average employment rates of older dislocated workers with no post-secondary schooling were at-

Table 4.17. **Estimated Dislocation Rates of Employed 55- to 64-Year-Olds During the January 1981–January 1986 Period, by Major Industrial Group (Numbers Per 100 Employees)**

Major Industrial Group	Dislocation Rate*
Agriculture, Forestry, Fishing	6.6
Mining	21.6
Construction	9.4
Durable Manufacturing	17.8
Nondurable Manufacturing	16.8
Transportation, Communications, Utilities	9.0
Wholesale Trade	12.0
Retail Trade	7.3
Finance, Insurance, Real Estate	2.9
Services	3.6
Public Administration	3.9
Total	8.7

*The dislocation rate for each industry group was obtained by dividing the number of 55- to 64-year-olds displaced from the industry over the previous five years by the sum of the displaced and those employed in that industry group at the time of the January 1986 survey.

Source: U.S. Bureau of the Census, Current Population Survey (January), 1986, public use tape.

tributable to a combination of lower rates of labor force attachment and higher unemployment rates.

The more severe unemployment problems encountered by the less educated older dislocated workers were associated with the occupational characteristics of the jobs from which they were displaced. A high fraction of the older unemployed with no post-secondary schooling had held semiskilled and un-

Table 4.18. **Estimated Dislocation Rates of Employed 55- to 64-Year-Olds Over the January 1981–January 1986 Period, by Major Occupational Group (Numbers Per 100 Employees)**

Major Occupational Group	Dislocation Rate*
Professional, Technical, Management	5.4
Sales	9.3
Administrative Support	4.2
Service Workers	4.4
Farming, Forestry, Fishing	2.5
Mechanics, Repair, Construction Trades	10.2
Extractive and Precision Production	17.7
Operators, Fabricators, Material Movers	19.1
Handlers, Cleaners, Laborers	16.8

*The dislocation rate for each major occupational group was obtained by dividing the number of 55-64 year olds displaced from that occupational group over the previous five years by the sum of the displaced and those employed in that occupational group at the time of the January 1986 survey.

Source: U.S. Bureau of the Census, Current Population Survey (January), 1986, public use tape.

Table 4.19. **Labor Force Participation Rates, Unemployment Rates, and Employment/Population Ratios for Older Dislocated Workers 55–64 Years Old, by Sex, Ethnic Group, and Educational Attainment, January 1986**

	Labor Force Participation Rate	Unemployment Rate	Employment/ Population Ratio
Total	67.2	25.8	49.9
Sex			
Male	69.4	22.5	53.8
Female	64.1	31.0	44.2
Race/Ethnic Group			
White, not Hispanic	66.9	23.9	50.9
Black, not Hispanic	71.5	31.0	49.3
Hispanic	73.9	41.4	43.4
Education			
High School Dropout	62.7	33.6	41.6
High School Graduate	68.1	24.9	51.2
Some College	72.2	21.7	56.5
College Graduate	76.0	8.7	69.4

Source: U.S. Bureau of the Census, Current Population Survey (January), 1986, public use tape.

skilled blue-collar jobs. In contrast, the college-educated, displaced older workers had held jobs in occupational areas (professional, managerial) and in industrial sectors (finance, services) that were experiencing above average rates of employment growth during the 1981–86 period.

Approximately one-third of older dislocated workers (ages 55 to 64) had withdrawn from active labor force participation by January 1986, as shown in Table 4.19. This represented a rate of withdrawal two to three times higher than that of their younger counterparts.[83] Clearly, some of the older workers not active in the labor force in January 1986 were individuals who chose to retire after being dislocated and were no longer interested in seeking paid employment. However, problems of high unemployment among older dislocated workers may have affected the propensity of some of the jobless to withdraw from active job search.

To determine whether the dislocated older workers not active in the labor force in January 1986 were interested in employment, their responses to the CPS survey questions on immediate job desires were analyzed (see Table 4.20).[84] The table clearly shows that the pool of older dislocated workers not attached to the labor force contain substantial fractions of individuals with an interest in reemployment. Economic dislocation clearly appears to reduce the labor force attachment of older workers.

Slightly more than 60% of the older dislocated workers with an interest in immediate employment cited "discouragement" reasons for not actively seeking employment, with economic discouragement factors being cited twice as often as personal discouragement factors ("too old" for consideration by

Table 4.20. **Job Desire Rate* of Dislocated Workers and All Other Adults (20 +) Who Were Not in the Labor Force During January 1986, by Age Subgroup (Percentages)**

Age Group	All Persons Not in the Labor Force	Dislocated Workers	All Others
All 20 +	7.6	27.1	7.0
20–24	20.8	42.4	20.1
25–34	16.7	24.7	16.1
35–44	15.6	29.0	14.9
45–54	10.0	24.3	9.1
55–64	5.4	31.0	4.5
65 +	1.3	10.3	1.3

*Those persons responding "yes" or "maybe" to the question "Do you want a job now?" were included in the count of those wanting immediate employment. The estimates represent the fraction of nonparticipants who expressed a desire for immediate employment.

Source: U.S. Bureau of the Census, Current Population Survey (January), 1986, public use tape.

employers). Of those expressing a desire for immediate employment, 84% indicated that they would seek work during the following year, while only 4% of those with no interest in immediate employment planned to look for a job during the following 12 months. Unfortunately, no information is available on the types of jobs older dislocated workers would like to obtain or the conditions that would have to be present for them to take advantage of potential job offers.[85]

Industrial/Occupational Mobility of Reemployed Older Dislocated Workers

The reemployment of dislocated workers is frequently accompanied by shifts to different industrial sectors and occupational groups.[86] Plant closings and major downsizings often make it necessary for displaced workers to seek employment in different industries, particularly when the industrial sector from which one is displaced is in decline in the local economy. Given the absolute declines in employment in key goods-producing industries during the early 1980s, one would expect workers displaced from such industries to experience greater difficulties in gaining reemployment in the same sector than those displaced from expanding industries.

The 1986 Bureau of Labor Statistics dislocated worker survey provides information on the industry from which workers were displaced and the industry in which they were employed at the time of the survey. A comparison of the combined industry groups from which workers were displaced with those in which they were currently employed revealed that only 37% of the reemployed older workers (55-64) had secured new jobs in the same broad group of industries from which they were displaced. This share was basically identical to that (37.3%) for all dislocated workers age 20 and older, indicating a high degree of industrial mobility for all age subgroups.

The industrial mobility rates of dislocated older workers did vary by industrial sector of displacement, however. A below-average share (31%) of the older workers displaced from manufacturing industries were able to be reabsorbed by a firm in the same industry group. Re-absorption rates were also quite low for older workers displaced from the transportation/utilities industries (23%) and from finance, insurance, and real estate (21%). Older workers displaced from the services industries were most likely to become reemployed in the same industrial area (60%). This last finding is in accord with expectations, given the explosive growth in employment in services industries during the 1980s.

The major occupational groups from which older workers were displaced were compared with those in which they had become reemployed by January 1986. Overall, 57% of reemployed older dislocated workers had been able to secure a job in the same major occupational category from which they were displaced, a ratio nearly six percentage points above that for all dislocated workers.

The ability of older dislocated workers to secure related employment, however, varied by major occupational group. Workers displaced from service occupations (70%) were most likely to become reemployed in the same major occupational group, followed by sales and administrative support workers (64%) and workers from professional and managerial occupations (61%). Only half of those older workers displaced from skilled and semiskilled blue-collar occupations were able to secure new employment in the same major occupational group. Given their greater rates of displacement during the 1981–85 period, many blue-collar workers would be expected to find themselves in a surplus labor situation in their local labor market.

Earnings Losses of Older Dislocated Workers

In addition to their problems in securing new jobs, older dislocated workers tended to encounter higher wage losses upon becoming reemployed than their younger counterparts. The weekly wages of the jobs from which dislocated workers were displaced were compared to those received from jobs held at the time of the January 1986 survey (see Table 4.21). Older dislocated workers incurred the largest relative weekly wage declines whether measured by the median or the mean weekly wage replacement ratio. Part of the difference is attributable to a greater shift to part-time employment among reemployed older workers. However, at least one-third of these shifts to part-time employment were due to economic factors rather than to a voluntary preference for part-time work. These lower weekly wages for older workers understate the true real earnings declines because they do not take into consideration the effects of inflation.[87]

The distribution of the replacement wage ratios for reemployed older dislocated workers is characterized by a substantial degree of dispersion. Among reemployed 55- to 64-year-olds, one of four experienced a weekly wage decline of 40% or more. On the other hand, 31% of the reemployed older

Table 4.21. **Current Weekly Wages of Employed Dislocated Workers as a Percentage of Weekly Wages on Job from Which Displaced, by Age Group (Median and Mean Values)**

Age Group	Median Weekly Wage Ratio	Mean Weekly Wage Ratio
All 20 +	100.0	114.8
20–24	114.3	130.4
25–34	102.5	119.2
35–44	100.0	111.1
45–54	100.0	105.9
55–64	87.5	87.1
65 +	75.0	85.4

Source: U.S. Bureau of the Census, Current Population Survey (January), 1986, public use tape.

dislocated workers were able to secure weekly wages in excess of those received on the jobs from which they were displaced. Overall, older dislocated workers were considerably more likely than their younger counterparts to suffer relatively large weekly wage declines. Only 25% to 30% of reemployed dislocated workers under 45 years of age incurred weekly wage declines of 20% or more versus 45% for dislocated workers in the 55–64 age group.

Receiving comparable replacement wages depends largely on the ability of reemployed older dislocated workers to secure employment in the same industrial sector or major occupational group from which they were displaced. Among those employed in the same industrial sector, the mean wage replacement ratio was 90%, versus 85% for those who were employed in a different industrial sector. Those obtaining employment in the same occupational group had a mean replacement wage ratio of 93%, versus 82% for those transferring to a new occupational group.

Improving the Preparedness and Utilization of Older Workers

Private Sector Role

Given that nearly 7 of every 10 employed older persons hold wage and salary jobs in private sector firms, future efforts to strengthen the preparedness and utilization of older workers will have to be focused primarily on the human resource management policies and practices of private sector firms and labor unions.[88] An array of training, work scheduling, recruitment, outplacement activities, and pension reforms by private sector firms can contribute to the attainment of important national workforce preparedness goals for older workers.

Increased training investments to update the skills of older workers and to assist them in acquiring new skills can play a critical role in improving the productivity of these workers and their ability to adapt to new technologies in the workplace.[89] A 1985 survey of full-time employees conducted by the Gallup Organization for the American Association of Retired Persons found that workers 50–62 years old were less likely than workers 40–49 years old to have received on-the-job training over the past three years and slightly less likely to have received employer-provided offsite training.[90] Older workers (age 50 to 62) were also less likely than their younger counterparts to have invested in their own training outside of work (12% versus 17%).

Human capital theory would predict some age differential due to the lower worklife available to recover the costs of the training investment. There are, however, steps that can be taken to increase such investments by older workers, including greater employer cost reimbursement for satisfactory performance in such programs, wage and salary improvements tied to completion of job-related courses, and tax deductibility of training expenses incurred by older workers in upgrading their skills. The same survey found a high level of interest among older workers in updating their existing skills (44%) and acquiring new skills that would qualify them for different jobs (33%).[91]

The likelihood of older workers receiving training from their employers varies widely by occupational area, however, with professionals and managers more likely to receive such training than laborers and other less-skilled workers. The lack of recent training investments in less-educated older workers combined with the greater tendency for their career jobs to end earlier in their worklife can create severe readjustment problems.[92] Dislocated workers with limited education tend to experience the most severe reemployment problems and suffer relatively greater losses in earnings upon reemployment.[93]

Given the frequent finding that many older workers would like to remain employed at least part-time following retirement from their career job, increased efforts should be made by private sector firms and unions to facilitate the ability of workers to retire gradually. A number of U.S. firms and Western European nations have developed innovative programs in this area, and a high fraction of older workers indicate that the availability of such partial retirement options would influence their retirement plan.[94]

The expansion of such partial retirement options will likely require reforms of existing pension plans to enable such workers to receive partial retirement benefits while they remain at work. More flexible compensation schemes may also be needed to encourage firms to offer more flexible part-time and part-year work arrangements. Research suggests, however, that the higher fixed costs and lower productivity often associated with part-time work inhibit greater adoption of such arrangements by employers of older workers.[95]

The potential for small employers to expand employment opportunities for older workers, especially those 65 and over, should be more actively promoted. Elderly workers are much more likely than those 55–64 years old to occupy jobs in small establishments (1–24 workers).[96] These smaller establishments, which have been increasing their share of total employment, are believed to possess more flexibility in meeting the flextime, part-time, and part-year employment desires of older workers.[97] They are also more likely to have greater flexibility in their compensation systems that allows them to facilitate the use of such variable work arrangements. Greater use of small employers by local networks serving the employment needs of older workers may well be desirable.

As noted earlier, changes in key provisions of private pension plans over the past decade have encouraged earlier retirement by workers. A reconsideration of early retirement incentives in private pension plans may well be called for to encourage continued employment by older workers. Among the provisions for which changes might be appropriate are those involving minimum age/service requirements for early retirement eligibility, the penalties attached to pension payments for early retirement, and the peaking of the actuarial values of defined benefit plans well before age 65.[98]

The economic impacts of dislocation associated with plant closings and downsizings have been felt by many older workers, especially those occupying blue-collar positions and those with no post-secondary schooling. In recent years, increasing concern has been expressed about the economic value of downsizing both to firms and to society at large. The adverse impacts of downsizing have included a reduction in the morale and loyalty of remaining employees, with attendant consequences for turnover and productivity. The reductions in the number of experienced older workers have also led to a loss of valuable skills and experience that often have to be reacquired through use of consultants or new hires.[99] Alternatives to downsizing include the development of new markets for existing products and services, more flexible work assignments, and retraining of existing workers to fill new skill requirements.[100]

When displacement cannot be avoided, greater efforts by management and labor unions to work together to facilitate the outplacement of dislocated workers should be promoted. A recent Government Accounting Office review of a series of Department of Labor demonstration projects involving joint labor/management committees to assist in the placement of workers affected by plant closings revealed that such committees can play an important role.[101] Among the benefits are an increased ability to provide adequate information on services to workers, increased access of displaced workers to services immediately before and after displacement, delivery of on-site services, and a personalization of the adjustment process. Older workers appear to have been better served by such programs than by regular JTPA Title III programs. Older workers accounted for 12% of the participants in the projects reviewed in the GAO study versus 8% in all JTPA dislocated worker programs.

The passage of the Economic Dislocation and Worker Adjustment Assistance Act of 1988 has the potential for expanding such initiatives. Among the provisions of the legislation are those calling for (1) the development of rapid response teams in each state to set up programs to assist in the placement of workers affected by plant closings and (2) the formation of joint labor/management committees to help in providing reemployment services for dislocated workers.

Public Policies and Programs

The public sector also has a number of important roles to play in improving the workforce preparedness and use of older workers. Federal, state, and local governments provide a diverse array of job placement, employment, and training programs for older workers. Through earned income tax credits, provisions limiting the allowable earnings of certain groups of Social Security retirement beneficiaries, and regulation of private pensions, the federal government also can influence the economic incentives for work by older persons and the willingness of employers to provide job opportunities for older workers.

A variety of government programs, including the labor exchange activities of the state Job Services, JTPA Title IIA job search training and placement programs, and dislocated worker programs, provide job placement assistance for unemployed older workers and those wishing to change jobs. However, unemployed older persons, particularly those over age 65, are less likely than their prime-aged counterparts to use the placement services of the state Job Services.[102] When older persons do use the Job Service, they tend to receive fewer services than their younger counterparts.[103] Improving the delivery of job placement services to older workers will likely require an increased emphasis by the U.S. Department of Labor and the state Job Services on targeting more services to older applicants, including counseling, testing, and individualized job development. The integration of Job Services activities for older workers with those of other community agencies serving the needs of this clientele, such as Operation ABLE, should also be promoted.[104]

Job training opportunities for economically disadvantaged older persons are available under various titles and sections of the Job Training Partnership Act.[105] Traditionally, older persons have been underrepresented in such programs relative to their estimated share of the eligible population.[106] The low level of services to the older disadvantaged under JTPA does not appear to be justified by concerns over limited placement prospects or poor returns to investment. Termination data for JTPA Title IIA programs for the first three quarters of Program Year 1988 indicate that 79% of all older terminees were placed in jobs versus 75% for all adults 22 and older.[107] Prior studies of the impacts of CETA job training programs on older participants (over age 45) revealed that such programs were successful in increasing employment rates and earnings in the first year following termination.[108]

States can also play a more active role in the retraining of displaced older workers through more aggressive marketing of training opportunities under Section 30 of the unemployment insurance laws. Unemployment insurance claimants permanently displaced from jobs in occupations in which reemployment prospects are bleak and those previously employed in low-wage jobs are eligible for an additional 18 weeks of unemployment benefits if they are enrolled in a state-approved training program. Recent Massachusetts experience with the program has been quite favorable, with a completion rate over 80% and an employment rate of 85% among program completers at the time of a 52-week followup survey.[109]

The role of public sector job creation as a tool for improving employment prospects for unemployed adult workers has been quite limited since the demise of such programs under the Comprehensive Employment and Training Act (CETA). Older persons living in households with incomes below 125% of the poverty line are, however, eligible for participation in the Senior Community Service Employment Program (SCSEP), a program that offers part-time jobs at the minimum wage in nonprofit and state agencies providing general community services or services to the elderly. The program has served nearly 100,000 persons per year over the past four years.

Given frequent shortages of staff in social service agencies oriented to the elderly, stronger ties between SCSEP employment activites, JTPA training, and Job Service placement offices should be promoted. The possibility of expanding eligibility for these programs to poor and near-poor adults in the 50–54 age group also should be examined.[110]

The federal government currently provides economic support for low-income working families through the Earned Income Tax Credit.[111] Families with at least one child under age 18 in the home can receive up to $874 in tax credits depending on their level of earnings during the year. Unfortunately, the bulk (85%) of older poor and near-poor workers do not reside in families containing a child under age 18. In 1989, the Congress reviewed and several committees approved legislation that would expand the tax credits provided under the current program.[112] Future legislation might well wish to include eligibility provisions for low-income, working older families that do not contain children under 18 years of age to encourage work effort among older adults and strengthen the real income position of their families.

Labor Market Environment

The attainment and maintenance of full employment conditions in national, state, and local labor markets are indispensable to sustained improvements in the labor market position of many older workers. The existence of full employment in state labor markets in the late 1980s has been associated with higher rates of labor force attachment among the older population, especially those in the 55–64 age group. Because it improves employment and earnings prospects, full employment may encourage older persons to remain more committed to the labor market and facilitate labor force reentry to take advantage of new job opportunities. Older workers' unemployment rates and the durations of their unemployment spells are sensitive to overall labor market conditions.[113] By reducing the incidence and durations of unemployment among older workers, a full-employment environment should indirectly influence labor force attachment, given the greater propensities of unemployed older workers to end their spells of unemployment by withdrawing from the labor force.

Strong labor market conditions also improve reemployment prospects for older dislocated workers and favorably affect their ability to regain earlier wage levels.[114] Full employment traditionally has reduced gaps between the employment rates and earnings of white and black men and has generally improved the relative labor market position of more disadvantaged workers.[115]

Full employment should also provide greater incentives for firms to retain their older workforces and to reach out to local employment and training agencies serving the employment needs of older workers. Even though full employment by itself will not solve all or even most of the labor market problems faced by older workers, it substantially enhances the effectiveness of all public and private workforce preparedness initiatives.

Notes

This chapter is primarily the responsibility of Andrew M. Sum and W. Neal Fogg.

1. In this chapter, "older workers" are individuals 55 years of age or older, and the "elderly" are those 65 and older. Our definition of older workers is in accord with that of the U.S. Congress in establishing eligibility criteria for participation in older worker employment and training programs funded under the Job Training Partnership Act and its predecessor, the Comprehensive Employment and Training Act. See 97th U.S. Congress, Public Law 97-300: Job Training Partnership Act of 1982.

2. For further details on the developments influencing the reforms of the Social Security Act in 1983, see Henry J. Aaron, Barry B. Bosworth, and Gary Burtless, _Can America Afford to Grow Old? Paying for Social Security_ (Washington, D.C.: Brookings Institution, 1989); Stephen Crystal, _America's Old Age Crisis: Public Policy and the Two Worlds of Aging_ (New York: Basic Books, 1982); and John A. Svahn and Mary Ross, "Social Security Amendments of 1983: Legislative History and Summary of Provisions," _Social Security Bulletin_ 46 (July 1983): 3–48.

3. Between 1970 and 1983, the number of beneficiaries under the Old Age, Survivors, and Disability Insurance programs increased from 26.2 million to 36.1 million, a gain of 9.9 million or 38%. Over the same time period, however, payments to these recipients increased more than five times as a result of rising average monthly payments fueled in part by the rapid rates of inflation that boosted nominal benefits automatically as a result of the indexation provisions built into the 1972 amendments to the Social Security Act. See Svahn and Ross, "Social Security Amendments of 1983"; U.S. Bureau of Census, _Statistical Abstract of the United States, 1989_ (Washington, D.C.: U.S. Government Printing Office, 1989).

4. The ratio of persons over 65 to those 18–64 years old is projected to rise from 19.8 per 100 in 1987 to 21.8 per 100 by the year 2010 and then jump dramatically to 38.0 per 100 by the year 2030 as the baby boom cohort fully enters the ranks of the nation's elderly population. U.S. Bureau of the Census, Current Population Reports, Series P-25, No. 1018, _Projections of the Population of the United States, by Age, Sex, and Race: 1988 to 2080_, by Gregory Spencer (Washington, D.C.: U.S. Government Printing Office, 1989).

5. Svahn and Ross, "Social Security Amendments of 1983."

6. The penalty for collection of Social Security retirement benefits at age 62 will be gradually raised from 20% to 30% over the 2000–30 period, and an increase in the delayed retirement credit from 3% to 8% per year will be fully effective in 2008.

7. See John Carey, "The Changing Face of a Restless Nation," _Business Week_, September 25, 1989, pp. 92–106; Peter B. Doeringer and Andrew M. Sum, _Job Markets and Human Resource Programs for Older Workers in New England_, Paper Prepared for the New England Board of Higher Education, Boston, 1984; Elizabeth Ehrlich and Susan B. Garland, "For American Business: A New World of Workers," _Business Week_, September 19, 1988, pp. 112–120; Malcolm H. Morrison, "The Aging of the U.S. Population: Human Resource Implications," _Monthly Labor Review_, May 1983, pp. 13–19; U.S. Department of Labor, _Older Worker Task Force: Key Policy Issues for the Future_, Washington, D.C., January 1989.

8. Howard H. Fullerton, "Labor Force Projections: 1986 to 2000," *Projections 2000* (Washington, D.C.: U.S. Government Printing Office, 1988), pp. 17–27.

9. William B. Johnston and Arnold E. Packer, *Workforce 2000: Work and Workers for the 21st Century* (Indianapolis: Hudson Institute, 1987).

10. See Kathleen Christensen, "Flexible Work Arrangements and Older Workers: Older Workers' Experiences with Part-Time, Temporary, Off-the-Books Jobs, and Self-Employment," Paper Written for the Commonwealth Fund Commission on Elderly People Living Alone, New York, 1988; Peter B. Doeringer (Ed.), *Bridges to Retirement: Older Workers in a Changing Labor Market* (Ithaca, N.Y.: ILR Press, 1990); Ehrlich and Garland, "For American Business"; Mark Muro, "Granny Is Soda Jerk of '80's as Firms Seek to Fill Jobs Void," *Boston Sunday Globe*, November 27, 1988, p. A23; Carolyn Paul, "Work Alternatives for Older Americans: A Management Perspective," in *The Problem Isn't Age: Work and Older Americans* (New York: Praeger, 1987), pp. 165–176; and Operation ABLE of Greater Boston, *1987 Annual Report*, Boston, 1988.

11. Ehrlich and Garland, "For American Business," p. 120.

12. Tomasko uses the term "demassing" to refer to a downsizing effort affecting at least 5 to 15% of a company's mid-level workforce, that cuts across multiple divisions or departments, that emphasizes staff reductions as the primary method for achieving cost savings, and that aims to achieve these cutbacks in a speedy fashion. See Robert M. Tomasko, *Downsizing: Reshaping the Corporation for the Future* (New York: Amacom, 1987).

13. See Paul O. Flaim and Ellen Sehgal, "Displaced Workers of 1979–1983: How Well Have They Fared?" *Monthly Labor Review*, June 1985, pp. 3–16; Francis W. Horvath, "The Pulse of Economic Change: Displaced Workers of 1981–85," *Monthly Labor Review*, June 1987, p. 3–12.

14. See John Byrne, "Caught in the Middle—Six Managers Speak Out on Corporate Life," *Business Week*, September 25, 1989, pp. 92–106; Peter Nulty, "Pushed Out at 45—Now What?" *Fortune* 115 (no. 5, 1987): 26–30; Tomasko, *Downsizing*.

15. Katherine S. Newman, *Falling from Grace: The Experience of Downward Mobility in the American Middle Class* (New York: Vintage Books, 1988).

16. See Commonwealth Fund Commission on Elderly People Living Alone and ICF, Inc., *Old, Alone and Poor*, New York, 1987; Sar A. Levitan and Isaac Shapiro, *Working but Poor: America's Contradiction* (Baltimore: Johns Hopkins University Press, 1987); Andrew M. Sum and Neal W. Fogg, "Labor Market and Poverty Problems of Older Workers and Their Families," in Peter B. Doeringer (Ed.), *Bridges to Retirement: Older Workers in a Changing Labor Market* (Ithaca, N.Y.: ILR Press, 1990), pp. 64–91.

17. See Philip L. Rones, "The Labor Market Problems of Older Workers," *Monthly Labor Review*, May 1983, pp. 3–12; Philip L. Rones, "Employment, Earnings, and Unemployment Characteristics of Older Workers," in *The Older Worker*, (Madison, Wisc.: Industrial Relations Research Association, 1988), pp. 25–53; Andrew M. Sum and Neal W. Fogg, "Trends in the Labor Force Behavior, Employment Patterns, and Labor Market/Income Inadequacy Problems of Older Persons (55 +) and Their Families," in Peter B. Doeringer (Ed.), *Work, Earnings, and Retirement: The Changing Labor Market for Older Workers*, Center for Applied Social Science/ Institute for Employment Policy, Boston University, June 1988.

18. See Herbert S. Parnes (Ed.), *Work and Retirement: A Longitudinal Study of Men* (Cambridge, Mass.: MIT Press, 1981); Herbert S. Parnes (Ed.), "Introduction and Overview," in *Policy Issues in Work and Retirement* (Kalamazoo, Mich.: Upjohn Institute for Employment Research, 1983), pp. 1–27; Herbert S. Parnes (Ed.), *Retire-*

ment Among American Men (Lexington, Mass.: D.C. Heath and Company, 1985); Christopher J. Ruhm, "Why Older Americans Stop Working," *Gerontologist* 29 (no. 3, 1989): 294–299.

19. In her 1988 *Washington Post* analysis of corporate restructuring, Cindy Skrzycki has argued that "downsizing is here to stay—a management prerogative that will be used not once but repeatedly in good times and bad." See Cindy Skrzycki, "Downsizing Isn't Just for Downturns," *Washington Post National Weekly Edition*, August 28–September 3, 1989, pp. 20–21.

20. See U.S. Department of Labor, Bureau of Labor Statistics, *Labor Force Statistics Derived from the Current Population Survey: A Databook, Volume 1*, BLS Bulletin 2096 (Washington, D.C.: U.S. Government Printing Office, 1983); U.S. Bureau of Labor Statistics, *Employment and Earnings*, January 1989.

21. U.S. Department of Labor, Bureau of Labor Statistics, *Projections 2000*, BLS Bulletin 2302 (Washington, D.C.: U.S. Government Printing Office, 1988).

22. See Barry Alan Mirkin, "Early Retirement As a Labor Force Policy: An International Overview," *Monthly Labor Review*, March 1987, pp. 19–33; Morrison, "Aging of the U.S. Population"; Newman, *Falling from Grace*; and Skrzycki, "Downsizing Isn't Just for Downsizing."

23. Between March 1952 and March 1968, the civilian labor force participation rate of married women ages 55–64 more than doubled, rising from 17% to 35%. Substantial gains in participation also occurred among separated, divorced, and widowed women; however, the participation rate of single women (though remaining the highest of these three groups) rose by less than two percentage points. See U.S. Department of Labor and U.S. Department of Health, Education, and Welfare, *Employment and Training Report of the President, 1979* (Washington, D.C.: U.S. Government Printing Office, 1979), Table D-2, pp. 292–293. For a longer-term perspective on the changing labor force participation patterns of 55- to 64-year-old women in various marital status groups, see Diane E. Herz, "Employment Characteristics of Older Women, 1987," *Monthly Labor Review*, September 1988, pp. 3–12; and Diane E. Herz, "Employment in Perspective: Women in the Labor Force," BLS Report 758, Washington, D.C., 1988.

24. Deaths and immigration will have altered somewhat the composition of each age cohort over the following decade. We believe, however, that these estimates are minimum estimates of labor force withdrawal rates because some of those participating in the civilian labor force in 1988 would not have been active participants in 1978. Gross withdrawal rates will thus exceed the net withdrawal rates appearing under the last column. For trends in the retirement behavior of different age cohorts over time, see Parnes, *Retirement Among American Men*, and Philip L. Rones, "Using the CPS to Track Retirement Trends Among Older Men," *Monthly Labor Review*, February 1985, pp. 46–49.

25. The March CPS survey includes a work experience supplement that is used to collect fairly detailed information on the labor force, employment, and earnings experiences of persons 15 and over in the preceding calendar year. Those with no work experience in the preceding year are asked to describe their reasons for not working. The CPS survey does allow for proxy respondents; thus, some of the answers of married older men may have been provided by their wives or other family members.

26. U.S. Department of Labor, Bureau of Labor Statistics, *Employment and Earnings*, January 1983 and January 1989.

27. See Parnes, *Retirement Among American Men*; Herbert S. Parnes, "The Retirement Decision," in Herbert S. Parnes (Ed.), *The Older Worker* (Madison: Wisc.:

Industrial Relations Research Association, 1988), pp. 115–150; Christopher J. Ruhm, "Why Older Persons Stop Working: A Review of the Literature," in *Work, Earnings and Retirement*, Report Prepared for the Commonwealth Fund Commission on Elderly People Living Alone, Boston University, Boston, 1988; and Ruhm, "Why Older Americans Stop Working."

28. Given the fact that many studies of retirement behavior depend on self-reported data on health status rather than more objective measures of health conditions, some critics have argued that health's role in early retirement is exaggerated because it is used as a socially acceptable excuse for not actively seeking work. For a further discussion of these issues, see Peter Diamond and Jerry Hausman, "The Retirement and Unemployment Behavior of Older Men," in Henry Aaron and Gary Burtless (Eds.), *Retirement and Economic Behavior* (Washington, D.C.: Brookings Institution, 1984); Robert J. Myers, "Why Do People Retire from Work Early?" *Social Security Bulletin*, September 1982, pp. 10–14; Parnes, "Introduction and Overview"; and Ruhm, "Why Older Persons Stop Working."

29. Carl Eisdorfer and Donna Cohen, "Health and Retirement, Retirement and Health," in Herbert S. Parnes (Ed.), *Policy Issues in Work and Retirement* (Kalamazoo, Mich.: Upjohn Institute for Employment Research, 1983), pp. 57–73.

30. See Eric R. Kingson, "The Health of Very Early Retirees," *Social Security Bulletin* 45 (September 1982): 3–9; Herbert S. Parnes and Gilbert Nestel, "Middle-Aged Job Changers," *The Pre-Retirement Years, Vol. 4*, U.S. Department of Labor R & D Monograph 15 (Washington, D.C.: U.S. Government Printing Office, 1975); and Parnes, *Retirement Among American Men*.

31. Gary Burtless and Robert Moffitt, "The Effects of Social Security Benefits on the Labor Supply of the Aged," in Henry Aaron and Gary Burtless (Eds.), *Retirement and Economic Behavior* (Washington, D.C.: Brookings Institution, 1984).

32. See Michael J. Boskin and Michael D. Hurd, "The Effects of Social Security on Retirement in the Early 1970's," *Quarterly Journal of Economics* 99 (no. 4 1984), 767–790; Herbert S. Parnes, "The Retirement Decision . . ."; and Ruhm, "Why Older Persons Stop Working."

33. Gary S. Fields and Olivia S. Mitchell, "Economic Determinants of the Optimal Retirement Age: An Empirical Investigation," *Journal of Human Resources* 19 (no. 2, 1984): 245–262.

34. See Aaron, Bosworth, and Burtless, *Can America Afford to Grow Old?*; Crystal, *America's Old Age Crisis*; Olivia S. Mitchell, "Pensions and Older Workers," in Michael E. Borus (Ed.), *The Older Worker* (Madison, Wisc.: Industrial Relations Research Association, 1988), pp. 151–168.

35. Crystal, *America's Old Age Crisis*.

36. Donald C. Snyder, "Pension Status of Recently Retired Workers on Their Longest Job: Findings from the New Beneficiary Survey," *Social Security Bulletin*, August 1986, pp. 5–21.

37. Snyder, "Pension Status."

38. Among the 1982 new beneficiaries who were private-sector wage and salary workers, 67% of the white males had pension coverage on their longest jobs versus only 43% of black and other nonwhite males, 41% of white women, and 25% of black and other nonwhite women.

39. Mirkin, "Early Retirement as a Labor Force Policy."

40. Donald Bell and William Marclay, "Trends in Retirement Eligibility and Pension Benefits, 1974–83," *Monthly Labor Review*, April 1987, pp. 18–25.

41. Elizabeth L. Meier, "Managing an Older Work Force," in Michael E. Borus (Ed.), *The Older Worker* (Madison, Wisc.: Industrial Relations Research Association, 1988), pp. 167–189.

42. Michael Beer, Bert Spector, Paul R. Lawrence, D. Quinn Mills, and Richard E. Walton, *Managing Human Assets: The Groundbreaking Harvard Business School Program* (New York: Free Press, 1984).

43. See Mirkin, "Early Retirement as a Labor Force Policy"; Jeanne M. Hogarth, "Accepting an Early Retirement Bonus," *Journal of Human Resources* 23 (Winter 1988): 21–33.

44. Shirley H. Rhine, *Managing Older Workers: Company Policies and Attitudes*, Report No. 860 (New York: Conference Board, 1984).

45. See Byrne, "Caught in the Middle"; Mirkin, "Early Retirement as a Labor Force Policy"; Bill Saporito, "Cutting Costs Without Cutting People," *Fortune*, May 25, 1987, pp. 27–32; Skrzycki, "Downsizing Isn't Just Downsizing"; and Tomasko, *Downsizing*.

46. See Parnes and Nestel, "Middle-Age Job Changers"; Parnes, *Retirement Among American Men*.

47. Joseph F. Quinn, "Job Characteristics and Early Retirement," *Industrial Relations* (October 1978): 315–323.

48. Joan E. Crowley, "Longitudinal Effects of Retirement on Men's Psychological and Physical Well-Being," in Herbert S. Parnes (Ed.), *Retirement Among American Men* (Lexington, Mass.: D.C. Heath and Company, 1985), pp. 147–173.

49. Crowley, "Longitudinal Effects of Retirement."

50. U.S. Department of Labor, *Older Worker Task Force: Key Policy Issues for the Future*, Washington, D.C., January 1989.

51. Sum and Fogg, "Trends in the Labor Force Behavior."

52. The industry and occupational employment data appearing in Tables 4.8 and 4.9 are estimates derived by the authors from the public use tapes of the Current Population Survey for March 1968, March 1980, and March 1988. The Current Population Survey is a national household survey conducted monthly by the Bureau of the Census for the U.S. Department of Labor's Bureau of Labor Statistics. The CPS employment data provide the most comprehensive count of the employed, including the self-employed and unpaid family workers as well as wage and salary workers and covering the agricultural sector as well as nonagricultural employment. See U.S. Bureau of Labor Statistics and U.S. Bureau of the Census, *Concepts and Methods Used in Labor Force Statistics Derived from the Current Population Survey*, BLS Report No. 463 (Washington, D.C.: U.S. Government Printing Office, 1976).

53. Bennett Harrison and Barry Bluestone, *The Great U-Turn: Corporate Restructuring and the Polarizing of America* (New York: Basic Books, 1988).

54. Frank Swoboda and Albert B. Crenshaw, "Assessing the Liabilities of Retirement Benefits," *Washington Post National Weekly Edition*, February 20–26, 1989, p. 19.

55. During March 1968, women accounted for 35.4% of employed older workers, but by March 1988 their share had risen to nearly 42%.

56. See Howard M. Iams, "Employment of Retired-Worker Women," *Social Security Bulletin*, March 1986, pp. 5–13; Parnes, *Retirement Among American Men*; Joseph F. Quinn, "Labor Force Participation Patterns of Older Self-Employed Workers," *Social Security Bulletin*, April 1980, pp. 17–28.

57. Valerie A. Personick, "Industry Output and Employment Through the End of the Century," in *Projections 2000*, BLS Bulletin 2302 (Washington, D.C.: U.S. Government Printing Office, 1988), pp. 28–43.

58. Due to changes in the occupational classification systems used in coding CPS employment data in the early 1980s, the occupational employment categories of the late 1960s and the 1970s are not directly comparable to those for 1983 onward. To enable reasonable comparisons of occupational employment patterns of older workers over time, we combined individual occupations into rather broad categories. For example, all professional, technical, and managerial positions are placed into one category. This practice minimizes the effects of occupational coding changes. For example, in the late 1960s, accountants and auditors were classified as professional workers while today they are included in the managers, executives, and administrators category. By combining professional and managerial occupations, such reclassifications have no impact on the estimated shares of older workers in the Professional, Technical, and Managerial category.

59. Andrew M. Sum, Lorraine Amico, and Paul Harrington, *Cracking the Labor Market: Human Resource Planning in the 1980s* (Washington, D.C.: National Governor's Association, 1985).

60. See Paul E. Harrington, Marilyn Boyle, and Andrew Sum, *High Technology Careers in Massachusetts* (Boston: Massachusetts Division of Employment Security, 1987); Richard W. Riche, Daniel E. Hecker, and John V. Burgan, "High Technology Today and Tomorrow: A Small Slice of the Employment Pie," *Monthly Labor Review*, November 1983, pp. 50–58.

61. Harrison and Bluestone, *Great U-Turn*.

62. Patricia M. Flynn, *Facilitating Technological Change: The Human Resource Challenge* (Cambridge, Mass.: Ballinger, 1988).

63. See Sum and Fogg, "Trends in the Labor Force Behavior"; Sum and Fogg, "Labor Market and Poverty Problems of Older Workers."

64. George T. Silvestri and John M. Lukasiewicz, "A Look at Occupational Employment Trends to the Year 2000," in *Projections 2000*, BLS Bulletin 2302 (Washington, D.C.: U.S. Government Printing Office, 1988), pp. 44–61.

65. Self-employment accounted for nearly 18% of all employed older persons (55 and older) in the United States in March 1968 versus only 15% in March 1988. Part-time employment increased from 25% to 30% over the same time period; however, a part of this gain was attributable to an increased frequency of part-time employment for economic reasons (e.g., slack work, material shortages, an inability to find full-time jobs). See Sum and Fogg, "Trends in the Labor Force Behavior."

66. See Iams, "Employment of Retired-Worker Women"; Joseph F. Quinn; "Labor Force Participation Patterns of Older Self-Employed Workers," *Social Security Bulletin*, April 1980, pp. 17–28; and Herbert S. Parnes and Lawrence J. Less, "Economic Well-Being in Retirement," in Herbert S. Parnes (Ed.), *Retirement Among American Men* (Lexington, Mass.: D.C. Heath and Company, 1985), pp. 95–118.

67. In 1967, some 40% of employed family heads aged 66 to 70 would have been members of poor or near-poor families in the absence of their earnings. Among employed family householders 71 or older, 30% needed their earnings to avoid such income inadequacy problems. By 1987, only 15% of employed 66- to 70-year-old family householders and 8% of those 71 and over needed their earnings to avoid being poor or near poor.

68. The concept of a labor force overhang was developed by Eli Ginzberg in the late 1970s. See Eli Ginzberg, "The Job Problem," *Scientific American*, November 1977, pp. 43–51.

69. The number of persons making up the labor force overhang is typically four to five times as large as the number of discouraged workers. See T. Aldrich Finegan, *The*

Measurement, Behavior, and Classification of Discouraged Workers (Washington, D.C.: National Commission on Employment and Unemployment Statistics, 1978); and Andrew M. Sum, "Estimating Potential Labor Force Participants Among the Older Population: Findings of Previous Research and Their Implications for the Design of Future Surveys," Paper Prepared for the Commonwealth Fund Commission on Elderly People Living Alone, Boston, 1988.

70. Although the first three labor force problems are mutually exclusive, there is some overlap between the working poor/near poor and those in the first three problem categories. The classification of one's status as a member of the working poor or near poor is based on employment experiences and family income during 1987, while the other three measures reflect one's status at the time of the March 1988 survey. Our analysis indicates that for all persons 55 and older approximately 21% of the working poor and near poor would have been unemployed, employed part-time for economic reaons, or a member of the labor force overhang in March 1988.

71. Sum and Fogg, "Trends in the Labor Force Behavior."

72. See Sum, "Estimating Potential Labor Force Participants"; Sum and Fogg, "Trends in the Labor Force Behavior."

73. U.S. Department of Labor, *Geographic Profile of Employment and Unemployment: 1988*, Bulletin 2327 (Washington, D.C.: U.S. Government Printing Office, 1989).

74. See Sally Bould "Unemployment as a Factor in Early Retirement Decisions," *American Journal of Economics and Sociology* 39 (1980): 124–136; Doeringer and Sum, *Job Markets and Human Resource Programs*; and Stuart H. Garfinkle, "The Outcome of a Spell of Unemployment," *Monthly Labor Review*, January 1977, pp. 54–57.

75. U.S. Bureau of the Census, Current Population Reports, Series P-70, No. 16-RD-2, *Spells of Job Search and Layoff and Their Outcomes* (Washington, D.C.: U.S. Government Printing Office, 1989).

76. See Flaim and Sehgal, "Displaced Workers of 1979–1983"; Horvath, "Pulse of Economic Change"; U.S. Department of Labor, Bureau of Labor Statistics, *BLS Reports on Worker Displacement*, December 9, 1988.

77. See Flaim and Sehgal, "Displaced Workers of 1979–1983"; Horvath, "Pulse of Economic Change"; U.S. Department of Labor, *BLS Reports*.

78. See Barry Bluestone and Bennett Harrison, *The Deindustrialization of America* (New York: Basic Books, 1982); Jeanne Prial Gordus, Paul Jarley, and Louis A. Ferman, *Plant Closings and Economic Dislocation* (Kalamazoo, Mich.: Upjohn Institute for Employment Research, 1981); Kevin Hollenback, Frank C. Pratzner, and Howard Rosen (Eds.), *Displaced Workers: Implications for Educational and Training Institutions* (Columbus, Ohio: National Center for Research in Vocational Education, Ohio State University, 1984); William Kolberg (Ed.), *The Dislocated Worker: Preparing America's Workforce for New Jobs* (Cabin John, Md.: Seven Locks Press, 1984); and Tomasko, *Downsizing*.

79. Dislocated workers are defined here as those who have lost a job over the past five years as the result of a plant closing, a major reduction in force, or abolition of one's shift or position. This is somewhat broader than the definition used by the Bureau of Labor Statistics which also has a minimum three-year tenure requirement. The dislocation rate is calculated by dividing the estimated number of dislocated workers over the 1981–86 period by the number of persons in the adjusted civilian labor force in January 1986. The adjusted civilian labor force for any subgroup is equal to the number of persons in that subgroup who were either employed or unemployed at the time of the January 1986 survey plus those dislocated workers who were not active labor force participants during that month.

80. Herbert S. Parnes, Mary G. Gagen, and Randall H. King, "Job Loss Among Long Service Workers," in Herbert S. Parnes (Ed.), *Work and Retirement* (Cambridge, Mass.: MIT Press, 1981), pp. 65–92.

81. The Parnes, Gagen, and King study's definition of a dislocated worker required the older worker to have been "involuntarily separated" from the job and to have been employed for five or more years with their last employer. Our findings on large interoccupational differences in dislocation rates for older workers held true for those with three or more years of tenure as well as for all those displaced.

82. The estimated reemployment rate for Hispanics needs to be interpreted with caution given the small number of observations upon which it is based. The estimated weighted number of older dislocated Hispanics is 39,000; however, there are fewer than 40 such Hispanics in the sample.

83. See Flaim and Sehgal, "Displaced Workers of 1979–1983"; Horvath, "Pulse of Economic Change"; U.S. Department of Labor, *BLS Reports*.

84. The CPS questions on current job desires and job-seeking intentions are asked of only one-fourth of the sample, those in the outgoing rotation groups four and eight. The estimates of the proportion of dislocated workers desiring immediate employment and their reasons for not actively seeking work are thus based on one-fourth of the dislocated workers not active in the civilian labor force during January 1986.

85. Sum, "Estimating Potential Labor Force Participants."

86. See Richard M. Devens, "Displaced Workers: One Year Later," *Monthly Labor Review*, January 1986, pp. 40–43; Flaim and Sehgal, "Displaced Workers of 1979 to 1983"; and Horvath, "Pulse of Economic Change."

87. U.S. Bureau of Labor Statistics, *Monthly Labor Review*, February 1988, p. 107.

88. The proportion of the older employed occupying private sector wage and salary jobs has been increasing slightly over the past 20 years as self-employment and unpaid family work have diminished in importance. The fraction of older workers that holds private-sector wage and salary positions tends to decline with age, however, as self-employment accounts for a rising share of the older employed. For example, in March 1987, the self-employed accounted for 11% of employed 55- to 59-year-olds, 13% of 60- to 62-year-olds, 19% of those 66–70, and 25% of those 71 and over. See Sum and Fogg, "Trends in the Labor Force Behavior."

89. See Meier, "Managing an Old Work Force"; and U.S. Department of Labor, *Older Worker Task Force*.

90. Meier, "Managing an Older Work Force."

91. U.S. Department of Labor, *Older Worker Task Force*.

92. Christopher J. Ruhm, "Career Jobs, Bridge Employment, and Retirement," in *Work, Earnings and Retirement*, Report Prepared for the Commonwealth Fund Commission on Elderly Persons Living Alone, Boston, 1988.

93. Paul Swaim and Michael Podgursky, "Do More-Educated Workers Fare Better Following Job Loss?" *Monthly Labor Review*, August 1989, pp. 43–45.

94. See Mirkin, "Early Retirement as a Labor Force Policy"; National Commission for Employment Policy, *Older Worker Employment Comes of Age: Practice and Potential* (Washington, D.C.: The Commission, 1984); and U.S. Department of Labor, *Older Worker Task Force*.

95. Jim Jondrow, Frank Brechling, and Alan Marcus, "Older Workers in the Market for Part-Time Employment," in Steven H. Sandell, (Ed.), *The Problem Isn't Age: Work and Older Americans* (New York: Praeger, 1987), pp. 84–99.

96. Report of the President, *The State of Small Business* (Washington, D.C.: U.S. Government Printing Office, 1986).

97. Peter B. Doeringer (Ed.), *Bridges to Retirement: Older Workers in a Changing Labor Market* (Ithaca, N.Y.: ILR Press, 1990).

98. See Doeringer, *Bridges to Retirement*; Ruhm, "Why Older Persons Stop Working"; and U.S. Department of Labor, *Older Worker Task Force*.

99. See Byrne, "Caught in the Middle"; Nulty, "Pushed Out at 45"; Saporito, "Cutting Costs Without Cutting People"; Skrzycki, "Downsizing Isn't Just for Downturns"; and Tomasko, *Downsizing*.

100. Saporito, "Cutting Costs Without Cutting People."

101. U.S. General Accounting Office, *Dislocated Workers: Labor-Management Committees Enhance Reemployment Assistance*, Washington, D.C., November 1989.

102. Our analysis of CPS survey findings on the job search methods used by the unemployed over the 1982–88 period revealed that only 22% of unemployed 55- to 64-year-olds and 14% of the elderly unemployed (age 65 and older) used the Job Service to find work. Among the prime-aged unemployed, 27% reported use of the Job Service.

103. See Donald E. Pursell and William D. Torrence, "Age and the Job-Hunting Methods of the Unemployed," *Monthly Labor Review*, January 1979, pp. 68–69; Terry R. Johnson, Katherine P. Dickinson, and Richard W. West, "Older Workers, Job Displacement, and the Employment Service," in Steven H. Sandell (Ed.), *The Problem Isn't Age: Work and Older Americans* (New York: Praeger, 1987), pp. 100–119.

104. See Shirley Brussell, "Prepared Statement of Shirley Brussell, Executive Director Operation ABLE Inc.," in Steven H. Sandell, (Ed.), *Retirement: The Broken Promise* (Washington, D.C.: U.S. Government Printing Office, 1981), pp. 76–81; James O. Gollub, "Increasing Employment Opportunities for Older Workers: Emerging State and Local Initiatives," in Steven H. Sandell (Ed.), *The Problem Isn't Age: Work and Older Americans* (New York: Praeger, 1987), pp. 143–164; and Operation ABLE of Greater Boston, *1987 Annual Report*, Boston, 1988.

105. Older persons could have received services under Title IIA programs, the 3% older worker set asides, and Title III dislocated worker programs.

106. See Kalman Rupp, Edward Bryant, Richard Mantovani, and Michael Rhoads, "Government Employment and Training Programs and Older Americans," in Steven H. Sandell (Ed.), *The Problem Isn't Age: Work and Older Americans* (New York: Praeger, 1987), pp. 121–142; Steven H. Sandell and Kalman Rupp, "Who Is Served in JTPA Programs? Patterns of Participation and Intergroup Equity," National Commission for Employment Policy, Washington, D.C., 1988; and Sum and Fogg, "Trends in the Labor Force Behavior."

107. U.S. Department of Labor, Division of Performance Management and Evaluation, Office of Strategic Planning and Policy Development, *Job Training Quarterly Survey: JTPA Title IIA and III Enrollments and Terminations During the First Three Quarters of PY 1988*, Washington, D.C., September 1989.

108. Rupp, Bryant, Mantovani, and Rhoads, "Government Employment and Training Programs."

109. Massachusetts Department of Employment and Training, *Section 30 Training Participation and Outcomes*, Boston, June 1989.

110. National Council for Employment Policy, *Labor Market Problems of Older Workers*, Washington, D.C., January 1987.

111. David Ellwood, *Poor Support: Poverty in the American Family* (New York: Basic Books, 1988); and Levitan and Shapiro, *Working but Poor*.

112. Thomas B. Edsall, "Extending a Helping Hand to the Working Poor," *Washington Post, National Weekly Edition*, August 28, 1989, p. 12.

113. Sum and Fogg, "Trends in the Labor Force Behavior."

114. David Shapiro and Steven H. Sandell, "Economic Conditions, Job Loss, and Induced Retirement," Paper Presented at the 37th Annual Meeting, Industrial Relations Research Association, Dallas, December 1984; and David Shapiro and Steven H. Sandell, "The Reduced Pay of Older Job Losers: Age Discrimination and Other Explanations," in Steven H. Sandell (Ed.), *The Problem Isn't Age: Work and Older Americans* (New York: Praeger, 1987), pp. 37–51.

115. Herbert S. Parnes, "Conclusions," in *Retirement Among American Men* (Lexington, Mass.: D. C. Heath and Company, 1985), pp. 209–224).

II

TURBULENCE AND WORKPLACE ADJUSTMENT

5

The Life-Cycle Model for Managing Technological Change

Technological change has historically been associated with employment growth, not employment decline.[1] By contributing to reduced production costs, providing for better products, stimulating demand for goods and services, creating capital to be invested in further production, and generating incomes for workers, technological change fosters economic expansion and prosperity. Although often labor-saving in its immediate impact, these labor-saving effects have not contributed significantly to worker displacement.[2] Indirect employment effects more than compensate in the long-run for initial job losses due to the adoption of new technologies. Indeed, the *failure* of U.S. firms to remain technologically competitive contributes more to worker displacement and job loss than does the adoption of new technologies.[3]

Aggregate studies suggest that technological change has been largely neutral with respect to skills mix.[4] Technological change has resulted in neither significant upgrading nor significant downgrading in overall skills requirements.

Furthermore, despite anecdotal evidence that the pace of technological change is accelerating, aggregate indicators do not support this conclusion. On average, measured rates of technological innovation and diffusion have not risen significantly over the past two decades.[5]

This benign view of technological change results from aggregate data that mask offsetting positive and negative disruptions in the labor market caused by such change. Technological change bolsters productivity, industrial competitiveness, and economic growth. However, it can also result in skill obsolescence, worker displacement, and unemployment. Individual firms, industries, and regions can therefore suffer significant, often irreparable, losses from technological change.

The skills and job impacts of technological change are fundamentally firm-level phenomena. Technology-induced shifts in skill requirements affect hiring and staffing practices of employers, organizational structures, and career paths. Case studies of individual firms, however often present a confusing mix of findings about how technological change affects employment and skill requirements.[6]

Depending on the case, technological change has been shown to contribute to an increase, a decrease, or no change in net employment at the firm. Similarly, the average level of skills has been shown to increase after the introduction of technological change in some firms but remains constant or decreases in others. Technological change also results in the upgrading or promotion of some workers, while others are downgraded or laid off.

This diversity is often viewed as a sign that anything can and will happen—that "uncertainty prevails."[7] Thus, there would appear to be little hope of predicting the impact of technological change at the workplace.

This chapter demonstrates, however, that when viewed in the framework of "production life cycles," the impacts of technological change on employment, skills requirements, and training needs are neither random nor inconsistent. Over a technology's development cycle, common patterns emerge affecting the larger environment in which firm-level decisions are made regarding the organization and allocation of work.

Technological Change at the Workplace

Technological change at the workplace almost always results in some restructuring in the organization of work. The simplification of certain tasks and the skills upgrading of others trigger changes in the content or in the structure of jobs. Internal movement, new training needs, and shifts in management and worker responsibilities follow from most technological adoptions. In addition, changes in traditional job classifications and pay structures often accompany the adoption of new technologies.[8]

A variety of mechanisms, including retraining, the recruitment of new workers, transfers, liberalized retirement plans, hiring freezes, the use of temporary workers, and layoffs, are used to integrate technological change at the workplace. Even adoptions of similar technologies generate dissimilar results in different work environments.[9] Nevertheless, some generalizations can be drawn about the critical role of organizational factors in determining how technological change affects skills requirements, jobs, and workers at particular workplaces.[10]

Existing Technology and Skill Levels

The types of skills at the firm prior to adoption influence the character of the adjustment needed to integrate technological change into the workplace. For example, the adoption of a technology that results in a shift in task focus from "setup and operation" to "monitoring and control" demonstrates how diverse results can emerge from technologies that trigger a need for workers to have new "traits," such as attention to speed, agility, and alertness. When relatively low-skill operative functions, such as those in apparel or printed circuit board assembly, become oriented more toward monitoring than setup, the result is usually enlarged and upgraded operative positions. When the shift toward monitoring affects highly skilled operatives, however, these jobs are often deskilled, as the new job attributes are viewed as less difficult than the types of skills previously needed.

Office automation further shows how the level of technology and skills and the scope of work influence the nature of adjustments. When word-processing technologies replaced sophisticated typing equipment, existing secretarial positions tended to be enlarged, but when word-processing equipment replaced traditional typewriters, new clerical positions were usually established. When word-processing was introduced in offices in which typing was done by "typists," new "word-processing operator" positions were generally created. In contrast, when typing had been just one component of a more diversified secretarial job, the new word-processing tasks generally became an additional part of the existing position.

Organization of New Tasks

The ways in which the new tasks generated by technological change are organized affect job structure and staffing practices at the firm. Newly created tasks can be integrated into the job structure in a variety of ways. Thus deskilling of tasks need not result in the deskilling of jobs or in the downgrading of workers. Tasks can often be regrouped to generate jobs requiring similar or more advanced skills than prior to the change, rather than allowing jobs to become narrower, easier, and less satisfying.

With the introduction of numerical control machines, operative jobs have been upgraded when new programming tasks were added, but downgraded when programming functions were assigned elsewhere. Similarly, when flexible manufacturing systems are adopted, some firms use job rotation and work teams, whereas others allocate the new tasks within the more traditional hierarchical structure of jobs. With word processing as well, firms differ as some divide and split tasks (e.g., entry, setup, correction, and supervision) among narrowly specialized jobs, while others generate more complex and diversified clerical positions.

The decision to centralize or decentralize various functions also influences jobs and staffing practices. Centralizing new activities such as data processing or word processing in a separate department, for example, rather than dispersing them throughout the firm, promotes a greater degree of job specialization. Centralization fosters the creation of new positions, rather than the "enlargement" of established jobs.

Absorption of Dislocated Workers Within the Firm

Technological change almost always results in the dislocation of some workers from their jobs. However, relatively few workers have been displaced from their firms as a result of the adoption of new technologies.

A variety of policies are used by firms to cushion the displacement impacts of technological change. Some employers implement hiring freezes or use temporary workers in the period prior to the adoption to minimize the amount of disruption among regular employees. In addition, employers generally try to integrate technological changes during periods of business expansion and economic prosperity. Growing demand within the firm increases the likelihood of internal job opportunities; high labor demand in the area fosters voluntary quits and reduces the internal amount of adjustment required.

A considerable amount of the readjustment to deskilling and skill obsoles-cence takes place at the workplace. With office automation, workers dislocated from their jobs due to technological changes have usually been absorbed by growth or replacement needs elsewhere in the firm. In manufacturing, except when mass layoffs and plant closings are involved, blue-collar workers whose jobs were eliminated have often been retrained, even at considerable time and expense, rather than having new recruits perform the tasks created by tech-nological changes.

Trouble Spots: Declining Industries and Relocations

Economic expansion eases adjustments to technological change; however, even a booming economy does not ensure against layoffs and redeployment diffi-culties in certain situations. When technological change occurs in "declining industries" or is associated with the geographical relocation of production, adjustment problems are often extensive, and they spill beyond the boundaries of the firm. In industries experiencing a long-term decline in output and demand, such as textiles, apparel, and coal mining, workers whose jobs were eliminated by technological change were often laid off. Considerable layoffs were also reported in case studies involving intrafirm consolidations or the relocation of a plant geographically far removed from the initial work site. In these instances, workers often refuse to accept a long commute or a relocation.

Blue Collar Versus White Collar

Workplace practices governing the allocation of jobs among workers influence the distribution of gains and losses from technological change. When newly emerging technologies are adopted, *current* employees are generally retrained by employers to perform the tasks created by the change. However, the pool from which these workers are drawn differs when blue-collar and white-collar workers are affected. In factories, job security and seniority provisions in collective bargaining agreements often weight the selection decision in favor of those blue-collar workers who have been displaced by the technology.

In contrast, clerical workers most directly affected by office automation have usually been laterally transferred rather than assigned the new, higher-skilled jobs. Based on criteria such as aptitude tests, interviews, and references from management, white-collar workers from *other* departments in the firm are often transferred into relatively high-skilled jobs created by office automation; these workers are subsequently taught the required skills in company-sponsored training programs.

Worker Support

Although a variety of factors facilitate the adoption of technological change (e.g., job security, good communication, extensive planning, and adequate retraining), worker support appears essential to a successful adoption. Case studies suggest that worker support for new technologies is often linked with job security at the firm.[11] Companies with a formal policy of no layoffs and no downgrading as a result of technological change rarely indicate employee opposition to new technologies. Expectations of promotions or expanded future advancement opportunities further enhance the level of worker support of such change.

In sharp contrast, when workers or supervisors are resistant to change, there may be difficulties in adopting technologies that generate even relatively minor modifications in skill requirements, job content, or training. Uncertainty regarding job security, in particular, can thwart technological changes even in cases characterized by extensive planning, workers sympathetic to the reasons for change, and ongoing communication between managers and workers.

Technology Life Cycles and Human Resources

One of the most useful tools for understanding the impacts of technological change at the workplace is the technology "life cycle." Technologies exhibit patterns of growth and development, characterized by sequential phases—introduction, rapid growth, diminished growth, and stability or decline.[12] Technologies are introduced slowly at first, become more widely adopted as intensive research and development efforts lead to improved performance, and then are replaced by a new, superior technology.

The life-cycle model emphasizes the evolutionary character of technological change.[13] As a technology evolves, so do its skill and training requirements. Viewed in this perspective, the seemingly contradictory empirical evidence reveals common patterns over the life of a technology. The life-cycle model can therefore be a useful guide to human resources policies for facilitating the adoption of new technologies.

Skill-Training Life Cycle (STLC)[14]

Extending the life-cycle model to human resource issues reveals the evolution of a skill-training life cycle (STLC) as the level of demand and standardization of skills change with the development of a technology. These patterns of skills and training requirements in turn affect the emergence of occupations, staffing patterns, and career paths. The four phases of the STLC are summarized in Table 5.1.

Phase 1. Introduction: New and Emerging Skills. The early stages of a technology, which are characterized by a high degree of product innovation, are relatively skill- and labor-intensive.[15] Engineers and scientists are needed to develop new products, construct pilot models, and implement design changes. These professionals also perform most of the tasks later assumed by production and marketing managers, technicians, and skilled craftsworkers. The general-purpose equipment that characterizes the early stages of product development requires skilled operatives able to perform a broad range of tasks and to adapt equipment to the company's needs. The unsettled environment surrounding emerging technologies and the lack of appropriately trained

Table 5.1. **Skill Training Life Cycle**

	I Introduction: New and Emerging Skills	II Growth: Increased Demand for Skills	III Maturity: Slower Growth in Demand for Skills	IV Decline: Skill Obsolescence
Nature of tasks	Complex	Increasingly routinized	Increasingly routinized	Narrowly defined
Type of job skills	Firm-specific	Increasingly general	General; transferable	General; transferable
Effects on job structure	Job enlargement; new positions created when significant change in skill needs occurs	Emergence of new occupations	Relatively rigid job hierarchy; occupations associated with formal education and related work experience requirements	Elimination of occupations
Skill-training provider	Employer or equipment manufacturer	Market-sensitive schools and colleges	Schools and colleges, more generally	Declining number of schools and colleges; some skills provided by employer

Source: Adapted from Patricia M. Flynn, *Facilitating Technological Change: The Human Resource Challenge* (New York: Ballinger, 1988), p. 19.

workers encourages "job enlargement," whereby employers incorporate newly created tasks into existing jobs.[16]

The firm-specific nature of skills required and the lack of appropriately trained workers in the initial stage of the STLC mean that employers at the cutting edge of new technologies must provide their own training or rely on equipment vendors to do so.

Phase 2. Growth: Increased Demand for Skills. As a technology becomes more widely adopted and equipment standardized, skills that were once firm-specific become general and transferable among employers. Employers are less able to capture the return on investments in training for general skills and usually prefer that such training be provided in the schools, where the government or students will assume the costs. Moreover, increased demand for and standardization of skills permit their "production" on a larger scale and at locations away from the R&D sites. Together these two forces encourage the shift of skill development from the workplace to the formal education system as technologies mature. Computer programming, keypunching, and word processing are classic examples of this transfer.

When skills become standardized as technologies mature, employers are less hesitant to add new positions. Unless job ladders and promotion patterns are relatively well defined, however, employees may be reluctant to move into newly created positions or departments for fear of being removed from the mainstream operations of the firm and known career ladders.[17]

Increasing levels of standardization and mass production foster the fragmentation of relatively complex tasks into more routine, less-skilled assignments.[18] For instance, whereas engineers performed maintenance and repair tasks as well as innovation and design functions during the early stage of development of a technology, adopters of similar technologies years later cite demands for technicians and maintenance workers to perform such tasks. When production processes mature to the point that most repairs involve simply replacing standardized components, operatives have been assigned these responsibilities.

With the diffusion of established technologies, the number of experienced workers increases, as does the supply of newly trained graduates from colleges and schools.[19] New occupations also emerge. These developments influence the hiring practices of firms. For example, as demands for electronic skills increased and colleges and schools expanded their curricular offerings in this field, firms adopting electronically controlled manufacturing processes expected new employees to have acquired their basic electronics skills prior to being hired. A similar pattern has subsequently occurred with computer-related skills.[20]

Skill shortages in new occupations result as growing demands for appropriately trained workers in these fields outpace their supply, which is constrained by implementation and training lags in the educational system. Newly emerging occupations are generally characterized by rapidly rising relative wages and high turnover, fostered in part by aggressive hiring practices of employers. These developments, in turn, encourage employers to narrow the scope of training they provide in these fields.

Phase 3. Maturity: Slower Growth in Demand for Skills. Schools and colleges emphasize different goals, face diverse constraints, and play disparate roles in preparing workers for employment.[21] As a result, types of training are diverse, as are the manner and time frame in which educational institutions respond to labor market changes. As the provision of job skills shifts from the workplace to the educational system, such training initially is offered by schools and colleges that are oriented toward meeting the needs of employers. Over time, training becomes more widely diffused among educational institutions, and demand and supply for skills come more into balance.

Moreover, with the growing supply of appropriately trained graduates, educational credentials become associated with particular occupations. Computer programmer positions, for example, increasingly require a bachelor's degree in a computer-related field; computer technicians, a two- or four-year degree in a computer or technical field; and computer analysts, a graduate degree in computer science.

Whereas there is much upgrading and job enlargement when new technologies are adopted, the introduction of relatively mature technologies fosters discontinuous job ladders and barriers to advancement at the firm. Employers adopting maturing technologies often fill their newly created needs with workers who received their job-related training at other firms or in school. This change suggests an increasing disparity over the technology life cycle between those who gain and those who lose from technological change at the workplace.

Phase 4. Decline: Skill Obsolescence. As technologies become obsolete, training focuses on replacement needs and on the retraining of workers for other fields. The market for skills becomes limited, resulting in declining student enrollments and the termination of school-based training programs. The responsibility for training to fill the relatively short-term skill needs that remain shifts back to the firm. In the declining shoe and apparel industries in New England, for example, school-based programs can no longer attract students, and employers now train their own stitchers.[22]

Anticipating and Planning for Technological Change

The life-cycle model suggests a variety of implications for employers, unions, educators and government officials seeking to facilitate technological change. It accentuates the need for policies for both the "upside" and the "downside" of such change. Failure to adapt to the newly created skill needs generated by new technologies can restrict the productivity of workers and of firms, undermining industrial competitiveness and economic growth.[23] Failure to minimize the negative impacts of technological change as jobs are simplified or eliminated can further constrain the benefits of technological progress.

The STLC underscores the interrelated and evolving nature of the roles of various skill providers at different stages of a technology's development (see Table 5.2). If they are to take an active role in integrating new technologies at the workplace, managers and workers need to understand better than in the past the human resource implications of technology life cycles.[24]

Management can facilitate technological change through planning that integrates the natural shifts in skills with training needs and by promoting ways in which workers expect and realize better job prospects as a result of such change. Unions can foster the adoption of new technologies by developing

Table 5.2. **Responsibilities over the Skill-Training Life Cycle**

Institution	I Introduction: New and Emerging Skills	II Growth: Increased Demand for Skills	III Maturity: Slower Growth in Demand for Skills	IV Decline: Skill Obsolescence
Employers	Provide training for new and emerging technologies	Provide training for firm-specific skills	Provide training for firm-specific skills	Provide training for replacement needs
Joint Labor- Management Efforts	Facilitate adoption of new technologies	Establish apprenticeship training programs, where appropriate	Establish retraining programs for internal transfers of workers whose skills are soon to become obsolete	Provide training and out-placement assistance for displaced workers
Schools	Provide basic skills training	Provide training for general, or transferable, job skills, as well as basic skills	Provide training for general, or transferable, job skills, as well as basic skills	Eliminate training programs for obsolete skills Provide basic skills
Government	Encourage adoptions of new technologies	Facilitate skill transfer from the workplace to the schools	Facilitate skill transfer from the workplace to the schools	Provide retraining for displaced workers Assist firms in meeting replacement needs

---

BOX 5.1

MANAGER'S CHECKLIST FOR ANTICIPATING THE EFFECTS OF
TECHNOLOGICAL CHANGE ON JOBS AND WORKERS

Characteristics of the Technology

- What is the stage of development of the technology: is it a newly emerging technology or a relatively mature technology? What other firms have adopted this technology?
- What skills are required to perform the tasks generated by the adoption? Are particular occupations or educational credentials associated with the new skill needs?
- Are appropriately trained workers available to perform these new tasks?
- What are the sources of related skill training?
- What types of tasks are deskilled or eliminated by the technology?

Organizational Structure

- What is the current skill mix at the firm, and how are skill requirements expected to change at the workplace?
- What is the current occupational mix at the firm, and how will the new skill needs be integrated into the job structure? Is "job enlargement" a feasible way to incorporate the new tasks? Will new positions have to be added to the job hierarchy?
- Does the firm have the capacity to provide the training for newly required skills if not available elsewhere?
- For which positions, if any, will workers be recruited externally?

---

ways to incorporate greater flexibility into the lives of workers and their organizations.

Management Options

To effectively manage technological change, employers need to evaluate various technolgical choices in the light of the firm's organizational structure and policies. A checklist of questions that will guide managers in anticipating the impacts of technological change on jobs and workers is provided in Box 5.1.

Although the STLC provides a tool for anticipating how technologies will impact the workplace, it does not provide a set of easy answers regarding the effects of such change. On the contrary, the life-cycle model suggests that firms will experience a diverse range of outcomes even when similar technologies are adopted.[25] The STLC does, however, help managers identify the human resource tradeoffs involved with adopting technologies at various

- What restrictions exist at the workplace that pertain to the restructuring of job classifications, compensation schemes, or the reassignment of workers?
- Are job openings available via replacement or growth needs for transfers within the firm? Will the technological change result in a relocation of the worksite? Are layoffs likely to occur?
- What is the unemployment rate in the local economy? Are job opportunities comparable to those of workers displaced available in the community?

Human Resource Impacts

- How much training/retraining is anticipated? Which workers will be retrained?
- Given the criteria for determining internal promotions and transfers, which workers, if any, will be transferred? Will anyone be downgraded?
- What are the characteristics of those likely to be displaced from their jobs due to the technological change? What are employee turnover rates in these areas?
- Which workers, if any, will be laid off? What provisions does the firm have for these workers?
- Can federal, state, or local public programs, such as JTPA or the Employment Service, help smooth the transition?
- What changes will occur in internal career paths at the firm? Which workers will experience diminished advancement opportunities due to the technological change?
- What morale problems are likely to surface from the introduction of the technological change? Which workers and managers will be directly and indirectly affected?

phases of their development and systematically assess the skill and training requirements likely to be generated at the firm when the technology is introduced.

Management usually decides when and where new technologies are to be adopted. The timing of the adoption relative to the stage of development of the technology influences not only the nature of the new skill needs but also the availability of appropriately trained workers. Firms that choose to adopt newly emerging technologies will experience considerable uncertainty regarding the nature of skills and training required and have to absorb the costs of new training. Adoptions in the second phase of the STLC, in which training is shifting from the workplace to the schools, raise the issue of whether the firm should "buy" or "make" the trained workers required by the change.[26]

As technologies become more widely adopted, appropriately trained workers are increasingly available from outside the firm. However, buying such workers can be quite costly given their rapidly rising wages and relatively high turnover rates. If firms choose to make their own skilled workers, training programs have to be developed and workers selected for training. This option has lower recruitment costs, but raises the firm's training bill. Whichever course is taken during this phase, firms will face stiff competition for these workers as their skills are becoming increasingly transferable among workplaces.

By the third phase of the STLC, skill needs are considerably clearer, and workers with the appropriate skills are more readily available from schools and other firms. Morale issues come to the fore for firms adopting technologies during this phase, as the hiring of trained and experienced workers in occupations that now exist in these fields can threaten traditional job structures and internal career paths. Current workers who see the better jobs being created going to outsiders while they or their co-workers are transferred, downgraded, or laid off are likely to resist the technological change. Workers not immediately affected by the change who envision their advancement opportunities diminished will also feel threatened by the technology.

Technological adoptions during the fourth phase of the STLC occur as schools phase out programs in these fields. Firms that continue to use outdated technologies will have to provide the training necessary for workers to fill skilled replacement needs unless they can hire trained workers from other firms.

Unions and Collective Bargaining

Facing a growing incidence of worker displacement in recent years due to plant closings and technological changes, unions in the manufacturing sector have sought to move beyond liberalized retirement plans and severance pay packages as solutions to such changes.[27] There have been concessions in work rules, often with a broadening of job classifications, in exchange for a greater commitment on the part of employers to support employment security measures.

Union-management agreements are beginning to reflect the more general trend away from job security at the firm, and toward employment security that may involve a job with another employer.[28] Unions have negotiated educational and retraining services for displaced, as well as active, workers. The Ford and General Motors contracts with the United Automobile Workers and the AT&T agreement with the Communications Workers of America provide for training, counseling, and relocation services to workers displaced from the firm. In addition, union-management agreements have resulted in a broadening of the scope of courses eligible under tuition remission programs.[29] For example, covered employees can be reimbursed by the firm for participation in courses providing job-related skills useful for employment outside the firm or more general personal development such as computer literacy, written and oral communication techniques, and goal setting and motivation.

Although still relatively few in number and too new to evaluate, these innovative agreements illustrate the potential for union-management cooperation to promote technological change at the workplace through measures designed to enhance flexibility and employment security.

Implications for Public Policy

To date, the dynamics of production life cycles and of technological change have not figured prominently in human resource policies in the United States. The life-cycle model helps to pinpoint places along the development path of technologies where public intervention is likely be most effective, namely, in facilitating techological change at the workplace.

Provision of Job-Related Skills

The life-cycle model suggests that demands for new, highly skilled labor created by the adoption of new technologies will be relatively small compared to total employment needs. However, the failure to meet these skill needs can hamper the diffusion of new technologies.

Anticipating new and emerging skill requirements is difficult; they do not appear in past employment trends, nor can they be identified by traditional forecasting techniques. Employment projections frequently used to guide occupational education in the schools are best able to indicate growth and replacement needs in more traditional industries with relatively stable products and technologies.[30] They are least effective in anticipating turning points in employment, training gaps in areas of emerging skill needs, or sudden spurts in employment growth.

Employer-sponsored training is critical for the acquisition of skills required in emerging fields; however, closer and earlier coordination between employers and educational institutions than has occurred in the past would facilitate the skills transfer process from the workplace to the schools as technologies mature. Studies show, for example, that active cooperative education programs help facilitate the skills transfer. Educators initiate and monitor the programs, but the acquisition of job-related skills takes place on equipment at the workplace. When the time comes for the schools to pick up more of the skill training, the process is relatively smooth because the educators and employers had been working together all along.

In recent years public policy has promoted greater understanding of how the changing skill needs of workers and employers can be better integrated. For example, the Perkins Vocational Education Act and the Job Training Partnership Act (JTPA) have actively promoted industry-school partnerships and public-private cooperation and coordination. Given their relatively low funding levels, however, it seems unlikely that these programs will bring about significant change.

Efforts to promote public-private cooperation in human resources development could be strengthened by modest funding for innovative programs designed to meet new and emerging employment needs.[31] Strong program monitoring and evaluation, and extensive dissemination of the results of these programs, would foster the diffusion of the lessons from such experiments.

Anticipating Plant Closings and Skill Obsolescence

In the life-cycle model, plant closings, worker displacement, and skill obsolescence are seen as natural consequences of technological progress. Public policies should be geared toward integrating change and facilitating the readjustment of workers caught in the transition.

The bulk of worker retraining in the United States occurs within firms; thus, plant closings and mass permanent layoffs impede the process whereby most workers acquire skills for alternative employment. Experience suggests that displaced workers who receive several months advance notice of permanent job loss have shorter periods of unemployment than do workers without such notice.[32] The Worker Adjustment and Retraining Notification Act (WARN) of 1988, mandating 60-day employer notice to workers before large-scale layoffs, provides more time for implementing adjustment programs but, as discussed in Chapter 3, this plant-closing legislation is not a panacea for worker displacement.[33]

The STLC provides guidance in assessing the likelihood and nature of skill obsolescence over time. It suggests that public officials must (1) better understand the firms and jobs in their local employment base and (2) anticipate major structural changes before being faced with large-scale layoffs and plant closings. Local planners should be addressing such questions as: What types of products and product lines are major employers involved with? What kinds of production activites (e.g., R&D, small batch runs of customized products, standardized mass production assembly) are taking place in local plants? Are local businesses company headquarters or branch plants? What kinds of firms are moving into, and out of, the area, and why? Which skill areas are experiencing declining demands, and why?

More generally, the life-cycle model suggests that education and training policies should be a cornerstone of a more broadly based economic development strategy that recognizes the importance of a diversified employment base.[34]

Balancing Short-Run and Long-Run Workforce Needs

The life-cycle model underscores the need for public policy that distinguishes short-run and long-run employment conditions. Such a two-pronged policy stance is necessary to guard against creating structures that are so "labor market responsive" as to undermine long-run economic growth and the ability of workers to adjust to structural changes over time.

Policy planners need to recognize that educators and employers use different time horizons when making planning and evaluation decisions—with those of employers generally far shorter than those of educators. Moving quickly in response to employer requests to alleviate skill shortages—rather than relying on employers to solve some of their immediate staffing difficulties through changes in recruitment and internal training practices—may foster future skill imbalances. Ample evidence suggests caution against rapid installment of programs to build up skill supplies unless the shortage is large and continued demand can be demonstrated.[35]

Publicly funded occupational education programs should focus on providing skills that are transferable among different workplaces. Programs for youths, particularly at the secondary level, need to be broad enough to enable them to work in a variety of situations and to adjust to structural change over the course of industrial development.

Notes

This chapter is primarily the responsibility of Patricia M. Flynn.

1. Richard Cyert and David C. Mowery (eds.), *Technology and Employment* (Washington, D.C.: National Academy Press, 1987); Office of Technology Assessment, *Automation of America's Offices* (Washington, D.C.: Government Printing Office, 1985); National Commission on Technology, Automation and Economic Progress, *Technology and the American Economy* (Washington, D.C.: Government Printing Office, 1966).

2. General Accounting Office, *Dislocated Workers: Business Closures, Layoffs, and the Public and Private Response* (Washington, D.C.: Government Printing Office, 1986).

3. Michael L. Dertouzos, Richard K. Lester, and Robert M. Solow, *Made in America* (Cambridge, Mass.: MIT Press, 1989); David C. Mowery, "The Diffusion of New Manufacturing Technologies," in Richard M. Cyert and David C. Mowery (eds.), *The Impact of Technological Change on Employment and Economic Growth* (New York: Ballinger, 1988), pp. 481–509; Kenneth Flamm, "The Changing Pattern of Industrial Robot Use," in Cyert and Mowery, *Impact of Technological Change,* pp. 267–328; Cyert and Mowery, *Technology and Employment;* Office of Technology Assessment, *Structural Unemployment: Reemploying Displaced Adults* (Washington, D.C.: Government Printing Office, 1986).

4. Kenneth I. Spenner, "Technological Change, Skill Requirements and Education: The Case for Uncertainty," in Cyert and Mowery, *Impact of Technological Change,* 131–184; Kenneth I. Spenner, "Deciphering Prometheus: Temporal Change in the Skill Level of Work," *American Sociological Review* 48 (1983): 824–837.

5. Cyert and Mowery, *Technology and Employment;* Edwin Mansfield, *The Economics of Technological Change* (New York: Norton, 1968).

6 Patricia M. Flynn, *Facilitating Technological Change: The Human Resource Challenge* (New York: Ballinger, 1988); Spenner, "Technological Change, Skill Requirements and Education"; Paul Attewell and James Rule, "Computing and Organizations: What We Know and What We Don't Know," *Communications of the ACM* 27, no. 12 (December 1984): 1184–1192.

7. Spenner, "Technological Change, Skill Requirements and Education."

8. Paul Osterman, *Employment Futures: Reorganization, Dislocation and Public Policy* (Cambridge, Mass.: MIT Press, 1988); National Research Council, *Human Resource Practices for Implementing Advanced Manufacturing Technology* (Wash-

ington, D.C.: National Academy Press, 1986); Office of Technology Assessment, *Technology and the American Economic Transition* (Washington, D.C.: Government Printing Office, 1988).

9. Maryellen R. Kelley and Harvey Brooks, "The State of Computerized Manufacturing in U.S. Manufacturing" (Cambridge, Mass.: Harvard University, John F. Kennedy School of Government, 1988); Flynn, *Facilitating Technological Change;* Spenner, "Technological Change, Skill Requirements and Education"; Ramchandran Jaikumar, "Postindustrial Manufacturing," *Harvard Business Review* 64, no. 6 (November–December 1986): 69–76; Maryellen R. Kelley, "Programmable Automation and the Skill Question: A Reinterpretation of the Cross-National Evidence," *Human Systems Management* 6, no. 3 (1986): 223–241

10. See *Flynn, Facilitating Technological Change,* for an annotated listing of approximately 200 enterprise-level case studies from which these generalizations are drawn.

11. For discussion of the importance of employment security in the acceptance of change at the workplace also see: Osterman, *Employment Futures;* Jeffrey Liker, David B. Roitman, and Ethel Roskies, "Changing Everything at Once: Worklife and Technological Change," *Sloan Management Review* 28 (Summer 1987): 29–46; Markley Roberts, "A Labor Perspective on Technological Change," in Eileen L. Collins and Lucretia Dewey (eds.), *American Jobs and the Changing Industrial Base* (New York: Ballinger, 1984), pp. 183–205; Paul Lawrence, "How to Deal with Resistance to Change," *Harvard Business Review* 32 (May–June 1954).

12. William L. Shanklin and John K. Ryans, Jr., *Marketing High Technology* (Lexington, Mass.; Lexington Books, 1984); Richard N. Foster, "A Call for Vision in Managing Technology," *Business Week* (May 24, 1982), pp. 24, 26, 28, and 33; David Ford and Chris Ryan, "Taking Technology to Market," *Harvard Business Review* 59 (March–April 1981): 117–126.

13. Richard R. Nelson and Sidney G. Winter, *An Evolutionary Theory of Economic Change* (Cambridge, Mass.: Harvard University Press, 1982); Nathan Rosenberg, *Inside the Black Box: Technology and Economics* (Cambridge, England: Cambridge University Press, 1982); Robert H. Hayes and Steven C. Wheelwright, "The Dynamics of Process-Product Life Cycles," *Harvard Business Review* 57 (March–April 1979): 127–136; Robert H. Hayes and Steven C. Wheelwright, "Link Manufacturing Process and Product Life Cycles," *Harvard Business Review* 57 (January–February 1979): 133–140; Richard R. Nelson and Victor D. Norman, "Technological Change and Factor Mix over the Product Cycle," *Journal of Developmental Economics* 4 (1977): 3–24; Gunter Krumme and Roger Hayter, "Implications of Corporate Strategies and Product Cycle Adjustments for Regional Employment Changes," in Lyndhurst Collins and David Walker (eds.), *Location Dynamics of Manufacturing Activities* (New York: Wiley, 1975), pp. 325–356; James Utterback and William J. Abernathy, "A Dynamic Model of Process and Product Innovation," *Omega* 3, no. 6 (1975): 639–656; Raymond Vernon, "International Investment and International Trade in the Product Cycle," *Quarterly Journal of Economics* 80, no. 2 (May 1966): 190–207.

14. This section draws heavily upon Flynn, *Facilitating Technological Change.*

15. Hayes and Wheelwright, "Link Manufacturing"; Hayes and Wheelwright, "Dynamics of Process-Product Life Cycles"; William J. Abernathy and James M. Utterback, "A General Model," in William J. Abernathy, *The Productivity Dilemma* (Baltimore, MD: Johns Hopkins University Press, 1978), pp. 68–84; Utterback and Abernathy, "Dynamic Model"; Nathan Rosenberg, "Factors Affecting the Diffusion of Technology," in Nathan Rosenberg, *Explorations in Economic History* (New York:

Academic Press, 1972); Seev Hirsch, "The United States Electronics Industry in International Trade," in Louis T. Wells, Jr. (ed.), *The Product Life Cycle and International Trade* (Cambridge, Mass.: Harvard University Press, 1972).

16. James R. Bright, *Automation and Management* (Boston: Harvard Graduate School of Business Administration, 1958); Rosenberg, "Factors Affecting the Diffusion of Technology."

17. Thomas A. Barocci and Kirsten R. Wever, "Information Systems Careers and Human Resource Management," Working Paper 1482, Sloan School of Management, MIT (September 1983); Thomas A. Barocci and Paul Cournoyer, "Make or Buy: Computer Professionals in a Demand-Driven Environment," Working Paper 1342, Sloan School of Management, MIT (September 1982); G.P. Schultz and T.L. Whisler (eds), *Management Organization and the Computer* (Glencoe, Ill: Free Press, 1960).

18. Joan Greenbaum, *In the Name of Efficiency* (Philadelphia: Temple University Press, 1979); Philip Kraft, *Programmers and Managers: The Routinization of Programming in the United States* (New York: Springer-Verlag, 1977); Harry Braverman, *Labor and Monopoly Capital: The Degradation of Work in the Twentieth Century* (New York: Monthly Review, 1974); James R. Bright, "Does Automation Raise Skill Requirements? *Harvard Business Review* 36 (1958): 84–98.

19. Robert E. Taylor, Howard Rosen, and Frank Pratzner (eds.), *Responsiveness of Training Institutions to Changing Labor Market Demands* (Columbus, Ohio: National Center for Research in Vocational Education, Ohio State University, 1983); Peter B. Doeringer and Patricia F. Pannell, "Manpower Strategies for Growth and Diversity in New England's High Technology Sector," in John C. Hoy and Melvin H. Bernstein (eds.), *New England's Vital Resource: The Labor Force* (Washington, D.C.: American Council on Education, 1982), pp. 11–35; Richard B. Freeman, *The Market for College-Trained Manpower* (Cambridge, Mass.: Harvard University Press, 1971).

20. Harold Goldstein and Bryna Shore Fraser, "Training for Work in the Computer Age: How Workers Who Use Computers Get Their Training," Research Report RR-85-09 (Washington, D.C.: National Commission for Employment Policy, 1985).

21. Taylor, Rosen, and Pratzner, *Responsiveness of Training Institutions;* Patricia F. Pannell, "Occupational Education and Training: Goals and Performance," in Peter B. Doeringer and Bruce Vermeulen (eds.), *Jobs and Training: Vocational Policy and the Labor Market* (Boston: Martinus Nijhoff Publishing, 1981), pp. 50–71; Wellford W. Wilms, "The Non-System of Education and Training," in Peter B. Doeringer and Bruce Vermeulen (eds), *Jobs and Training in the 1980s* (Boston: Martinus Nijhoff Publishing, 1981), pp. 19–49.

22. Patricia M. Flynn, "Lowell: A High Technology Success Story," *New England Economic Review* (September–October 1984): 39–49.

23. Although changes in the global economy suggest modifications to the international product life cycle, levels of uncertainty, standardization of product and process, and product demand—the key features of the life-cycle models—will continue to play critical roles in determining production and employment trends. See Raymond Vernon, "The Product Life Cycle Hypothesis in a New International Environment," *Oxford Bulletin of Economics and Statistics* 41, no. 4 (1979): 255–267. Also see Edward M. Bergman and Harvey A. Goldstein, "Dynamics, Structural Change and Economic Development Paths," in Edward M. Bergman (ed.), *Local Economies in Transition* (Durham, N.C.: Duke University Press, 1986), pp. 84–110; Krumme and Hayter, "Implications of Corporate Strategies."

24. Stephen S. Cohen and John Zysman, *Manufacturing Matters* (New York: Basic Books, 1989); Dertouzos, Lester, and Solow, *Made in America;* Peter F. Drucker, "The

Coming of the New Organization," *Harvard Business Review,* 66 (January–February, 1988): 45–53; Robert H. Hayes and Ramchandran Jaikumar, "Manufacturing's Crisis: New Technologies, Old Organizations," *Harvard Business Review* 66 (September–October 1988): 77–85; Robert H. Hayes and William J. Abernathy, "Managing Our Way to Decline," *Harvard Business Review* (July–August 1980): 67–77.

25. As discussed earlier, employer experiences will vary due to adoptions occurring at different phases of a technology's development. The STLC model further accentuates that a firm's product mix will influence the nature of the technology-induced skill needs. More specifically, consistent with life-cycle models of products and technologies, a variety of skill development paths are possible; in each case the timing and shape of individual cycles depend on levels of uncertainty, standardization, and demand. (See Shanklin and Ryans, *Marketing High Technology*; Ford and Ryan, "Taking Technology to Market"; Chester R. Wasson, *Dynamic Competitive Strategy and Product Life Cycles,* 3rd ed. (Austin, Tex.: Austin Press, 1978); Utterback, "General Model"; Theodore Levitt, "Exploit the Product Life Cycle," *Harvard Business Review* 43 (November–December 1965): 81–94.)

For example, for firms in which production remains in small-batch jobs, skill requirements may remain quite high. Similarly, a technology such as flexible manufacturing systems that suppresses the benefits of exploiting economies of scale in production would be expected to experience an extended phase in which competitive advantage remains a function of innovation and product design and quality, rather than of cost minimization. See Peter B. Doeringer, David G. Terkla, and Gregory C. Topakian, *Invisible Factors in Local Economic Development* (New York: Oxford University Press, 1987); Michael J. Piore and Charies J. Sabel, *The Great Industrial Divide* (New York: Basic Books, 1984); Charles J. Sable, Gary Herrigel, Richard Kazis, and Richard Deeg, "How to Keep Mature Industries Innovative," *Technology Review* 90, no. 3 (April 1987): 26–35; Wasson, *Dynamic Competitive Strategy.*

26. Barocci and Cournoyer, "Make or Buy."

27. Everett Kassalow, "Employee Training and Development: A Joint Union-Management Response to Structural and Technological Change," *Proceedings of the Industrial Relations Research Association* (December 1987): 107–117; Harry Katz, *Shifting Gears* (Cambridge, Mass.: MIT Press, 1985); Thomas A. Kochan, Harry C. Katz, and Nancy Mower, *Worker Participation and American Unions: Threat or Opportunity?* (Kalamazoo, Mich.: Upjohn Institute for Employment Research, 1984); Thomas A. Kochan and Harry C. Katz, "Collective Bargaining, Work Organization and Worker Participation: The Return to Plant Level Bargaining," *Labor Law Journal* 34 (August 1983): 524–530; Peter Cappelli, "Union Gains Under Concession Bargaining" (1983), unpublished manuscript.

28. Jill Casner-Lotto and Associates, *Successful Training Strategies* (San Francisco: Jossey-Bass 1988); Kassalow, "Employee Training and Development"; Katz, *Shifting Gears.*

29. See Chapter 6 for more details on changes occurring in industrial relations systems.

30. Patricia M. Flynn, "Introducing New Technology into the Workplace: The Dynamics of Technological and Organizational Change," *Investing in People: A Strategy to Address America's Workforce Crisis, Background Papers* (Washington D.C.: Commission on Workforce Quality and Labor Market Efficiency, U.S. Department of Labor, 1989), pp. 411–456; David W. Stevens, *Employment Projections for Planning Vocational and Technical Educational Curricula: Mission Impossible* (Columbia, Mo.: University of Missouri, Human Resources Research Program, 1976).

31. Flynn, *Facilitating Technological Change*.

32. Cyert and Mowery, *Technology and Employment*.

33. Office of Technology Assessment, *Plant Closings: Advance Notice and Rapid Response* (Washington, D.C.: Government Printing Office, 1986); General Accounting Office, *Plant Closings: Information on Advance Notice and Assistance to Dislocated Workers* (Washington, D.C.: Government Printing Office, 1987).

34. Lawrence Ingrassia, "Recession Haunts City That Believed It Was Saved by High-Tech," *Wall Street Journal,* January 25, 1990, pp. 1 and A8; Flynn, *Facilitating Technological Change;* Office of Technology Assessment, *Technology and the American Economic Transition*; Edward J. Malecki, "High Technology Sectors and Local Economic Development," in Edward M. Bergman (ed.), *Local Economies in Transition* (Durham, N.C.: Duke University Press, 1986), pp. 129–142; Edward J. Malecki, "Technology and Regional Development. A Survey," *International Regional Science Review* 8, no. 2 (1983): 89–125; Benjamin Chinitz, "Contrasts in Agglomeration: New York and Pittsburgh," *American Economics Association, Papers and Proceedings* 50, no. 3 (1961): 279–289.

35. Norton W. Grubb, "The Bandwagon Once More: Vocational Preparation for High Tech Occupations," *Harvard Educational Review* 54, no. 4 (November 1984): 429–451; Harold Goldstein, "The Accuracy and Utilization of Occupational Forecasts," in Robert E. Taylor, Howard Rosen, and Frank C. Pratzner (eds.), *Responsiveness of Training Institutions to Changing Labor Market Demands* (Columbus, Ohio: National Center for Research in Vocational Education, Ohio State University, 1983), pp. 39–70; Richard B. Freeman and John A. Hanson, "Forecasting the Changing Market for College-Trained Workers," in Robert E. Taylor, Howard Rosen, and Frank C. Pratzner (eds.), *Responsiveness of Training Institutions to Changing Labor Market Demands* (Columbus, Ohio: National Center for Research in Vocational Education, Ohio State University), pp. 79–99; Freeman, *Market for College-Trained Manpower.*

6

Industrial Restructuring and Human Resource Preparedness in Unionized Settings

Human resource preparedness and development policies have become a major issue in U.S. collective bargaining. Under pressure from rapid corporate and workplace reorganization, labor and management are taking novel steps to adjust and prepare the workforce. This chapter analyzes current approaches and examines the policies issues posed by new endeavors.

To understand the limits and potentials of new programs, the traditional approaches to workforce preparedness in U.S. industrial relations are reviewed and the enormous changes under way in this area are examined. The evidence suggests that labor and management are experimenting with a new system of industrial relations, one that shifts activity away from traditional collective bargaining and toward the strategic and workplace levels. This transformation in industrial relations, along with extensive industrial restructuring, provides the impetus and context for current preparedness and adjustment policies.

Traditional Collective Bargaining Approaches

In traditional collective bargaining, much of the concern surrounding worker training focused on the development of appropriately trained skilled trades workers, with apprenticeship training programs playing a critical role in the development and certification of skilled trades workers. These apprenticeship programs usually required four years for the attainment of journeyman status.

For production workers, most training was acquired on the job or in short preparatory courses. In manufacturing, the training required to operate new equipment was often provided by vendors or through hands-on training. There was often little advance planning to project either current skill availability or future needs for the production workforce. Planning of this sort, where it occurred, concerned skilled trades, as management most often adjusted to production worker needs through the external labor market or emergency action.

Management could rely on the external labor market to substitute for advance planning of blue-collar needs because of the availability of well-trained workers there. The external market was particularly attractive to high-wage employers (often large firms), who could bid qualified employees away from smaller firms. As will be described in more detail later, this training strategy is becoming less and less viable in the face of rapid technological change and the high skill demands of many new jobs.

Although training was one part of traditional human resource preparedness policies, downside adjustment policies were another. Downside adjustments in the traditional system used layoffs, either temporary or indefinite. The most advanced collective bargaining agreements provided supplementary unemployment benefits coupled to the unemployment insurance benefits provided by the government. Typically, negotiated severance payments were provided where layoffs became permanent.

Again, policies fit with the economic environment. Layoffs were an acceptable adjustment device because the growth in most firms made the scale of such layoffs small and their duration often limited. Growth in the economy also made location of new employment relatively easy for most laid-off workers. Here too, the pace and extent of recent restructuring have made this traditional approach less acceptable.

In traditional collective bargaining, extensive adjustment policies occurred where technological changes precipitated major employment adjustments or where a firm faced sudden financial problems. In the longshoring industry in the 1960s and 1970s, for example, labor and management negotiated special programs to address the major employment displacements that occurred when containerization brought a major decline in the need for labor. On the West Coast, a novel agreement was negotiated that facilitated the introduction of new container technologies and established a fund to pay compensation to dock workers.[1] One of the features of this agreement was its two-tier form, whereby workers above a given level of seniority qualified for benefits while low seniority workers were not eligible. This agreement is particularly interesting because it foreshadows the sort of two-tier pay agreements negotiated at many firms in the 1980s.

This traditional adjustment approach has been modified substantially in recent years. The impetus for change has come from the corporate restructuring, layoffs, and plant closings, discussed in Chapter 3. The extent of worker dislocation has led a number of leading firms to provide permanently displaced workers with various forms of assistance.[2] In some cases this assistance is triggered by the occurrence of a plant closing; in other firms, any permanently displaced employee qualifies for the assistance.

In some unionized companies, the new adjustment programs include

---

BOX 6.1

ARMOUR AUTOMATION FUND

In the 1950s Armour & Co. faced competition in its core meat processing business from nonunion competitors located in small, modern plants in rural areas. Armour's plants, in contrast, were located in traditional urban meatpacking centers, and many were obsolete. By the late 1950s Armour had closed nine of its plants and was planning to close six more. At the same time, the company was opening a number of smaller automated plants in rural areas.

In 1959 Armour and its two unions, the Amalgamated Meat Cutters and Butcher Workmen and the United Packing, Food, and Allied Workers, reached an agreement to aid displaced workers. The agreement called for a nine-member automation fund committee comprising four members from the company, two members from each of the unions, and a neutral chair (later expanded to two co-chairs). The committee's only specified responsibility was to initiate a training and interplant transfer program.

The committee, financed by a $500,000 company fund, encouraged interplant transfers, relocation allowances, advance notice, and planning. Displaced senior employees were offered early retirement. Initially, the program had difficulty getting workers to accept interplant transfers, as many workers, facing a choice between transferring and accepting a lump sum severance payment, opted for payment.

Many workers were reluctant to transfer because they did not want to sever their family and community ties. This was particularly true for minority

---

efforts to improve employment opportunities inside the firm by meshing improvements in employee skills with efforts to bring new business in-house. Whether they are focused on employees who leave the firm or employees who move within the firm, these programs represent some of the most extensive human resource preparedness policies adopted in the private sector in the United States. We now describe three such pathbreaking programs: at Armour, AT&T, and General Motors.

Labor-Management Joint Adjustment Programs

We start with the program launched at the Armour Corporation in the late 1950s, described in Box 6.1. The Armour program is not a recent initiative, but it was so novel and has so many lessons for current efforts that it is worthwhile to review its nature and consequences.

workers, a significant segment of the work force. Many of these workers were being asked to transfer into all-white rural communities. To address, this problem, flowback rights were adopted, permitting workers to return to a former location after several months on the new job and to retain severance eligibility.

Finding new jobs for workers permanently displaced by the plant closings proved difficult. The workforce was characterized by low levels of education, advanced age, and long attachment to the industry. Most workers were unskilled, but even skilled meat packers usually did not possess skills that were transferable to other industries. The urban labor markets where these older plants were located had high unemployment rates. Most plant closings displaced all employees at the same time, so that a large number entered a local labor market where workers with similar characteristics were already experiencing high levels of joblessness.

The committee tried several approaches: skills assessment, retraining programs, active campaigns to find jobs, and placement programs. Despite these efforts, many displaced workers did not find jobs or were forced to accept work at wages below their prior earnings.

Shultz and Weber identified obstacles the committee encountered: (1) reluctance to hire Armour workers because of their union background;[3] (2) the relatively high wages of the displaced workers, causing potential employers to fear that these workers, if hired at lower wages, would be dissatisfied and call for unionization; and (3) racial, ethnic, and age discrimination.[4]

The Armour program received mixed reviews. Shultz and Weber concluded that the committee's efforts were "marked by disappointment and by some modest achievements."[5]

The Armour Automation Fund was one of the earliest and largest labor-management efforts to manage workforce adjustment. The program was unusual not only because of its scale but also because of the wide range of tactics used to assist displaced workers. These tactics included both outplacement assistance to workers who left and efforts to locate company openings into which workers could be shifted. The Fund also provided an early effort at the labor-management-neutral tripartite governance of retraining and outplacement assistance.

As the case shows, the Armour Fund encountered many difficulties. Although well intentioned, and even with the extensive resources and planning associated with the Fund, there was great difficulty finding employment with comparable earnings for many of the displaced workers.

Another early adjustment effort is described in Box 6.2, which discusses the programs adopted by AT&T and the CWA when they confronted major technological changes in the 1950s and 1960s. The early AT&T and CWA

BOX 6.2

AT&T AND CWA PROGRAMS IN THE 1950S AND 1960S

The conversion to long distance direct dialing drastically reduced the need for operators in local offices throughout the country in the 1950s. Many local offices were closed as operator services became more centralized. The Bell System implemented human resource plans that anticipated the effects of the changes and avoided layoffs of operators, represented by the Communications Workers of America (CWA).

Contracts negotiated between AT&T and CWA provided for advance notice and consultation over workforce reductions. The reduction process relied on attrition, intracompany transfers, the hiring of temporary workers, and advance notice both to employees and to the union. In addition to accomplishing the workforce reduction, other objectives of the planning process were to retain as many employees as possible, provide adequate transfer opportunities, and avoid downgrading. Attrition worked well because of the high level of turnover among operators.

Changeovers to direct dial technology were planned two years in advance. Each office was required to estimate the number of operators it would need after the switch was accomplished and how many operators would need transfers. Hiring of permanent employees stopped one year before the conversion. As the workforce was reduced by turnover, temporary employees were hired to fill in the gaps, overtime was scheduled, and vacations were postponed until after the cut over. Because the company relied on attrition one year before the conversion, the number of employees who needed transfers was minimized. Because other segments of the industry were growing and expanding staff levels, transfers could be offered to all regular employees. All employees were counseled about transfer and training opportunities. However, not all operators took transfers, particularly where relocation was required, as many had family responsibilities. Those operators who did not accept transfers were given severance pay and terminated, although they were given preference for rehiring.

---

programs illustrate the advantages that forward planning can provide where economic factors (in this case a high turnover rate among operators) can assist adaptation. The parties here also benefited from the availability of expanding opportunities in other parts of the Bell system.

AT&T and the CWA faced even greater challenges in recent years when they confronted the problems associated with the restructuring of the entire industry. Box 6.3 describes recent joint adjustment programs.

The major innovation created by AT&T and the CWA was the Alliance, a jointly administered program funded by company contributions. The Alliance's objectives are roughly similar to those of the Armour Automation

BOX 6.3

Post-Divestiture AT&T and CWA Programs

On January 1, 1984, more than a million employees of the Bell System were divided into eight companies: 385,000 were assigned to AT&T, 588,000 remained with the seven regional operating companies, and 125,000 were transferred from Bell companies to AT&T. In this reorganization, AT&T stepped back from its traditional commitment to long-term employment security for nonmanufacturing employees.

During the first two years of post-divestiture operation, AT&T reduced its headcount by 40,000, with approximately one third of these cuts in management. Of the total reduction, however, only about one fourth were laid off. The remainder left through attrition, voluntary programs offering incentives to resign or retire early, or transfers to other AT&T companies and Bell operating companies.

In August 1985, AT&T announced a further 24,000 job reduction in an effort to cut $800 million from its operating losses at AT&T Information Systems. In response to vigorous protests, including a nationwide CWA strike vote, the company scaled back the reduction. As of mid-January 1986, the reductions amounted to 8,625, of which 3,100 were layoffs. Of the 8,625, some 2,200 were transferred to jobs elsewhere in AT&T. A major issue in the dispute with the CWA over these layoffs was the continued use of subcontractors and temporary workers while permanent positions were being eliminated, an issue that remains a major concern for the union.

Employment security was a central issue in the 1986 CWA–AT&T negotiations. To address the issue, the settlement created a new joint venture known as the Alliance for Employee Growth and Development. The Alliance has two objectives: (1) to aid workers displaced because of AT&T's changing business and (2) to support and encourage employee career development to increase the adaptability of the current workforce to changing skill demands. The Alliance is a nonprofit corporation receiving its funding mainly from the collective bargaining agreement. The company contributes $3.75 per month for each bargaining unit member currently employed at AT&T.

Since the Alliance became operational in early 1987, approximately 20,500 bargaining unit employees (about 14% of the 1988 eligible workforce) have been involved in its programs. Approximately 30% of the 500 CWA locals representing AT&T workers have established local joint labor-management committees involved in Alliance programs. Recently, the International Brotherhood of Electrical Workers (IBEW) (representing other workers at AT&T) joined the Alliance, and approximately one third of the IBEW's 30 locals are now active in Alliance activity.

The Alliance has provided assistance in several facility closings. Its services have included career counseling, relocation assistance, financial planning, and job search assistance. To further career development, the Alliance supports correspondence courses to prepare employees for the changing technical skills demanded by new telecommunications technology and customer service concerns.

BOX 6.4

GM/UAW AND GM/IUE PROGRAMS

GM and the UAW launched new training and income support programs in the national contracts negotiated in 1982. The new income support program provides payments that rise as a function of senority to permanently displaced workers, and these payments can be as great as 75% of the final year's earnings.

Additional income security is provided through the Jobs Bank program. The Jobs Bank provides full income support to workers displaced by new technology, outsourcing, corporate reorganizations, and negotiated productivity improvements.[6] Workers do not qualify for the Bank if they are displaced due to a decline in sales. In 1987 the company also agreed to replace 50% of the workers lost by attrition.

The Jobs Bank program is important because it provides a new measure of security to the workforce. Yet its most far-reaching effects derive from the pressure it creates for the company to engage in retraining and human resource planning. The Jobs Bank creates a sizable incentive for the company to redeploy the existing workforce in productive endeavors rather than have workers receive payments while in a Jobs Bank slot.

GM has now had extensive experience with the programs. In some plants, voluntary early retirement buyouts have reduced the number of workers qualifying for the Jobs Bank program.[7] In other plants, the program has been used as part of an extensive effort to upgrade the skills of the existing workforce.

Fund, although the Alliance's administrative and funding structure is novel. The Alliance is also different from the Armour Fund in the way it relies on plant-level committees. These local committees initiate both outplacement assistance programs and efforts to find new job opportunities within the AT&T system for displaced employees. It will take time before researchers will be able to tell if the Alliance proves to be successful. At this point, it is an interesting example of how labor and management in a unionized setting are struggling to meet corporate and employee needs simultaneously.

Like many other cases involving unions, the new training and outplacement assistance programs negotiated by General Motors and the UAW, described in Box 6.4, were introduced along with a number of other novel collective bargaining arrangements. At GM, these other arrangements included profit sharing, pay concessions, and, in some plants, new work practices involving team systems.

Perhaps the most interesting aspect of the GM/UAW retraining and adjustment programs is the extent to which they are linked to other changes occurring on the shop floor. For example, the Jobs Bank program discussed in Box 6.4

Coping with the extensive corporate and workplace restructuring now under way requires new ways of thinking. To address this need, GM and the UAW created a Paid Educational Leave Program (PEL) in 1984. The program provides local union officers with four weeks of off-site training in an array of economic, technological, and auto industry developments. In a number of GM plants, local PELs have begun providing a week of such instruction to the hourly workforce.

The Packard-Electric division of GM provides another good illustration of how the workforce and union (Packard workers are represented by the International Union of Electrical Workers (IUE)) can become involved in business reorganization. Packard-Electric has confronted substantial competitive challenges from lower cost foreign and non-union competitors and has developed a business strategy to shift to high-technology work. Labor and management created joint planning boards to oversee plant operations as part of the negotiation of an extensive employment security and multitiered wage program adopted in 1984. Over the last five years, workers and the IUE have played a critical role in generating new business.

Training and adjustment programs are an important part of Packard's success story. Training is needed to facilitate the reorganizations that have enabled Packard to bid on new products. Training has also played a major role in enabling the workforce to operate the new, often more flexible machinery associated with the complex technologies being introduced. Successful bids on new work has at times included the use of temporary and part-time employees, another subject matter in the domain of the joint planning boards that oversee operations.[8]

uses displaced employees to fill in for employees being retrained. In some plants, training and development funds are used to assist plants in bidding on new work. The new training efforts also extend to education programs for local union officers and hourly workers. The latter programs are intended to provide a better understanding of the economic changes under way in the auto industry and the possibilities available to the union.

In this case, as with the Alliance, it is too early to tell how successful the new programs will be. Yet it is clear that GM and the UAW have created a number of innovative funding and administrative structures in these new programs.

Effective Outplacement Efforts

A number of lessons can be drawn from previous experience regarding how best to assist employees who must make the transition to work opportunities outside the firm.[9] For one thing, the success of any program closely depends on the state of the labor market. Firms can improve adjustments by notifying workers, the union, and the appropriate government and community agencies as early as possible about any major employee displacement. Severance payments can also play a constructive role.

In multiplant companies, attrition can be a useful instrument in any interplant transfer plan. The option of interplant transfer is more likely to be selected by workers if each individual is allowed a trial period in the new location. It is important to give workers the option to return within six months without sacrificing severance pay.

Careful assessment of the abilities of employees about to be displaced can be used to identify retraining and skill development. In pursuit of this option, however, it should be realized that bad training is worse than no training. Poorly equipped private training programs seeking quick returns at the expense of displaced workers do damage to the workers and to the basic concept of retraining. Occupational training programs must also provide adequate financial support and incentives for potential retrainees. The failure to enroll retrainees rapidly in vocational programs can have serious consequences. Too often, displaced workers awaiting training find menial jobs and become reluctant to give up such jobs for retraining and the promise of future employment.

Programs for aiding displaced workers cannot be a one-shot affair; they must be closely supervised over a long period of time. An important objective of any displaced worker program should be to cultivate a sense of mobility among the displaced. Mobility has become particularly difficult given the presence of many dual-earner couples. The most successful programs have been those that remain flexible and deal with the person within the framework of individual problems.

Current Restructuring in Industrial Relations

The preparedness and adjustment policies adopted in three innovative firms give some sense of the lessons that have been learned about outplacement. But why is the need for such policies so intense today, and why is it so hard to develop successful approaches? To answer those questions, it is important to step back from specific cases and examine the broad changes under way in U.S. industrial relations.

In union settings, adjustment policies have been affected by a broad transformation occurring in industrial relations. This transformation is a product of deregulation in some industries and of intensified international and nonunion competition in others. Intensified competition has been accompanied by increased volatility and uncertainty in the economic environment. Major changes in corporate structure and in the organization of work on the shop floor have ensued, and these changes have led to major changes in human resource utilization and adjustment policies.

Labor and management in the United States are experimenting with a new system of industrial relations, a system that differs markedly from traditional collective bargaining practices and procedures.[10] The new system includes contingent compensation, team systems of work organization, employment security programs, and enhanced worker and union participation in decision making.

Contingent compensation links pay directly to firm or worker performance. In some cases this concept has been introduced in unionized firms through profit sharing or stock ownership. On the shop floor, contingent pay has been introduced through gain-sharing programs that tie worker pay to work area or plant performance and through "pay-for-knowledge" arrangements that provide pay increases as the employee proves competence in a wider variety of jobs.

Team systems are associated with reductions in the number of job classifications. In some manufacturing worksites, the number of job classifications has dropped from more than 100 to a single "production worker" classification. Team members often take on some inspection, material handling, repair, and housekeeping tasks. In the more advanced teams, workers assume responsibility for some production control and planning tasks, and hourly (unionized) team leaders perform job responsibilities formerly under the control of supervisors.

Employment security often provides the glue that binds the new system together. New programs range from explicit employment guarantees to retraining and income support. The negotiation of such programs is typically linked to the introduction of more flexible work rules and other work practices associated with team systems.

Team systems allow wider roles for hourly workers as they become involved in production control tasks. Teams systems go hand in hand with statistical quality control and other quality programs that often entail worker participation in production decisions. The team systems and the administration of new employment security are often associated with a broadening of worker and union involvement in strategic business decisions. In part this involvement arises as a consequence of the major corporate reorganizations that confront the workforce. After watching plants close and work being outsourced, workers and unions have sought avenues to affect the decisions that weigh so heavily on their future.

Strategic participation by workers and unions also expands by the very nature of the bargain being drafted in the new industrial relations system. Workers and unions are often initially hesitant to adopt contingent pay, teams, and flexible work rules. They fear potentially lower and more volatile pay associated with contingent compensation and the possibility of increases in work pace and loss in protections associated with the modification of work practices. In response, labor has asked for greater shop floor and strategic involvement in decisions along with employment security provisions as both a form of compensation and a form of insurance for the protection of employee and union rights.

The new industrial relations involves a shift in the level of industrial relations activity. Traditional collective bargaining concerned the negotiation and implementation of a contractual agreement. The new system de-emphasizes negotiated procedures and shifts activity to the workplace and strategic levels. At the workplace there is greater emphasis on new communication policies, flexible work practices, and direct worker involvement. Where the new procedures work well, continual and informal discussion between labor and management replace traditional arm's-length relations.

Need for More Extensive Human Resource Development

Industry has always had to adjust to new technology, yet it is the scale of recent changes that has led to the current focus on preparedness and adjustment policies. Corporations are under pressure to restructure their production processes and internal operations, and this restructuring places demands on their human resource systems. For example, throughout U.S. industry there is a sustained push for improved product quality. Statistical production control (SPC) techniques and other control procedures have been expanded as part of these efforts. But to implement SPC on the shop floor requires a workforce that can engage in mathematical and computer analysis. Training programs are therefore needed not only to convey the SPC skills but also to provide the mathematical and statistical skills necessary to carry out SPC and other quality programs.

The economic environment has put a premium on industry's ability to produce goods using batch rather than traditional mass production techniques and to shift more rapidly across the types of products produced. More flexible manufacturing processes often entail the introduction of sophisticated electronically directed machinery and automated storage and retrieval systems. These systems, like SPC, can be most effectively operated by a workforce skilled in fairly advanced mathematics and statistics. Team systems fit into this network of new production techniques as the organizational vehicle through which hourly workers take on the responsibilities to monitor and often direct quality control and production processes.

The human resource needs generated by these production and control systems go beyond traditional requirements. Not only must workers have quantitative analytic skills, they must also be skilled in the use of computer and other electronic technologies. Furthermore, because team systems are often associated with the new work practices, workers need communication and group skills.

The extent of corporate and economic restructuring associated with new competitive pressures has led some leading firms to create educational programs that address the broad nature of these economic changes, as well as their implications for the shop floor. The GM/UAW Paid Educational Leave Program described in Box 6.4 provides a good illustration of how union officers and workers can analyze the far-reaching economic and technological challenges confronting their industry. Unions and the workforce also are now continually provided with more extensive information regarding the financial and economic changes under way in their firm and industry. Such information exchange requires educational programs that enable the parties to understand and utilize the complex business and technological information they confront.

In the last decade, many firms accustomed to offering employment security through human resource planning were faced with substantial employment contractions. Because these firms were no longer able to generate sufficient openings to offer transfers to all surplus employees, a number of labor-management agreements have moved toward comprehensive adjustment programs. The new programs combine human resource planning with outplacement assistance for those workers who are displaced.

Linking Adjustment Policies to Work Reorganization

A whole set of other problems arise in those cases in which the focus of human resource adjustment policies is on assisting internal reorganization and the redeployment of workers within the firm. The major challenge confronting these efforts is making adjustment programs forward looking and to coordinate them with the reorganization plan. In the long run, employment security can best be provided through production that is competitive in world markets. The ultimate test for training and adjustment policies is whether they help labor and management move their organizations to that competitive level. To accomplish this objective, training and adjustment programs need to be linked to changes in organizational structure and industrial relations practice.

The experience of AT&T and other workplaces suggests that several conditions must be met if human resource planning for new technology is to operate effectively. First, there must be coordination between those planning new technology on the one hand and labor relations and human resource staffs on the other. Without advance knowledge about when new technology is to be introduced, and about its projected staffing levels, human resource planning is impossible. Second, if transfer opportunities are to be offered to all affected employees, there must be an adequate balance between turnover and new positions becoming available.

As they struggle to link training and adjustment policies to competitive challenges, labor and management are confronted by a number of specific problems. For one thing, reorganizations on the shop floor are pushing toward work systems that blur the distinction between blue- and white-collar workers. The challenge for training and adjustment programs is to keep up with these changes in employee roles. In many corporations there have traditionally been sharp distinctions between the training received by blue- and white-collar employees and a sharp differentiation in the adjustment benefits to which various employees are entitled. Often separate corporate staffs dealt with blue-collar and white-collar training. These distinctions no longer make sense. Furthermore, continuing to differentiate among employees in training or adjustment benefits thwarts ongoing efforts on the shop floor to narrow task and role distinctions.

Another problem is created by the simultaneous nature of the economic pressures confronting most businesses. Corporations face extreme uncertainty in their labor demand at the same time that they are committing themselves to more extensive employment or income security guarantees. The obligations acquired under the employment security commitments can be managed if organizations can make accurate assessments of their current skill availability and their future skill needs. This sort of information requires extensive human resource planning and information. The problem is that more extensive planning is needed when corporations are under competitive cost pressures that lead them to reduce personnel staffs. Just when they need to engage in more extensive human resource planning, organizations are hard pressed to free up the resources to carry out such planning.

In addition, many corporations are shifting the composition of their human resource staffs so as to involve operating managers more extensively in personnel and training decisions. As discussed above, this shift is all for the better in an environment in which companies are rapidly altering their business and human resource management (HRM) strategies. The solution appears to lie in the development of cost-effective planning and information systems and the linking of operational and planning functions in corporate and union staff jobs.

Summary and Policy Recommendations

Throughout the adjustment process, labor and management need to keep in mind the following issues:

- The context in which radical changes in training and adjustment policies are occurring in union settings in the United States includes the emergence of a new system of industrial relations involving contingent compensation, work teams, employee and union participation in business decisions, and employment security commitments.
- Economic pressures and rapid technological changes have markedly increased the level of training needed and shifted the composition of that training. Blue-collar employees now need to be provided with both quantitative and communication skills along with the skills to help them understand the wide-ranging business and financial information they now confront in their work lives.
- Employment security commitments have raised the penalty for poor human resource planning and adjustment. Organizations must develop programs to assist redeployment and career movements. As blue- and white-collar distinctions become less prevalent on the shop floor, they should become less important in training and adjustment policies.
- Corporate restructuring has increased the frequency of plant closings and displacement at the same time organizations have taken on greater responsibility to assist employees in career adjustments. Organizations must develop cost-effective ways to provide such assistance.

- Training and adjustment policies should be linked to workplace and corporate reorganizations.
- The pace of reorganization and the uncertainty concerning future business demand more active human resource management planning. The training should be decentralized and placed under the control of those aware of operating needs.

Labor and management confront a full agenda in union settings. Although their task may appear daunting, it also is important for them to recognize the long record of innovation in collective bargaining they can draw on. To encourage effective human resource preparedness in union settings management, labor, and the government should adopt the following policies.

Management

Firms need to create inventories of the skills held by their workforces and project any gaps between future skill needs and availability. These skill inventories also should be used to assist current employee redeployments. The development of career planning and training programs should be shifted downward because work groups can most clearly identify where technology is headed and how the workforce can be best prepared.

Management must take steps to convince the workforce that reorganizations will lead to corporate growth rather than further downsizing. Employment security and corporate reinvestment policies must be used to help convince employees that enhanced internal flexibility can yield positive payouts and enhance the career opportunities of the workforce.

Unions

Mechanisms should be developed to bridge the gap between training efforts for the skilled and "production" workforces. Formal apprenticeship programs can no longer be provided only to those moving into skilled trades occupations. The distinctions between skilled trades and production work are blurring, and so must the distinctions in training programs.

Union members and leaders need to become more aware of current and future reorganizations, corporate structure, and technology. Unions need to become equipped to anticipate workplace changes rather than merely react to their consequences.

Joint Labor and Management Efforts

Human resource preparedness programs and policies should be jointly designed and administered. As collective bargaining in the United States moves away from its traditional formal and arm's-length approach and toward more informal and continuous accommodation, so must the development of human resources adjustment policies.

Education programs regarding the broad nature of changes confronting firms and the workforce should be jointly designed and presented in forums that allow labor and management dialogue.

The administration and allocation of human resource development and training funds should be decentralized wherever feasible. Technological and skill needs are being identified on the shop floor and at local levels in the organization. Plant and shop floor workers should be the ones to target expenditures on needs identified through local action.

Joint programs are needed to make better use of community colleges and equipment suppliers in workforce training programs.

Intervention by a third party such as the Cornell Programs for Employment and Workplace Systems (PEWS) or area labor-management committees can provide assistance to distressed facilities. A third party can play a valuable role in reassessing alternatives and can provide information regarding successful strategies adopted in other locations.

Government

Greater governmental financial and technical assistance is needed for mature industrial workers who confront the consequences of corporate and technological reorganization.

Federal and state governments need to expand their assistance to apprenticeship programs and also create subsidies for emerging programs to upgrade production employees. Apprenticeship and other training should be designed to give employees skills that are portable across employers, a necessary requirement in the face of continued corporate reorganization.

The federal government needs to create training and redeployment networks that assist communication across firms and between firms and key parts of the vocational and technical education system, including community colleges.[11]

Notes

This chapter is primarily the responsibility of Harry C. Katz and Jeffrey H. Keefe.

1. The containerization agreement and the events surrounding its negotiation are described in Paul T. Hartman, *Collective Bargaining and Productivity* (Berkeley: University of California Press, 1973).

2. Joint labor-management programs that provide assistance to workers displaced during plant closings are described in Ruth H. Fedrau and Kevin P. Balfe, "A Case Study Monograph on Labor-Management Worker Adjustment Programs" (Washington, D.C.: Bureau of Labor-Management Relations and Cooperative Programs, U.S. Department of Labor, 1987).

3. Refusing to hire individuals because of their past union affiliation is a violation of Section 8(a)(3) of the National Labor Relations Act. This problem is considerably worse today than it was in the early 1960s.

4. See George P. Shultz and Arnold Weber, *Strategies for the Displaced Worker* (New York: Harper & Row, 1966), p. 112.

5. Shultz and Weber, *Strategies for the Displaced Worker*, p. 188.

6. There are similar programs in Ford Motor Company and the Chrysler Corporation.

7. For example, after a major retrofit for a new model and the introduction of new technology at GM's Linden, New Jersey, plant, a large number of workers chose an early retirement option rather than enter the Jobs Bank. See Ruth Milkman, "Technological Change and Job Security: A Case Study from the Auto Industry," unpublished paper, Department of Sociology, CUNY Graduate Center, April 1988.

8. Other good illustrations of how training policies can be linked to the identification of new business opportunities are provided in Work in America, *Training for New Technology* (White Plains, N.Y.: Work in America, 1985–1987), Parts 1–5.

9. This discussion draws heavily from Schultz and Weber, *Strategies for the Displaced Worker,* pp. 189–201.

10. The transformation underway in American industrial relations is described more fully in Thomas A. Kochan, Harry C. Katz, and Robert B. McKersie, *The Transformation of American Industrial Relations* (New York: Basic Books, 1986).

11. Examples of the positive new roles played by community colleges in industrial restructuring are provided in William E. Schmidt, "Community Colleges Emerge as Centers for Job Training," *New York Times,* June 20, 1988, pp. A1 and B8.

7

The Two-Tiered Workforce
in U.S. Corporations

Firms in the United States, particularly in the large enterprise sector, have undergone profound changes in the last decade as a result of downsizing, mergers and acquisitions, and the need to stay competitive in an increasingly global economy. For example, Fortune 500 companies reduced their work-forces by 3.1 million between the beginning of 1980 and the end of 1987, going from an aggregate of 16.2 million employees to 13.1 million.[1]

This type of labor market turbulence has prompted many companies to rethink their staffing attitudes and practices. The traditional attitude of a firm toward its white-collar workforce called for permanent, or at least relatively secure, employment with some notion of career advancement. Yet current staffing practices challenge that attitude. Many companies now think of their personnel in the same manner as they do their inventories, striving for a just-in-time staffing strategy to parallel their just-in-time inventory systems.

This desire for elasticity in staffing has resulted in a two-tiered workforce in many U.S. firms. The first tier consists of a core of salaried employees on the company payroll toward whom the traditional attitude still holds. These core employees are accorded a relatively high degree of job security, per-quisites, health and pension benefits, and opportunities for training and skill upgrading.

The second tier includes a cadre of workers, many of whom are not on the company payroll, who have weak ties to the company, are generally hired for finite periods (often in a nonsystematic fashion), and typically receive no benefits. They are hired as part-time workers, self-employed independent contractors, agency temporaries, or temporaries working in a pool internal to the firm. Many workers in the second tier previously worked for the firm as core employees.

This second tier workforce goes by many names, including the contingent workforce, peripheral or secondary workers, and even the informal work-force.[2] Although this tier has always existed in the United States and elsewhere, recent evidence indicates that its numbers are growing.[3] Examples abound in the publishing, television, insurance, and advertising industries of employees laid off from the core and hired back as independent contractors, or sup-planted by temporary workers. Yet in-depth studies of this trend have been lacking, and a critical question remains as to what individual firms now do with regard to contingent staffing.

Contingent Workforce

The primary purpose of this chapter is to address questions regarding con-tingent labor from the perspective of management—what drives the use of this type of worker, what are the corporate costs and benefits of the arrangement, and what are the future trends? These management-driven questions will be answered from the perspectives of two data bases: a national Conference Board survey of contingent labor in 521 of the largest U.S. corporations[4] and in-depth case studies of two firms that have relied on these arrangements.[5] A more limited purpose of the chapter is to lay a foundation for thinking about the policy consequences of contingent work.

Defining Contingent Work

For purposes of this chapter, contingent employment arrangements include workers hired as part-timers, temporary agency hires, independent contrac-tors, and workers in internal temporary pools (see Box 7.1). Common to all these arrangements is the degree of permanence of the work agreement. Most contingent workers are hired on a limited basis, frequently with no guarantee of future employment. Despite numerous attempts, there is no commonly agreed upon definition of contingent labor.[6] Polivka and Nardone, however, provide the most complete definition. Based on a review of existing research, they define contingent work as "any job in which an individual does not have an explicit or implicit contract for long term employment and one in which the minimum hours worked can vary in a non-systematic manner."[7]

Drive Toward Contingent Work

Corporate motives for turning to contingent staffing are varied: to cut labor costs, to staff for peak periods without increasing permanent workforces, and to respond to slack demand without incurring layoffs. In addition, contingent hiring can provide a way to attract valuable skills.

BOX 7.1

DEFINITIONS

Contingent Staffing Arrangements—Workers typically have weak, nonpermanent ties to the employer and perform short-term assignments with no guarantee of future employment.

- Part-time Work: Less than full-time work by employees on company's regular payroll; benefits may or may not be available.
- Temporary Agency Hires: Persons hired through a temporary service firm who are employees of that agency, not of the firm contracting for the service.
- Independent Contractors: Self-employed workers hired for a finite period of time as, for example, free-lancers or consultants.
- Internal Temporary Pool: Persons enrolled in the pool on call as needed. The pool is managed internally by the company and may consist of former employees or external hires or both.

Contingent staffing cuts labor costs in that employers pay only for work done and not for any lag time between projects, as they do when paying employees by annual salary or wage arrangements. Furthermore, employers pay few or no discretionary benefits for temporaries, independent contractors, and many part-time workers. They can also avoid contributing to pension plans in the case of temporaries and contract workers, although federal law requires their contributions to pension coverage for part-timers working more than 1,000 hours annually.

Contingent staffing also provides flexibility for those employers who want to avoid layoffs due to recessions or seasonal fluctuations in demand. Contingent staffs constitute a workforce that can be contracted, expanded, or redeployed according to demand. By hiring workers on these flexible arrangements, companies can protect the job security of core employees. The contingent workers, in effect, absorb the vicissitudes of the marketplace.

A contingent workforce also provides a way for company officials to circumvent rigid headcount limitations, even though top management may not support the practice. In a situation where a company officer may be allocated an insufficient number of employees (headcount) to handle the workload, temporaries or independent contractors can be brought in to meet work demands because they fall outside headcount systems.

Although a number of economic forces fuel the use of contingent work from the perspective of employers, some companies responding to The Conference Board survey expressed concern that heavy reliance on a contingent workforce can result in decreased loyalty, productivity, and quality of work.

Although a contingent work staff may be profitable in some senses, it can be costly in others.

Corporate Experience with Contingent Staffing

The turbulence affecting U.S. corporations in recent years is reflected in the survey responses on contingent staffing. Over the 1985–1987 period, more than a third of the responding companies were involved in major acquisitions or divestitures, nearly a quarter instituted significant layoffs, and one fifth introduced early retirement programs (see Table 7.1). Among those surveyed, manufacturing was more severely affected by these restructurings than firms in the financial and nonfinancial services sectors.

Contingent Staffing Practices

Of the 521 respondents to the survey, 91% hire contingent workers (defined as part-time workers, temporary agency hires, internal temporary workers, and self-employed independent contractors). As Table 7.2 shows, firms are most likely to use part-time labor as a contingent staffing alternative, followed closely by temporary workers: 457 firms hire part-timers, while 451 rely on temporary workers hired through agencies. In addition, 321 firms use independent contractors, and 186 companies established internal temporary pools.

The data suggest that internal temporary pools may become more prevalent in the future, because they represent the arrangement most likely to be under consideration by the firms surveyed, as shown in Table 7.2. According to survey responses, however, internal pools also seem more susceptible to being discontinued than other contingent staffing arrangements. This ambivalence may be due in part to problems inherent to a temporary workforce and to the realization that, because they are small, many internal pools work best in informal arrangements.

Table 7.1. **Business Restructuring: 1985-87**

	Percentage of Firms Experiencing Major Changes between 1985 and 1987		
	Significant Layoffs	Early Retirement Incentives	Major Acquisitions and Divestitures
Total sample	24%	20%	35%
Manufacturing	32	25	45
Nonfinancial services	28	28	29
Finance and insurance	14	9	31

Source: Kathleen Christensen, *Flexible Staffing and Scheduling in U.S. Corporations*, Research Bulletin No. 240 (New York: The Conference Board, 1989).

Table 7.2 **Flexible Staffing Arrangements in U.S. Companies**

	Temporary Agency Hires	Part-Time Workers	Independent Contracting	Internal Temporary Pool
Respondents (number)	465	508	412	379
Firms using	451 (97%)	457 (90%)	321 (78%)	186 (49%)
Firms no longer using	4 (1%)	5 (1%)	33 (8%)	46 (12%)
Firms who considered and rejected	—	8 (1.5%)	4 (1%)	30 (8%)
Firms currently researching	—	8 (1.5%)	5 (1.3%)	34 (9%)
Firms who have never considered	10 (2%)	30 (6%)	49 (12%)	83 (22%)

Source: Kathleen Christensen, *Flexible Staffing and Scheduling in U.S. Corporations*, Research Bulletin No. 240 (New York: The Conference Board, 1989).

Types of Contingent Staffing

Part-Time Employment. The 457 firms offering some type of part-time work typically limit it to clerical and administrative support jobs. The degree of reliance on part-time labor, however, varies by industry. Firms in manufacturing and nonfinancial services hire, respectively, on a median basis, 25 and 28 part-time workers. On the other hand, companies in the finance/insurance sector rely more intensively on part-time workers, with a median hiring level of 130 part-timers per firm.

Over half (56%) of surveyed companies indicate that part-time employment is the most advantageous way to cut labor costs (see Table 7.3), while

Table 7.3. **Advantages and Disadvantages of Contingent Labor for Controlling Costs, Productivity, and Work Quality**

	Percentage of Firms Citing
ADVANTAGES	
Cut Labor Costs	
Regular part-time	56%
Temporary agency hires	30
Internal temporary pool	29
Buffer Downturns in the Economy	
Temporary agency hires	34
Regular part-time	33
Internal temporary pools	19
DISADVANTAGES	
Inconsistent Work Quality	
Temporary agency hires	55
Internal temporary pools	10
Lower Productivity	
Temporary agency hires	26

Source: Kathleen Christensen, *Flexible Staffing and Scheduling in U.S. Corporations*, Research Bulletin No. 240 (New York: The Conference Board, 1989).

48% report that reduced schedules are an important skills retention strategy (see Table 7.4). The majority of firms that value part-timers as a cost-cutting device hire part-time workers primarily from the outside, while firms that use part-time jobs to retain skills rely much less frequently on outside part-timers.

Firms often report difficulty in filling part-time jobs. An officer at a regional bank states: "We need good part-time employees to staff for peak periods, vacation, and absenteeism, but most applicants want full-time jobs." As will be discussed later, the availability of labor for part-time jobs may be a function of the types of compensation packages typically available to these workers on reduced workloads.

Temporary Agency Hires. Temporary agency hires proved to be the second most popular contingent staffing alternative (see Table 7.2), although survey results indicate that, as a result of perceived problems with high costs and uneven quality of work, the rate of growth in the use of temporary agencies may decline. In 1987 the median dollar figure that firms responding to the survey spent on temporary agency hires was $2.2 million. The responsibility for these agency hires is typically centralized in one department, usually

Table 7.4. **Advantages and Disadvantages of Contingent Labor for Workforce Quality**

	Percentage of Firms Citing
ADVANTAGES	
Retain Valuable Skills	
Regular part-time	48%
Internal temporary pool	22
Acquire Special Skills	
Independent contractors	45
Temporary agency hires	29
Regular part-time	18
Enhance Corporate Image	
Regular part-time	19
Offset Labor Shortage	
Temporary agency hires	36
Regular part-time	26
Internal temporary	19
Audition Job Candidates	
Temporary agency hires	30
Internal temporary pool	14
Regular part-time	13
DISADVANTAGES	
High Turnover and Absenteeism	
Regular part-time	10
Reduced Loyalty	
Temporary agency hires	36
Independent contractors	18
Regular part-time	13

Source: Kathleen Christensen, *Flexible Staffing and Scheduling in U.S. Corporations*, Research Bulletin No. 240 (New York: The Conference Board, 1989).

human resources. In fact, 57% of all surveyed firms do not permit local managers to contact the temporary agencies directly. Only 16% of the firms do give local managers this power, but require some form of higher approval. The remaining 27% allow local managers to hire from temporary agencies without higher level approval.

Most firms do not negotiate company-wide contracts with individual temporary agencies. Among the 40% that do have such contracts, nearly three quarters of the companies authorize their human resources departments to negotiate contracts, while the other quarter rely on other departments, most typically purchasing. Whether contracts are negotiated through human resources or purchasing may be a function of contract size—the larger the contract, the more likely it is to go through the purchasing department.[8]

From satisfaction ratings, it appears that line managers who work directly with temporary hires expressed dissatisfaction with the costs of temporary agency hires (see Tables 7.3, 7.4, 7.5, and 7.9). As a result, the human resources departments anticipate increased reliance on internal temporary pools.

Independent Contractors. Of the surveyed firms, 321 hired independent contractors—individuals working under limited-term contracts. The number

Table 7.5. **Advantages and Disadvantages of Contingent Labor for Routine Administration and Management Tasks**

	Percentage of Firms Citing
ADVANTAGES	
Cover During Absences and Vacation	
Temporary agency hires	69%
Regular part-time	44
Internal temporary pool	36
Staff for Peak Time	
Temporary agency hires	29
Regular part-time	18
Internal temporary pools	32
Reduce Absenteeism/Turnover	
Regular part-time	26
Avoid Head Count Problems	
Temporary agency hires	35
Independent contractors	20
Regular part-time	17
DISADVANTAGES	
Difficulties in Supervision	
Temporary agency hires	24
Regular part-time	12
Jobs Not Appropriate for Arrangement	
Regular part-time	*10*

Source: Kathleen Christensen, *Flexible Staffing and Scheduling in U.S. Corporations*, Research Bulletin No. 240 (New York: The Conference Board, 1989).

of contractors who worked within each firm was relatively small, however, with 75% of the firms reporting 20 or fewer independent contract workers. These contractors were typically brought in to handle professional, managerial, or technical tasks.

Firms are fairly discriminate in their use of contract labor, typically hiring such independent contractors for special skills not available in the firm. For example, a manufacturing firm in New York that hired five contractors in 1987 had no interest in expanding its use of contract labor. The firm recognized that its line managers were troubled over the lack of supervision they felt they had with contractors versus full-time employees.

In some companies, firms hire as independent contractors former employees who have been laid off, taken early retirement, or left the firm to go out on their own. Exactly how common this practice is is virtually impossible to determine since only a little more than a quarter of the firms keep centralized records on contractors. Similarly, the absence of centralized recordkeeping prevents the identification of annual expenditures on independent contractors. As a result, many larger firms do not know exactly how much of their workload has been shifted from core employees to outside contractors.

The typical arrangement regarding contractors is to allow local managers to hire contractors but to impose annual dollar limits on such authority. The median budget cited by ten firms that provided such figures was $100,000. A Northeastern utilities company sums up its experience with contractors as being effective, but notes that, "As temporary help, contractors can be used excessively unless reporting and budget controls are in place."

Internal Temporary Pools. Of the firms surveyed, 186 have established some type of internal temporary pool, or floater system, to cover short-term staffing needs. As a cost-cutting device, a northeastern pharmaceutical company developed a large internal temporary pool staffed by people between jobs, retirees, homemakers returning to the workforce, former employees, and students. In responding to the survey, the company's director of human resources reported: "Our costs for using temporary help from agencies were tremendous. In our case, the use of part-time employees and internal floating employees has helped significantly in reducing the cost of temporary agencies." This company draws on its floater system to cover all types of jobs—managerial, technical, clerical, and production and labor.

The pharmaceutical firm is unusual both in the size of its internal pool and in the scope of the services offered by the pool. Most firms with internal temporary pools are more like GTE of Connecticut, which has a small pool of 18 internal temporaries who handle clerical and administrative support jobs. As a rule, internal pools are small. In 1987, the median number of enrollees in an internal pool was 17, and they are typically targeted for clerical, administrative support, and sales jobs.

Many firms find the ideal internal temporary staffing arrangement to be one in which temps are former company employees. A nonfinancial service company in Chicago surveyed by The Conference Board exemplifies this.

According to a senior executive, "Almost all applicants selected for our internal temporary pool are ex-full-time employees or carefully screened prospects who want full-time work. This has been quite successful. By using this system, we have avoided temporary agency problems due to poor quality or inadequate performance."

But not all firms that need internal temps have such a rich pool of applications from which to choose. Companies in tight labor markets face a widespread staffing problem, and internal temporary pools are not exempt. For example, Xerox Corporation of Connecticut has trouble keeping its in-house temporary pool fully staffed, mainly because incumbents in the pool are quickly placed into full-time positions. As a result, Xerox, like The Travelers in nearby Hartford, has had to run "open houses" to recruit a steady stream of applicants for its pool.

The typical composition of internal temporary pools, in rank order of frequency of use, are shown in Table 7.6. Although retirees are now the least likely source of labor for internal pools, they are frequently mentioned as an untapped source for future temporary job assignments. For example, a midwestern manufacturing firm finds that retirees are particularly helpful in clerical work. "We get the advantage of their knowledge of the company—and they like to come back for short periods." The Travelers Corporation's internal pool is built on the same philosophy. A recent study details the experiences of major U.S. businesses that have established internal pools for older workers, including internal tempory pools.[9]

Only 31 of the 379 firms that have an internal temporary system provided figures on annual administrative costs for this arrangement. On average, each firm spent $66,000 in 1987. Whether that figure included any of the labor costs for the internal temps or simply reflected the costs for administering the program is unclear.

Industry Patterns

Having examined the four specific types of contingent labor, we need to ask what are the broader trends in these arrangements by industry, satisfaction

Table 7.6. **Composition of Internal Temporary Pools**

Rank	Type/Source of Worker	Percentage of Firms Using Source
1	Former employees other than retirees	62%
2	Homemakers returning to the workforce	56
3	Students	50
4	Retirees	44

*Numbers do not add up to 100% because companies may use multiple types of workers.

Source: Kathleen Christensen, *Flexible Staffing and Scheduling in U.S. Corporations*, Research Bulletin No. 240 (New York: The Conference Board, 1989).

Table 7.7. **Percentage of Firms by Industry Who Use Contingent Staffing Arrangements**

	Percentage of Industry Using Each Type of Contingent Labor			
	Part-Time Workers	Temporary Agency Hires	Independent Contractors	Internal Temporary Pool
Manufacturing	89%	90%	72%	40%
Nonfinancial services	84	86	65	31
Finance and insurance	98	87	53	38

Source: Kathleen Christensen, *Flexible Staffing and Scheduling in U.S. Corporations*, Research Bulletin No. 240 (New York: The Conference Board, 1989).

levels, and future prospects? Although management's use of temporary agency hires is relatively consistent across the three industry groupings—manufacturing, nonfinancial services, and finance/insurance—there are some interesting, albeit not dramatic, industry variations in the use of other forms of contingent labor—independent contractors, internal temporary pools, and part-time workers. Manufacturing firms show greater reliance on independent contracting and internal temporary pools than do firms in the finance/insurance and nonfinancial sectors (see Table 7.7). This may be due to the fact that manufacturing firms have experienced proportionately more layoffs, mergers, and divestitures than have firms in other industries. In addition, firms in finance/insurance are more likely to rely on part-time workers than firms in other industries, for reasons not entirely clear.

Survey results indicate that specific types of contingent staffing arrangements are closely linked to particular tasks (see Table 7.8). Although firms typically turn to both internal and agency temporaries for clerical work and to a lesser extent for production jobs, they rely on independent contractors for

Table 7.8. **Percentage of Contingent Workers Hired as Professionals/Managers/ Technicals, Clerical, and Production Workers**

	Type of Occupation		
Type of Contingent Arrangement*	Professional/ Managerial/ Technical (Percentage)	Clerical/ Administrative Support (Percentage)	Production (Percentage)
Temporary agency hires	5%	81%	14%
Part-time workers	8	76	16
Independent contractors	80	13	7
Internal temporary pool	4	83	13

*For each individual contingent staffing arrangement, the percentages equal 100%.

Source: Kathleen Christensen, *Flexible Staffing and Scheduling in U.S. Corporations*, Research Bulletin No. 240 (New York: The Conference Board, 1989).

short-term professional, managerial, or technical assignments. Despite the recent public attention to the growth of technical and managerial temporary agency workers, available evidence suggests minimal reliance by large corporations on temporaries for these skills.[10]

Satisfaction with Staffing Arrangements

The company officials surveyed were asked to rate their satisfaction with each of the four staffing arrangements—temporary agency hires, part-time workers, independent contractors, and internal pools—with respect to job performance, administrative costs, and ease of supervision. It is not possible, however, to discern from this survey the extent to which the advantages and disadvantages are real or merely the degree of familiarity the respondents have with the arrangements (see Box 7.2).

BOX 7.2

CONTINGENT LABOR AND SEASONAL WORK

Company U is a major food processor and marketer and has always had to think in seasonal terms. Yet the human resources implications of many seasonal factors had not been fully exploited by the company. Increased competition from low-priced warehouse supermarkets and high-priced boutique food stores led the company to intensify marketing and sales efforts and to devise new policies for reducing labor costs. Between improved revenue from marketing and cost minimization efforts from human resources, top company executives felt they had a good plan to bolster corporate profitability.

Seasonal Temporaries

The company's human resources people wanted to minimize labor costs, but they also wanted to minimize the pain inflicted on core employees. Consequently, they became interested in the potential for using seasonal employees. Because it is a food processor, the company has always had seasonal workers, but if more jobs could be made seasonal by bunching other tasks, then the company could expand its use of temporary workers.

Human resources executives and line managers felt that company jobs could be done by teachers and other workers who had an off-season from their regular job. The firm assumed that teachers would be looking for seasonal employment and would have no desire to enter the ranks of the

---

Table 7.9. **Management Satisfaction with Job Performance, Administrative Costs, and Ease of Supervision by Contingent Staff**

	(Percentage of firms reporting "very satisfactory" or "somewhat satisfactory" in each category for each arrangement)*		
	Job Performance	Administrative Cost	Ease of Supervision
Temporary agency hires	60%	44%	49%
Part-time workers	88	80	77
Independent contractors	82	61	68
Internal temporaries	87	82	72

*Equivalent to points 1 and 2 in a 5-point satisfaction scale.

Source: Kathleen Christensen, *Flexible Staffing and Scheduling in U.S. Corporations*, Research Bulletin No. 240 (New York: The Conference Board, 1989).

company's core workforce. The company's core workers would realize that seasonal teachers would work only for several months and would not view these temporaries as a threat to their jobs and advancement. Teachers would also be highly educated and self-starters, would not require much supervision, and would not require fringe benefits to supplement those already provided by their school systems. Thus, human resources people believed that their flexible employment systems could be staffed with quality workers at moderate costs.

What has been the actual experience? In general, the company has failed to attract the types of seasonal temporary workers it was looking to hire. Instead of teachers, the company attracted mostly temporaries who viewed the contingent work as a backdoor entrance into the company's core force. When many contingent workers realized that the seasonal work would not lead to permanent employment, various problems developed, including attitudinal and motivational issues. Many contingent workers wanted employee benefits, were not self-starters, and required a good deal of supervision. Even with intense supervision, these workers often did not have the same productivity and work ethic demonstrated by core workers. Many of these contingent workers did not mix well with the company's core workers, and some core workers expressed resentment toward the growing use of contingents.

As one of the company' senior human resources executives explains: "Our increased use of temporaries might have been a false economy. All I know is that if we go this route again, it will have to be managed much better."

Adapted from Richard S. Belous, *The Contingent Economy*, NPA Report No. 239 (Washington, D.C.: National Planning Association, 1989).

Satisfaction levels were highest for part-time workers and internal temporary employees on all three dimensions (see Table 7.9). Temporary agency hires, which represent the most prevalent staffing arrangement, received the lowest satisfaction ratings on all three dimensions. Differences in ratings may be related to the presence or absence of quality controls in the hiring process. People hired for internal pools or as contractors are often former employees who have been carefully selected. Although tested for certain tasks by their agencies, agency temporaries may be inappropriate for the demands of the jobs to which they are assigned or for the culture of the organization. In addition, consistent quality may be hard to obtain in the temporary service industry, given its rapid rate of growth. Although major temporary help agencies, such as Manpower, Inc. and Kelly Services, have built their businesses on improving quality by providing clerical temps with training on different types of word-processing software, not all temporary agencies provide that level of training.

Participating executives were asked to check off the advantages and disadvantages associated with various scheduling and staffing arrangements. On the whole, the respondents emphasized more advantages than disadvantages (see Tables 7.3, 7.4, and 7.5). It is evident from the data, moreover, that once an arrangement is in place, the tendency is to continue it (see Table 7.2).

Trends in Contingent Staffing

In the mid-1980s, a third of the companies using part-time workers, over half of those using temporary agency hires, and nearly all with internal temporary pools reported growth in their use of these types of temporary workers (see Box 7.3). On the other hand, only a third of the 412 firms hiring independent contractors cited recent increases in the use of this staffing arrangement.

For the future, 126 firms—more than two thirds of those responding—predict growth in their use of internal temporary pools, while approximately two thirds of respondents anticipated stabilization or cutbacks of part-time workers, independent contractors, or temporary agnecy hires. The cutbacks of temporary agency hires may reflect the lower level of satisfaction with quality and cost of these work arrangements, and the difficulties of managing a workforce with limited affiliation to the firm. Stabilization in the use of part-time workers is likely due to the fact that the majority of firms already hire part-timers. Expected growth in internal temporary pools may be related to the less extensive use of these staffing arrangement at the present time, as well as to their generally higher approval ratings.

Policy Outlook

In summary, U.S. businesses have entered an era in which flexibility constitutes a valued norm in how positions are staffed. Contingent staffing has

BOX 7.3

AD HOC VERSUS STRATEGIC USES OF CONTINGENT LABOR

Company A is a major natural resources and manufacturing corporation that was very profitable in the 1970s. Company executives speak of that era as one in which the corporation was a "paternalistic" employer: both wages and benefits were generous, and career development was predictable.

The company estimates that in 1980 its workforce consisted of 90% core workers and 10% contingent workers. By 1987, however, the workforce was 75% core worker and 25% contingent workers. In the 1980s, the company experienced a significant downsizing in its number of core workers. The image of the firm as a paternalistic employer became a thing of the past, and contingent workers were assigned to jobs—engineering, computer-related occupations, maintenance, and marketing positions—that formerly went only to core workers.

In light of this change, senior executives became concerned about exactly how this human resources transformation had occurred. The main finding was that they had ignored strategic thinking—the growth of the company's contingent workforce was an *ad hoc* response to dramatic shifts in business conditions. In the 1980s many of the markets for the company's leading products turned soft. To counter this development, management at many levels discovered that labor costs could be transformed from fixed to variable.

The real level of key decision-making in this context appeared to be on the line or divisional level. As corporate staff was being reduced, line and division managers often filled the vacuum with contingent workers. Given corporate performance standards based on bottom-line profit figures and corporate regulation concerning employee headcounts, it was often in the line manager's and division manager's interests to tilt the system toward more contingent workers and fewer core workers.

Long-Run Issues

The company is now considering the long-run implications of contingent staffing. The feeling seems to be that the company will continue to use a mix of 75% core and 25% contingent. But more of the company's human resources decisions will be strategic, that is, part of a conscious decision, and fewer will be reactive, *ad hoc* responses to problems.

The company goal is that if a line or division manager has a problem with a contingent workforce, the manager will be able to turn to other company line and division managers who have faced similar problems. As one company executive noted: "As it stands now, our people have to keep on reinventing the wheel.

Adapted from Richard S. Belous, *The Contingent Economy*, NPA Report No. 239 (Washington, D.C.: National Planning Association, 1989).

been driven largely by the need to cut costs, to buffer downturns in the economy, and to protect the security of core employees.

The potential for, as well as the difficulties of, flexible staffing has just begun to be documented. Yet one point stands out clearly from the existing data: firms must think of contingent staffing in strategic ways, not simply as *ad hoc* reactions to prevailing circumstances. Furthermore, effective methods of managing contingent workers, particularly if these workers are to work alongside core employees, must be developed if the arrangements are to meet company needs.

Notes

This chapter is primarily the responsibility of Kathleen Christensen. Richard S. Belous is primarily responsible for the case materials.

1. David Birch, "The Hidden Economy," *Wall Street Journal,* June 10, 1988.

2. Richard S. Belous, *The Contingent Economy: The Growth of the Temporary, Part-time and Subcontracted Workforce.* NPA Report 239 (Washington, D.C.: National Planning Association, 1989); Kathleen Christensen, Testimony Before the Committee on Government Operations, U.S. House of Representatives: *Rising Use of Part-time and Temporary Workers: Who Benefits and Who Loses?* (Washington, D.C.: Government Printing Office, 1988), pp. 82–83; Kathleen Christensen and Mary Murphree, "Introduction," in *Flexible Workstyles: A Look at Contingent Labor* (Washington, D.C.: U.S. Department of Labor, Women's Bureau, 1988); and Alejandro Portes and Saskia Sassen-Koob, "Making It Underground: Comparative Material on the Informal Sector in Western Market Economies," *American Journal of Sociology* 93 (1987): 53.

3. Bureau of National Affairs, *The Changing Workplace: New Directions in Staffing and Scheduling: A BNA Report* (Washington, D.C.: Bureau of National Affairs, 1986).

4. Kathleen Christensen, *Flexible Staffing and Scheduling in U.S. Corporations,* Research Bulletin No. 240 (New York: The Conference Board, 1989).

In April 1988, a survey concerning flexible staffing and scheduling was mailed to human resources executives in 2,775 U.S. companies in nine industries. A total of 521 companies sent back usable responses, of which 502 identified their industry: 169 manufacturing, 154 nonfinancial services, and 179 finance/insurance. The manufacturing category includes industrial and consumer manufacturing as well as extraction, including mining. Finance/insurance encompasses banks, insurance companies, and other financial services, while nonfinancial services include transportation, diversified services, construction, wholesale and retail trade, and utilities.

The executives were questioned regarding their firms' use in 1987 of three staffing arrangements (internal temporary pools, temporary agency hires, and independent contractors) and six scheduling arrangements (flextime, regular part-time, job sharing, compressed work week, phased retirement, and home-based work). For purposes of this chapter, part-time work is considered part of contingent staffing because survey responses indicated that companies were likely to use part-time work as a contingent arrangement more than a flexible scheduling one.

Flexible schedules are driven by motives different from those of contingent staffing and are available only to core employees. Consequently, they represent a phenomenon very different from contingent staffing and are therefore not covered in this chapter. For further information on flexible schedules, see Christensen, *Flexible Staffing.*

The sample is not representative of all U.S. businesses, or even of very large corporations. In fact, the responses may be skewed in favor of firms that provide flexible scheduling and staffing alternatives, since these firms may be more likely to have participated in the survey. The existence or extent of such bias is not known because no attempt was made to analyze the nonrespondent population.

The survey was directed by Kathleen Christensen and sponsored by The Conference Board, in conjunction with New Ways to Work. For a full report on the survey, see Christensen, *Flexible Staffing.*

5. Belous, *Contingent Economy.* The two case studies were conducted as part of a survey of 50 case studies directed by Richard S. Belous of the National Planning Association. The 50 case studies were of firms in five major economic sectors: 3 from natural resources and agriculture, 19 from manufacturing, 16 from services, 8 from private nonprofit, 2 from government, and 2 from unions. These firms were geographically dispersed throughout the continental United States, although many of them are involved in the global economy. See Belous, *Contingent Economy,* for more information.

6. Audrey Freedman, *The New Look in Wage Policy and Employee Relations,* Report No. 865 (New York: The Conference Board, 1985); Audrey Freedman, Testimony Before the Committee on Government Operations, U.S. House of Representatives: *Rising Use of Part-time and Temporary Workers: Who Benefits and Who Loses?* (Washington, D.C.: Government Printing Office, 1988), p. 35; Anne Polivka and Thomas Nardone, "On the Definition of Contingent Work," *Monthly Labor Review* 112 (December 1989), pp. 9–16; Belous, *Contingent Economy*; Christensen, Testimony; Christensen and Murphree, "Introduction."

7. Polivka and Nardone, "On the Definition," p. 11.

8. Mitchell Fromstein, personal communication (1988).

9. Helen Axel (ed.), *Employing Older Americans: Opportunities and Constraints,* Research Bulletin No. 916 (New York: The Conference Board, 1988); and Helen Axel, *Job Banks for Older Workers,* Research Bulletin No. 929 (New York: The Conference Board, 1989).

10. Lynn Asinof, "Rent-An-Exec Firm" in Labor Letter, *Wall Street Journal,* August 4, 1988, p. 1; and Selwyn Feinstein, "More Small Firms Get Help from Rent-A-Boss Service," *Wall Street Journal,* January 5, 1989.

8

Restructuring Managerial and Professional Work in Large Corporations

Managers and professionals working for major U.S. corporations enjoyed a prolonged period of company growth and employment security from the 1950s through the early 1970s. The pressures for individual performance were intense, to be sure, as chronicled in David Riesman's *The Lonely Crowd* and William H. Whyte's *The Organization Man*. Still, there was an implicit *quid pro quo* for the long work week and personal sacrifice: a sense of entitlement to a good job as long as it was wanted. Because many companies had steadily expanded, managers and professionals had often come to expect continuous salary growth, regular career promotions, and lifelong company employment.

The 1980s, by contrast, brought a far less certain employment environment. The sources of the uncertainty were several: increased competition from foreign firms, heightened pressures from domestic competitors in newly deregulated environments, and intensified threats of acquisition and takeover. Each company faced its own unique blend of pressures, but most shared in the general business plight of steadily declining profitability.[1]

As companies resorted to a range of cost-cutting strategies, the hitherto sacrosanct ranks of managers and professional were not spared. The actions have varied from massive terminations to retraining and redeployment, from "resizing" to "restructuring." But the actions have also had ramifications far beyond the immediate changes in personnel. They reach into the organization of corporate careers, the structure of managerial and professional work, and the educational preparation for both.

This chapter identifies what is known about the incidence of company resizing in recent years and how it has affected managers and professionals. It then turns to three related consequences of the corporate restructuring: (1) the altering of traditional career structures for managerial and professional employees, making career paths more horizontally diverse; (2) the reduction of opportunities for upward mobility; and (3) the increasing responsibilities of mid-level managers and professionals. Finally, the chapter considers the implications of company restructuring for management recruitment and the preparation of managers for flexible movement and redeployment.

Company Resizing and the Redeployment of Managers and Professionals

Company strategies for managing the impact of resizing on managers and professionals varied little by sector but considerably by size during the mid-1980s. A survey of 1,100 companies by the American Management Association in mid-1987, for example, found that similar proportions of manufacturing and service companies planned to redeploy their exempt employees in the event of downsizing (see Table 8.1). By contrast, more than half of the large corporations reported that they would use job redeployment and retraining for exempt employees in the event of downsizing, but only two fifths of the mid-size companies and just over a quarter of the small firms would plan to do so. Large corporations were twice as likely as small firms to anticipate the use of early retirement and selective outplacement schemes for their exempt employees.[2]

Managers and professionals in manufacturing were more likely to be affected by reductions in force. A cross-sectional sample study of companies

Table 8.1. **Downsizing Among U.S. Companies, by Company Size and Sector, 1987**

	All Companies	Company Size*			Industry	
		Large	Mid-size	Small	Manufacturing	Service
Percentage of Companies Downsizing						
Downsized during past 18 months	45%	58%	49%	40%	57%	43%
Expect to downsize during next 18 months	17	34	19	11	16	19
Percentage of Companies Using Policy for Exempt Employees in Event of Downsizing						
Job redeployment/ retraining	36%	51%	40%	28%	36%	36%
Early retirement	44	70	51	33	50	40
Selective outplacement	41	57	51	30	48	41

*Large companies are those with annual sales exceeding $500 million; mid-size companies have annual sales from $50 to $500; small companies have annual sales of less than $50 million. The number of companies on which figures are based varies from 1,067 to 1,080.

Source: American Management Association, *Responsible Reduction in Force* (New York: American Management Association, 1988).

with 50 or more employees by the General Accounting Office (GAO) found that closures and permanent layoffs were three to four times more prevalent among manufacturing establishments than among service and trade firms. Durable goods industries—producers in such areas as steel, autos, and machinery—were particularly hard hit.[3] Similarly, a Conference Board study of 512 corporations in 1985 reported that more than three quarters of the manufacturing companies had closed a facility or significantly reduced the workforce during a three-year period ending in December 1984. By contrast, under half of the financial firms and just over a third of the utility companies had taken such steps.[4]

These studies confirm that competitive pressures were the driving force behind the workforce resizings. The GAO survey asked the responding companies to identify the major factors accounting for their closure or layoff decisions, and the three leading factors were reduced product demand (cited by 60%), increased competition (56%), and high labor costs (45%). Among the 210 companies in the Conference Board survey that had closed a facility, the leading factor, identified by nearly half of the firms, was change in company markets, including increased domestic or foreign competition and production or process obsolescence.[5]

Large numbers of professionals and managers were affected by the downsizing, and some observers have suggested that the middle ranks were particularly subject to reduction. One widely cited estimate, for instance, indicated that as many as half a million middle management and professional positions were eliminated by some 300 companies between 1984 and 1986.[6] The one study that explicitly compares rates of job loss among various occupational groups, however, finds that managers and professionals have been *less* vulnerable than blue-collar groups.[7] Some 80% of the establishment closures and permanent layoffs identified in this study had affected both groups of employees, but blue-collar workers lost their jobs at twice the rate of white-collar employees.

Despite the relatively lower vulnerability to displacement or white-collar workers, companies were more likely to offer special assistance to affected white-collar than blue-collar workers in a range of areas, including the continuation of health and life insurance coverage, income maintenance assistance, early retirement benefits, relocation assistance, counseling, and assistance in searching for a new job. Also, managers and professionals may be relatively more protected during the corporate restructuring of the mid-1980s than during a general recession a decade earlier. Three fifths of the 500 largest manufacturing companies underwent personnel reductions during the mid-1970s, according to one study, and then the rate of job loss was greater among white-collar than blue-collar employes.[8]

Still, for managers and professionals who have been dismissed, the event often marks a watershed in their career development. Substantial numbers are likely to suffer a period of unemployment, and even larger proportions will find new employment outside the managerial and professional fields.

This is evident in a study by the U.S. Bureau of Labor Statistics of displaced employees who had lost their jobs because of plant closings and employment cutbacks between January 1979 and December 1983.[9] Focusing on relatively well-established employees, defined as those who had held the job from which they were displaced for at least three years, the survey found that a quarter of the 703,000 displaced managers and professionals did not hold a job in January 1985. Two thirds of these were looking for jobs, and one third had left the labor force. Of those who had found employment, only half had located alternative employment as managers and professionals, while the remainder were scattered throughout the occupational structure where neither status nor income was likely to equal their predisplacement position (see Table 8.2). Although managers and professionals displayed the lowest rate of unemployment of the five major occupational groupings, they had the highest rate of occupational change among those who were reemployed. On the other hand, further analysis of the displaced worker data reveals that white-collar employees suffered fewer overall economic losses than did blue-collar workers when the local economy was growing.[10]

Although downward mobility has harsh economic consequences for all occupational groups, it can be particularly difficult socially for managers and professionals. The U.S. culture of meritocracy offers little solace for those who fall short of its norms. Blame for failure is more often placed on the individual than on the impersonal market forces that account for the downward movement. Managers and professionals share more strongly in the ethos of individual success than do other groups, and when they do not meet its standards, the sense of failure is more acutely felt. In a detailed study of the personal consequences of downward mobility among company managers who lost their jobs during the 1980s, many because of corporate restructurings, one analyst reported that "downwardly mobile managers are left hanging and socially isolated with no stable sense of who they are," a consequence also noted in studies of managers and professionals out of work during the 1970s.[11]

Table 8.2. **Subsequent Employment Status of Displaced Managers and Professionals, January 1984**

Subsequent Employment Status	Percentage*
Managerial, professional	38%
Technical, sales, and administrative support	22
Service	4
Precision production, craft, and repair	5
Operators, fabricators, and laborers	2
Unemployed	17
Not in labor force	9
Other	3

*Based on 703,000 managers and professionals who lost or left a job between January 1979 and December 1983 due to plant closing or move, slack work, or the abolishment of their positions.

Source: Paul O. Flaim and Ellen Sehgal, "Reemployment and Earnings," in Paul D. Staudohar and Holly E. Brown (eds.), *Deindustrialization and Plant Closure* (Lexington, Mass.: Lexington Books, 1987).

Managerial Turbulence at the Workplace

Corporate downsizing and the subsequent redeployment of managers and professionals are restructuring the careers of these workers. Lateral mobility, both within and between companies, appears to have increased while vertical mobility within firms has decreased.

Increased Horizontal Mobility

Conventional career structures among managers and professionals working at many large corporations entail regular increases in salary and periodic promotions in responsibility. The upward movement, however, is generally confined not only to a single company but also to a single functional area or diversion within the company. New employees tend to enter the firm through a limited set of relatively low-level points and progress up well-defined career ladders within a specific area or division of the corporation. Entry-level and mid-career training by the firm is often extensive, and employees are expected—and expect—to remain with a single corporation and within an area or division of the company for most if not all of their career. Strong traditions of job security and loyalty to the company discourage mobility between firms, and even movement among the company's major divisions is often limited.

The prolonged period of steady growth experienced by many corporations during the 1960s and early 1970s permitted a number of companies to evolve stable employment systems built around divisional ladders and long-term employment entitlement. The equation balanced company commitment to managerial and professional employees with their loyalty to the company. Company downsizing and internal personnel redeployment have, however, undermined these conventional career principles. With downsizing, managers and professionals are more often being forced to leave their company and to seek their fortunes with new employers. As a result, loyalty to a company is being overshadowed by commitment to one's own career. The concept of the corporate career for many managers and professionals is being replaced by that of the "self-oriented career" in which skills and commitments are transferred from company to company.

The intensification of interorganizational mobility is having greater impact on managers than professionals, since the former have always been less likely to switch companies than the latter. A study of 100 employment sites in California, for example, reveals that the internal employment markets for managers are considerably stronger than for professional and technical employees. Compared to professional and technical positions, managerial positions are far more often filled by promotion from within the company than by recruitment from the outside. Similarly, a study of 12 largely white-collar firms found that middle and top managerial positions were almost completely closed to those from outside the firm. By contrast, nearly half of the positions of one of the professional groups in the companies—computer programmers—was filled by outsiders. Entry-level managers required twice as long as program-

---

BOX 8.1

COMPANY A: RETRENCHMENT AND RETRAINING

This manufacturing and service corporation, a major U.S. employer, had encountered severe competitive problems in the early 1980s because of a newly deregulated environment. As a result, the company reduced a labor force that had numbered several hundred thousand by more than 20% during a four-year period in the mid-1980s. Five major manufacturing facilities were closed, and a major division was phased out as well. Managerial and professional jobs were initially more protected than nonexempt positions, but they too were soon eliminated in large numbers as competitive pressures redoubled. Job freezes, early retirement schemes, and reassignment to openings in other locations absorbed some of the retraction, but for the first time in its long history the company laid off several thousand employees. Managers were permitted to protect the top-rated 10% of their staffs, but all others were fair game for the downsizing.

The previously unused step in this company's retrenchment was to offer managers and professionals an opportunity to retrain for very different positions within the corporation. The company had concluded that it had too few people in direct contact with customers and too many in other management and technical areas. Accordingly, it opened a program to retrain employees, largely college educated, for new openings in its sales force. Because many of the candidates for the program had worked for the company for 10 to 15 years with virtually no customer contact, an aptitude test for sales potential was applied, screening out about half of the applicants. The 3,000 accepted into the program were passed through an extensive retraining course. The evolving corporate philosophy, in the words of a divisional manager of education and training, was to transform the content of job entitlement: "We used to have lifetime employment [in one functional area], but now we have [lifetime] employment across boundaries and job categories."

---

mers to reach early proficiency within these companies, and managers were only half as likely as programmers to leave the company over a given time period.[12]

The intensifying redeployment of employees within major corporations has also meant that traditional career structures inside the firm have been eroded. Conventional boundaries have become more permeable, increasing the likelihood that managers and professionals may be required to cross both organizational and occupational divisions within the company. The increased movement across boundaries within a company can be seen in three large industrial companies whose policies we observed in mid-1988 (see Boxes 8.1, 8.2, and 8.3). Though facing different competitive pressures, all had initiated extensive

---

BOX 8.2

Company B: Downsizing and Redeployment

This industrial company specializing in office equipment had grown rapidly in the 1960s and early 1970s. By the late 1970s, however, Japanese makers had severely undercut the company's share of the office product market, leading to several rounds of layoffs and other downsizing steps during the decade. The company scrapped a longstanding written policy that no person with at least eight years of experience could be terminated without the chairman's permission. Because Japanese manufacturing costs were considerably lower, the U.S. company focused on cutting its production costs, significantly reducing employee rolls in manufacturing, materials handling, and inventory control. The personnel rolls at one manufacturing site, for example, were reduced from 11,000 to fewer than 6,000 employees. But the company also increasingly looked to redeployment as a companion strategy. Initially it retrained managers and professionals for comparatively short lateral moves, such as from mechanical to electrical engineering, but with growing confidence it initiated retraining for more remote lateral moves as well.

---

redeployments of their managerial and professional personnel in response to the pressures.

Although the increased horizontal mobility within these and other companies is a direct product of the downsizings and redeployment pressures of the era, the main underlying cause appears to be in part rapid change, not just competitive restructuring. Frequent boundary crossings are also characteristic of companies undergoing rapid expansion.

This can be seen, for example, in a study of five rapidly growing high-technology firms. Managerial careers were characterized by limited managerial identification with a particular functional area, frequent movement across units, and career arenas transcending many of a company's divisions and groups. Certain features observed among these companies were not shared, however, by firms undergoing downsizing and redeployment: promotions were more frequent, and successful managers acquired general positions of authority relatively early in their careers.[13] Companies undergoing rapid change—whether expansion or contraction—thus tend to reduce traditional career ladders and boundaries, though for different reasons. Expanding firms are overcoming shortages in experienced managers and professionals, while contracting firms are coping with employee surpluses. Whatever the source of change, companies often use the opportunity to flexibly restructure their workforces from within.

BOX 8.3

COMPANY C: REBALANCING THE WORKFORCE

This large manufacturer of information systems managed to avoid layoffs entirely when competition from other U.S. companies cut sharply into its revenue growth during the mid-1980s. A central feature of its strategy was to move people out of headquarters functions back to branch offices, reflecting the belief that the company must reduce its indirect costs while at the same time strengthening its customer service. Also at stake was the company's no-layoff policy that had engendered deep employee loyalty. Some 8,000 employees left headquarters to join branches during a two-year period, a redeployment with a "bright silver lining," according to the manager of personnel planning, since "people who came with a broader base of skills are now closer to the customer base." This rebalancing of the workforce thus saw a reduction of headquarters staff and general managers and an expansion of the company's district service personnel and its sales staff. Involuntary separations were successfully avoided altogether.

The company viewed loyalty and employee flexibility as indispensable ingredients of its successful long-term development. Its regular employee surveys had indeed shown that they remained highly flexible: three-quarters were prepared to change areas of work within the company, half would accept a move to a new location, and more than a third would do both. Moreover, the company's annual surveys of employee morale revealed that there had been no overall slippage during the period of workforce restructuring, testimony to the no-layoff strategy's general effectiveness for retaining employee loyalty.

Reduced Vertical Mobility

A second consequence of corporate resizing and redeployment is the truncation of career mobility among managers and professionals. Traditional patterns of upward movement entailed reasonably regular promotions, as can be seen in internal mobility data for one large corporation. Drawing on an extensive analysis of personnel records, the researcher found that managers could expect a promotion every three years during the early phases of a career, far more frequently than nonexempt employees, and that their salaries increased at a comparatively rapid rate as well.[14] Even after 15 to 25 years with the company, when promotion prospects and wage increases for most nonexempt employees had flattened, managers were still enjoying upward mobility, albeit at a pace slowed from the early years. Similar patterns of career mobility are recorded in a longitudinal study of managers hired in the 1950s by American Telephone and Telegraph.[15]

In corporations whose managerial and professional ranks had been thinned, however, the upward career mobility rates can be substantially reduced. Salary growth is slowed or even stopped as fiscal austerity limits the funds available for annual salary reviews and year-end bonuses. Career opportunities are lessened as fewer openings are available, and job plateauing comes sooner, though the specific impact varies significantly with the individual's age, education, and other characteristics.[16]

Longitudinal studies of earnings profiles and career outlooks confirm such changes. One study, for example, examined the earnings profiles of young men who entered the labor market in 1966, 1970, and 1974. Among those who had acquired a college business degree (and thus those who had presumably entered the private sector as managers or professionals), the rate of growth in earnings was considerably higher for the 1966 group than for the 1974 group. After 12 years of work experience, the 1966 group earned annual salaries that averaged more than twice their starting salaries in constant dollars. By contrast, the 1974 group was earning only about 14% more than its starting salary after a decade of experience. Those with engineering degrees, the great bulk of whom also entered private industry, suffered less but nonetheless substantial salary flattening as well. The salaries of engineers with 12 years of experience were 53% above the starting salaries for the 1966 engineering cohort, but only 17% above starting salaries for the 1974 group.[17]

Corroborating this finding of flattening career structures, direct study of managerial and professional outlook on career prospects reveals that managers and professionals see their company opportunity structures as more limited than did an earlier generation. Comparison of new managers hired at AT&T in the mid-1950s and late 1970s reveals, for instance, that even by the late 1970s (long before the breakup of AT&T at the start of 1984 and subsequent downsizing) new managers viewed their career prospects in considerably less sanguine terms than did the earlier cohort when they were beginning.[18]

Similarly, general surveys of managers and professionals reveal a prolonged decline in the confidence with which they view their own future. Ths is evident, for instance, in data collected by Opinion Research Corporation in the course of conducting contract studies of hundreds of companies of various sizes. Although the trend figures must be interpreted cautiously because they are based on different managers and companies at different time points, the broad outlines of a decline are unmistakable: middle managers were significantly less optimistic about their job security, benefits, and opportunities for advancement in 1980 than had been those in the early 1960s.

The trends for professionals followed much the same pattern. And although managers and professionals consistently gave their workplace opportunities higher marks than nonexempt employees, the outlooks of exempt and nonexempt employees were converging. Hourly and clerical workers have traditionally expressed less confidence in their job security than managers, for instance, but by 1980 there was little difference in their expectations.[19] A more recent study of employee attitudes reveals that managerial reading of employment opportunities continued to decline through the mid-1980s: middle managers were found to be significantly less optimistic about their opportunties for advancement and employment security in 1985 than in 1975.[20]

The decline of career optimism among managers and professionals can be directly linked in part to restructuring actions taken by corporations. A 1981–83 study of employee attitudes, for instance, shows that the deterioration in attitudes was most pronounced among the slower- or negative-growth companies whose personnel policies had presumably been under greatest downsizing pressures.[21]

Corporate restructuring, then, is expanding the rate of lateral movement and contracting opportunities for upward movement. As a result managers and professionals entering the workforce now may expect to work for more companies and for more divisions within a company. Also, corporations hiring managers and professionals may anticipate less managerial and professional loyalty to the firm and more privatized commitment to individual career development.

Although lower job security may improve job performance among managers and professionals, it may also make it more difficult for companies to foster flexibility in these employees or even retain their services. During an era of restructuring in which change often presages downsizing, company reorganization may face more internal resistance and less cooperation from employees concerned about their job futures. And companies may find it more difficult to retain high-performance managers and professionals, who view their uncertain job prospects within the firm as ample reason to be considering employment elsewhere.

Reskilling of Managerial and Professional Work

When the ranks of managers and professionals are thinned through redeployments and reductions, additional managerial responsibilities necessarily devolve upon those who remain. The experience of Company B is a case in point. Pressed by vigorous competition from Japanese manufacturers, the company carefully studied the supervisory structures of its Japanese counterparts. It found that the Japanese competitors often had only a single supervisor for as many as 100 workers, while it had a ratio of about one to 17.

In its manufacturing organization, Company B estimated that it had two support people for every one employee directly engaged in manufacturing, an indirect cost structure considerably higher than that of its Japanese competitors. As a consequence, Company B cut the ratio of indirect to direct staff by more than half between 1980 and 1988, and it more than doubled the span of control. The challenge, noted the manager of the company's employee involvement program, was to create "a culture in which the workers accept more responsibility" and are able to structure tasks in "more integrated, cross-functional ways so that engineers, sales and marketing, and manufacturing people all work together."

Case studies of companies A and C and other corporations reveal analogous developments, though such studies also indicate that middle managers are often poorly equipped or positioned to exercise their enhanced responsibilities. Two analysts studied a large manufacturer and a producer of consumer durables, both of which had experienced static or declining employment rolls, and they report that middle managers in both companies expressed relatively high rates of dissatisfaction, and some actively resisted delegation of authority to them. The analysts attribute much of the problem to inadequate communication and working relations across the company's functions. The increased responsibilities required middle managers to coordinate with their counterparts in other company divisions and units, but previous structures and policies of both companies had provided little opportunity for such networks to form.[22]

Similarly, a detailed study of the restructuring of one of the nation's leading banks reported that middle managers were subject to sharply conflicting demands. Because the bank's downsizing had been occasioned by poor profit performance, the remaining middle managers were expected to intensify the motivation of their employees and increase productivity. Yet the austerity conditions of the moment allowed them few resources with which to achieve either. They were unable to assure job security, promotion opportunities, or pay increases to those they supervised who did produce.[23]

Although many companies are thus placing greater responsibility on the shoulders of middle managers, in some cases the formation of organizational support systems has not kept pace with the increasing responsibilities. More generally, success in managing rapid retrenchment depends on a host of special strategies for overcoming organizational conflicts and shortcomings occasioned by the changes.[24] New information technologies may be particularly important for facilitating organizational adjustment. The introduction of computer systems can encourage broader spans of control, more rapid data retrieval, and faster communication across organizational boundaries, thereby reducing the number of managerial and professional positions required to achieve the same results. Corroborating evidence comes from a mid-1970s study of 40 industries in which it was found that a 10% increase in company computing power led to a 1% reduction in managerial employment.[25]

Whatever the problems and process of implementation, the pattern of increasing responsibility may be reversing a historic trend in U.S. industry toward more hierarchic and specialized forms of internal authority systems. According to one study, the ratio of supervisory to nonsupervisory employees in the U.S. economy increased from 13:100 in the late 1940s to 23:100 in the late 1960s; the proportion of total wage and salary earnings acquired by supervisory and nonproduction employees rose from 22% in 1963 to 34% in 1983.[26]

In manufacturing, recent decades have seen a sharp increase in the proportion of the workforce employed in managerial and professional positions and a steady or declining proportion of those employed directly in production. Managers and professionals constituted 9.6% of the manufacturing workforce in 1950, but 19.5% in 1980 and 20.7% in 1982. The proportion classified as managers and professionals in 1983 stood at 21.0% (the classification scheme was altered that year, making direct comparison with previous years problematic), and this rose to 22.8% by 1988.[27] However, the overall growth of managerial and professional employment in manufacturing may well have slowed or plateaued during the mid-1980s, particularly among large firms. Managerial, professional, and technical employees constituted a slightly higher proportion of manufacturing employees in 1988 than 1983 (overall manufacturing employment hovered at 21 million throughout the 1980s), but the growth in the proportion had slowed from earlier decades.

Although workforce reductions have been observed among many major corporations, the aggregate effects have not yet become manifest in trend data on the overall composition of the workforce. Still, in the large number of companies where the ranks of managers and professionals have been trimmed, the remaining managers and professionals can be expected to shoulder more responsibility and carry out more complex tasks. Thus, for at least certain cadres of managerial and professional employees, the period may be one of skill broadening rather than the workforce deskilling seen in some past eras.[28]

Job enrichment generally improves employee commitment. The reskilling of managerial and professional positions could thus be expected to heighten work attachment. Still, the upgrading of responsibilities is coming in an era of declining opportunity for upward mobility, and the latter may cancel any positive effect of upgrading. Although there is no direct evidence bearing on the net effect of these opposing tendencies, surveys of managers and professionals generally confirm that work interest is not declining but that confidence in the company is.

The study of new managers hired by AT&T in the 1950s and 1970s, for instance, reports that both groups were highly involved in and committed to quality work performance. Young male managers hired in the late 1970s, however, were less motivated to exert leadership and were more pessimistic about the qulity of life of a manager. Moreover, the younger generation was found to be significantly less loyal and emotionally invested in the company than had been the earlier generation at the equivalent career point.[29] Other studies of middle managers and professionals at various times between the early 1960s and the mid-1980s find diminishing loyalty in, and trust of, the employing corporation.[30]

Part of the decline of managerial and professional confidence in the employer is traceable not to the changing quality of work or the actions of specific firms but rather to the general drop of public confidence in business during the past several decades. The latter was itself part of a more general loss of confidence in the nation's major institutions.[31]

Turbulence and Managerial Recruitment

The turbulence in managerial and professional employment may be offering discouraging signals to college students. Reports of corporate restructurings and the thinning of middle-management and professional ranks circulate widely, and there is ample evidence that the decision to enroll in college, the choice of college major, and the development of career objectives are importantly shaped by student perceptions of short- and long-term opportunities, albeit in highly imperfect and, at times, lagging fashion.[32] The flattening of earnings and career opportunities for managers and professionals may thus make it more difficult for corporations to recruit college graduates.

The evidence to date, however, indicates that longer-term changes in the economic value of education and campus cultures, as well as heightened turbulence in the entry-level labor market for young adults with no post-secondary schooling, are still more than compensating for any negative impact of the corporate restructuring. If anything, more young people than ever are interested in a college education and a career in business. A college education is the key starting credential for the latter: whereas only 25% of the overall young workforce (aged 25 to 34) in manufacturing companies in 1986 was college educated, 63% of those in managerial, professional, and technical positions held college degrees.[33]

Enrollments in colleges and universities remained stable during the 1980s, with nearly 1 million students graduating from college with bachelor's degrees each year. Fueling the sustained enrollments during the 1980s, despite the declining size of the college-age cohort, was a strong increase in the relative value of a college degree.[34] As indicated in Chapter 2, changes in the relative earnings of high-school and college graduates during the 1980s was a joint product of declining real wages of high-school graduates and rising real wages of college graduates.[35] Moreover, for those entering managerial, professional, and technical occupations, the college premium became even greater.[36]

A more career-directed and income-conscious culture on campus also oriented more students toward a future in business. The political activism and concern with social issues of the 1960s and early 1970s gave way to a more self-focused concern of "getting ahead" and "making money," a reversal starkly illustrated by two key barometers of college freshmen values. In 1970, some 39% of the nation's entering college students endorsed "being very well off financially" as one of their primary life goals. By 1987, this number had risen to 76%. Conversely, although 80% of the freshmen in 1970 endorsed "developing a meaningful philosophy in life" as a major goal, this percentage dropped to 39% by 1987.[37]

College student aspirations also became more explicitly focused on a future in the private sector (see Table 8.3). Changing career interests were reflected in the undergraduate majors of choice among college students: the fraction of freshmen intending to major in business rose from 16% in 1970 to 27% in 1987, and the proportion graduating grew from 14 to 24% during the same period.[38]

Engineering enrollments, however, flattened during the mid-1980s. In 1970, engineering represented 6% of all bachelor degrees, and after a momentary decline in the early 1970s following the recession in engineering employment, the proportion climbed steadily to 10% by 1986 (aided by an infusion of women and foreign students). Shifts in the educational preferences of college

Table 8.3. **Percentage of First-Year College Graduates Endorsing Business-Related Career Goals, 1970–87**

	1970	1975	1980	1985	1987
Business is a probable career occupation.	11%	14%	20%	24%	25%
Having administrative responsibility for others is essential or very important.	22	31	39	43	45
Intend to major in business	16	19	24	27	27

Source: Alexander W. Astin, Kenneth C. Green, and William S. Korn, *The American Freshman: Twenty-Year Trends* (Los Angeles: Cooperative Institutional Research Program: University of California, Los Angeles, 1987); Alexander W. Astin, Kenneth C. Green, William S. Korn, and Marilyn Schalit, *The American Freshman: National Norms for Fall 1987* (Los Angeles: Cooperative Institutional Research Program, University of California, Los Angeles, 1987).

freshmen, however, suggest that the engineering interest may have at least temporarily plateaued: while 9% of all first-year college students reported plans to major in engineering in 1970, and 13% planned to do so in 1982, the proportion dropped back (despite improvements in relative earnings) to 9% in 1987.

Although engineers represented a growing proportion of new corporate employees during the 1980s, the number of college students preparing for careers in engineering may have momentarily peaked. Previous studies, however, suggest that student interest in engineering generally lags trends in employment opportunities, and student interest may later be revitalized if openings and competitive salaries for engineers remain strong.[39]

Increasingly recognizing that engineers play a central role in the management of many corporations, a number of college engineering programs initiated efforts during the 1980s to broaden the education received by their students. The faculty of the Massachusetts Institute of Technology, for instance, adopted a new set of undergraduate requirements in 1987 intended to increase significantly the exposure of its engineering students to the humanities and social sciences. Among the goals was an effort to enhance the engineering graduate's prospects for promotion into the managerial ranks of business. Said one Institute official: "Too many M.I.T. graduates end up working for too many Princeton and Harvard graduates." To expand the breadth and depth of exposure of engineering students to social science and humanities coursework, the Association of American Colleges and the Accrediting Board for Engineering and Technology initiated national efforts in 1988 to strengthen the role of liberal arts in engineering education.[40]

Preparing Managers for Redeployment

The changes in managerial and professional employment identified here point to several implications for the educational preparation of those who may enter the managerial and professional ranks of large firms. A new premium is placed on employees' flexibility and capacity to move quickly into new areas of responsibility within the firm. Similarly, as some employees face career paths with fewer upward opportunities and more outplacement experiences, company-specific and occupation-specific knowledge and information are less important, and transportable and boundary-spanning abilities become more salient.

The heightened demand for flexibly educated managers and professionals builds on an already substantial corporate need and preference for broadly trained entry-level hires. The need for a broad education, however, is often poorly communicated to prospective entry-level managers and professionals. Instead, the corporate stress on entry-level skills tends to bring into the company new college-educated managers and professionals who are poorly prepared for redeployment during their careers.

A range of studies confirm that corporations require employees who possess not only entry-level job skills, but also a broad enough educational background to permit ready movement into other positions and different companies. One comprehensive study of U.S. manufacturing, for instance, concluded that a well-educated workforce is a prerequisite for industrial firms to take advantage of market opportunities requiring rapid redeployment of employees.[41] Similarly, drawing on comparative studies of on-the-job training and personnel rotation in the United States, Japan, Germany, and elsewhere, a university-backed productivity commission concluded that company educational programs engendering breadth in skills and greater flexibility should improve both workplace organization and company performance.[42]

Another detailed study of corporate innovation reports that managers who "are broader-gauged, more able to move across specialist boundaries, [and] comfortable working in teams that may include many disciplines" are generally more effective in managing change.[43] Finally, in tracking the impact of technological change on future workplace demands for education and training, a general education emphasizing flexibility and adaptability is likely to be increasingly valued in an economy whose specific work requirements cannot be readily forecast and whose employment markets increasingly invite job- and career-changing.[44]

A 1987 study of company practices in hiring college graduates, based on surveys of 535 large and mid-size corporations and 505 middle and senior managers, confirms a widespread emphasis on generic skills. A major stress was on combining the liberal arts and the "useful arts," a general education and a specific specialty. College graduates, in the assessment of many companies and managers, need the finite, job-specific skills that are required for entry-level positions, but they also need the general analytic and communication skills that accompany a general education, particularly for movement into more responsible positions. Two thirds of the managers asserted that liberal arts students looking into careers in the private sector should acquire more business and technical courses, but two thirds also stated that business and engineering majors should acquire additional liberal-arts coursework.[45]

General communication, leadership, and analytic abilities, however, become salient only as managerial and professional careers mature. An AT&T tracking study, for example, followed a set of college-educated managers hired during the 1950s over much of their careers until 1984. In such critical areas of creativity, leadership, communication, and problem solving, liberal arts graduates scored higher on average than those with professional undergraduate degrees.

Yet the liberal arts graduates moved up the corporate ladder in their early years no faster than those with business and engineering degrees. Only later did their different potentials for long-term career development become apparent. After two decades with AT&T, 21% of the engineering graduates and 32% of the business graduates had reached at least the top levels of middle management, but 45% of the liberal arts graduates had done so.[46] Study of the application of a college background in company settings confirms that the need for technical skills declines and the demand for general talents increases as graduates acquire greater work experience.[47] Even among those who have earned a master's degree in business administration, general organizational skills gain in salience over technical business skills as their careers develop.[48]

Despite these findings, corporate recruitment frequently fails to stress educational preparation for longer-term career development and flexibility, focusing largely on entry-level skills. Front-line supervisors usually seek individuals with the specialized skills required to perform specific tasks. That the new college graduates they hire may lack the skills and educational background needed for work performance ten years later is not of immediate concern. Many entry-level managers and professionals will, of course, never reach middle levels of responsibility, and they need not necessarily be recruited into the company with the broad and flexible foundation required for later ascent to higher levels. Still, it is often difficult to identify in advance which entry-level recruits will later advance up the organizational chart.

The conflict between the focus of front-line recruiters and supervisors on specific skills on the one hand and the preference of senior managers for broad capacities on the other is confirmed in several studies. Senior managers are reported at some corporations to be extrolling the virtues of liberal learning while their own college recruiters are at the very same time stressing technical specialization. Directors of college placement offices often complain that corporate recruiters seldom seem interested in whether candidates possess additional skills that might be used for the next step upward.[49]

A study of company managers and business-school faculty and administrators in the mid-1980s found widespread campus misperceptions of corporate recruiting priorities. Corporate executives were asked whether their company preferred to recruit newly graduated business majors (1) who are well prepared to perform on the first job but whose preparation for eventual leadership is uncertain, or (2) those who are well prepared for later leadership positions but are of uncertain preparedness for the first job. Approximately two thirds of the company managers indicated that their organizations preferred to recruit business graduates with the second set of qualities. Yet some two thirds of the business-school faculty and administrators who were also surveyed on this question believed that companies were more likely to seek those with the first set of qualities.[50]

Policy Implications: A Permanent Restructuring

As major corporations have restructured in response to competitive and take-over pressures, the implicit contract of employment security and employee loyalty between the managerial-professional workforce and the company has been undermined. Managers and professionals remain as personally engaged in their work as ever, but they have become more pessimistic about their career prospects and less committed to their function or employing organization. With more career mobility within and among companies expected, a broad educational foundation has become particularly important.

Greater career flexibility has intensified the need for the recruitment of new managers and professionals who are capable of not only moving up within conventional career ladders, but also across traditional career boundaries. Some of the narrowness can be overcome by mid-career management and professional development programs. Although it might be tempting in a period of stringency to reduce such training or to focus it on highly specific skills, just the opposite is implied by the consequences of restructuring. Career development programs engendering breadth will make for a more flexible and re-deployable cadre of managers and professionals.

Rather than leaving career movement among corporations entirely to the market, many companies are acting to manage the process, at least in periods of rapid workforce reduction. For example, selective outplacement services were made available to exempt employees by more than two fifths of the downsizing companies surveyed in the 1987 American Management Association study. If heightened intercorporate mobility is not just a passing by-product of momentary restructuring, however, companies may move to institutionalize its management.

Permanent outplacement services would facilitate future resizings and could, ironically, enhance employee commitment among those who remain. Because white-collar workers seeking employment often rely on informal networks, such services would most effectively capitalize on the numerous informal ties that a company's managers and professionals have with their counterparts in other firms.[51] This service may be particularly important in an era in which employment relocation often requires movement of a working spouse as well. Research on the effectiveness of outplacement services for professionals, however, suggests that unless carefully designed, such programs can prove of little real value.[52]

To more fully understand the impact of corporate restructuring on managers and professionals and on educational strategies for entering these fields, a number of critical pieces of information are still needed. First, baseline data are required on the rates of downsizing and redeployment among the major subgroups of managers and professionals. Second, tracking information is needed on those who are redeployed within the organization, focusing on which groups are most effectively redeployed, how they are best retrained, and whether they adapt well to the new assignments. Third, although we know from many specific instances that the span of managerial control has increased, the ratio of indirect to direct staffing has decreased, and the emphasis on customer service and relations in training and staffing has intensified, the extent and effectiveness of these developments among leading U.S. corporations is yet to be established.

Although the most prominent form of corporate restructuring in many firms during the 1980s was downsizing, this may be a largely transient phenomenon that could well give way during the 1990s to significant expansion among a number of corporations. We have seen from at least one study that rapid expansion generates many of the same demands for flexibility as does rapid contraction.[53] Managerial responsibilities and careers in either case are forced to transcend traditional functional lines. As individuals and companies prepare for greater flexibility in managerial and professional career structures, that preparation should thus be oriented toward both downsizing and upsizing. What is critical here is institutionalizing the capacity to transfer and redeploy quickly, whatever the requisite direction.

Preparation of managers and professionals for a prolonged period of employment turbulence will depend on corresponding changes in four critical areas: higher education, the organization of early career paths, company training programs, and corporate cultures. College curricula need to offer opportunities for both general education and professional preparation to those intent on entering the private sector. For those who do enter, companies should structure early career paths for young managers and professionals to maximize opportunities for specialization in several diverse areas, an essential learning foundation for both future redeployment and later entry into general management.

For managers and professionals who stay with the company, corporate training programs are a critical facilitating vehicle for both immediate redeployment and future reassignment. They should be structured in ways that address both needs, if episodic cycles of layoffs and rehirings are to be avoided in an era of employment turbulence. And, finally, for all managers and professionals, a permanent redefinition of prevailing values is required. The emphasis on linear career progression, embedded in the cultures of achievement so aptly characterized during the 1950s by David Riesman and William H. Whyte, must give way during the 1990s to more complex ways of viewing and valuing managerial and professional work. The new cultures should move beyond the traditional conception of a career line as a straight ascent of a single lifelong ladder in one corporation. It should come to be viewed instead as an often unpredictable interplay between vertical and horizontal movement within and among firms.

Notes

This chapter is primarily the responsibility of Michael Useem.

1. Average annual rates of after-tax returns by U.S. nonfinancial corporations reached a postwar high of approximately 9% in the 1960s, but earnings dropped to 6% by the late 1970s, a comparatively low level cf return that continued into the early 1980s. See Daniel M. Holland and Stewart C. Myers, "Profitability and Capital Costs for Manufacturing Corporations and All Nonfinancial Corporations," *American Economic Review* 70 (1980): 320–325; Bennett Harrison and Barry Bluestone, *The Great U-Turn: Corporate Restructuring and the Polarizing of America* (New York: Basic Books, 1989).

2. American Management Association, *Responsible Reductions in Force* (New York: American Management Association, 1988).

3. General Accounting Office, *Plant Closings: Limited Advance Notice and Assistance Provided Dislocated Workers* (Washington, D.C.: General Accounting Office, 1987).

4. Ronald E. Berenbeim, *Company Programs to Ease the Impact of Shutdowns* (New York: The Conference Board, 1986).

5. Berenbeim, *Company Programs;* General Accounting Office, *Plant Closings.*

6. Rod Willis, "What's Happened to America's Middle Managers?" *Management Review* 76 (January 1987): 24–33; Paul Hirsch, *Pack Your Own Parachute: How to Survive Mergers, Takeovers, and Other Corporate Disasters* (Reading, Mass.: Addison-Wesley, 1987); Susan R. Sanderson and Lawrence Schein, "Sizing Up the Down-Sizing Era," *Across the Board* 23 (November 1986): 15–23.

7. General Accounting Office, *Plant Closings,* p. 82.

8. H.G. Kaufman, *Professionals in Search of Work: Coping with the Stress of Job Loss and Underemployment* (New York: Wiley, 1982), pp. 1–2.

9. Paul O. Flaim and Ellen Sehgal, "Reemployment and Earnings," in Paul D. Staudohar and Holly E. Brown (eds.), *Deindustrialization and Plant Closure* (Lexington, Mass.: Lexington Books, 1987), pp. 101–130.

10. General Accounting Office, *Plant Closings;* Flaim and Sehgal, "Reemployment and Earnings"; Marie Howland and George E. Peterson, "Labor Market Conditions and the Reemployment of Displaced Workers," *Industrial and Labor Relations Review* 42 (1988): 109–122.

11. Katherine S. Newman, *Falling from Grace: The Experience of Downward Mobility in the American Middle Class* (New York: Free Press, 1988), p. 93; Paula Goldman Leventman, *Professionals Out of Work* (New York: Free Press, 1981); Kaufman, *Professionals in Search of Work.*

12. James N. Baron, Alison Davis-Blake, and William T. Bielby, "The Structure of Opportunity: How Promotion Ladders Vary Within and among Organizations," *Administrative Science Quarterly* 31 (1986): 248–273; Paul Osterman, "White-Collar Internal Labor Markets," in Paul Osterman (ed.), *Internal Labor Markets* (Cambridge, Mass.: MIT Press, 1984), pp. 163–189.

13. Rosabeth Moss Kanter, "Variations in Managerial Career Structures in High-Technology Firms: The Impact of Organizational Characteristics on Internal Labor Market Patterns," in Paul Osterman (ed.), *Internal Labor Markets* (Cambridge, Mass.: MIT Press, 1984), pp. 109–131.

14. James E. Rosenbaum, *Career Mobility in a Corporate Hierarchy* (New York: Academic Press, 1984).

15. Ann Howard and Douglas W. Bray, *Managerial Lives in Transition: Advancing Age and Changing Times* (New York: Guilford Press, 1988), p. 129.

16. James E. Rosenbaum, "Organizational Career Mobility: Promotion Chances in a Corporation During Periods of Growth and Contraction," *American Journal of Sociology* 85 (1979): 21–48; Judith M. Bardwick, *The Plateauing Trap* (New York: Bantam, 1988).

17. Mark C. Berger, "Predicted Future Earnings and Choice of College Major," *Industrial and Labor Relations Review* 41 (1988): 418–429.

18. Howard and Bray, *Managerial Lives in Transition*.

19. M.R. Cooper, P. Morgan, M. Foley, and L.B. Kaplan, "Changing Employee Values: Deepening Discontent?" *Harvard Business Review* 57 (January–February 1979): 117–125; Opinion Research Corporation, *Changing Employee Values in America: Strategic Planning for Human Resources* (Princeton, N.J.: Opinion Research Corporation, 1981); William A. Schiemann and Brian S. Morgan, "Managing Human Resources: Employee Discontent and Declining Productivity" (Princeton, N.J.: Opinion Research Corporation, 1982); M.R. Cooper, "Changing Employee Attitudes: Fast Growth vs. Slow Growth Organizations" (Wellesley, Mass.: Hay Management Consultants, n.d.)

20. Hay Group, *Achieving Competitive Advantage Through the Effective Management of People, 1986–87* (Wellesley, Mass.: Center for Management Research, Hay Group, 1987).

21. Cooper, "Changing Employee Attitudes."

22. Leonard Johnson and Alan Frohman, "Identifying and Closing the Gap in the Middle of Organizations," *Academy of Management Executive* 3 (May 1989).

23. Vicki A. Smith, "Restructuring Management and Restructuring: The Role of Managers in Corporate Change," in Joyce Rothschild and Michael Wallace (ed.), *Research in Politics and Society* (Greenwich, Conn.: JAI Press, 1989); Vicki A. Smith, *Managing in the Corporate Interest: Control and Resistance in an American Bank* (Berkeley, Ca.: University of California Press, 1990).

24. Thomas Gilmore and Larry Hirschhorn, "Management Challenges Under Conditions of Retrenchment," *Human Resource Management* 22 (1983): 341–357; Kim Cameron and Raymond Zammuto, "Matching Managerial Strategies to Conditions of Decline," *Human Resource Management* 22 (1983): 359–375; John R. Kimberly and Robert E. Quinn (eds.), *Managing Organizational Transitions* (Homewood, Ill.: Irwin, 1984); Deborah Smith Cook and Gerald R. Ferris, "Strategic Human Resource Management and Firm Performance in Industries in Decline," *Human Resource Management* 25 (1986): 441–458; The Conference Board, "Managing Restructuring" (New York: The Conference Board, 1987); Anthony F. Buono and James L. Bowditch, *The Human Side of Mergers and Acquisitions: Managing Collisions Between People, Cultures, and Organizations* (San Francisco: Jossey-Bass, 1989); Nancy K. Napier, "Mergers and Acquisitions, Human Resource Issues and Outcomes: A Review and Suggested Typology," *Journal of Management Studies* 26 (May 1989): 271–289; Robert M. Tomasko, *Downsizing: Reshaping the Corporation for the Future* (New York: American Management Association, 1990).

25. Paul Osterman, "The Impact of Computers on the Employment of Clerks and Managers," *Industrial and Labor Relations Review* 39 (1986): 175–186; Paul Osterman, *Employment Futures: Reorganization, Dislocation, and Public Policy* (New York: Oxford University Press, 1988).

26. David M. Gordon, Richard Edwards, and Michael Reich, *Segmented Work, Divided Workers: The Historical Transformation of Labor in the United States* (New

York: Cambridge University Press, 1982); Myron Roomkin, "United States," in Myron J. Roomkin (ed.), *Managers as Employees: An International Comparison of the Changing Character of Managerial Employment* (New York: Oxford University Press, 1989), pp. 61–62.

27. U.S. Bureau of Labor Statistics, *Employment and Earnings* 35 (Washington, D.C.: Government Printing Office, July 1988 and earlier years); Arne L. Kalleberg and Ivar Berg, *Work and Industry: Structures, Markets, and Processes* (New York: Plenum, 1987), p. 111.

28. Arthur Francis, *New Technology at Work* (New York: Oxford University Press, 1986); William Form, "On the Degradation of Skills," *Annual Review of Sociology* 13 (1987): 29–47; William Form, Robert L. Kaufman, Toby L. Parcel, and Michael Wallace, "The Impact of Technology on Work Organization and Work Outcomes," in George Farkas and Paula England (eds.), *Industries, Firms, and Jobs: Sociological and Economic Approaches* (New York: Plenum, 1988).

29. Howard and Bray, *Managerial Lives in Transition*, p. 424.

30. Hay Group, *Achieving Competitive Advantage;* Cooper, Morgan, Foley, and Kaplan, "Changing Employee Values"; Opinion Research Corporation, *Changing Employee Values in America*.

31. Seymour Martin Lipset and William Schneider, *The Confidence Gap: Business, Labor, and Government in the Public Mind* (New York: Free Press, 1983); Louis Harris, *Inside America* (New York: Vintage Books, 1987); Donald L. Kanter and Philip H. Mirvis, *Cynicism at Work* (San Francisco: Jossey-Bass, 1989).

32. Berger, "Predicted Future Earnings"; Richard B. Freeman, *The Market for College-Trained Manpower: A Study of the Economics of Career Choice* (Cambridge, Mass.: Harvard University Press, 1971); Richard B. Freeman, "A Cobweb Model of the Supply and Starting Salary of New Engineers," *Industrial and Labor Relations Review* 30 (1976): 236–248.

33. U.S. Bureau of the Census, *Current Population Survey, 1987 March Supplement* (Washington, D.C.: U.S. Bureau of the Census, 1987).

34. U.S. Bureau of the Census, *Money Income of Households* (Washington, D.C.: U.S. Bureau of the Census, 1987 and earlier years).

35. Kevin Murphy and Finis Welch, "Wage Premiums for College Graduates: Recent Growth and Possible Explanations," *Educational Researcher* 18 (1989): 17–26.

36. Paul E. Harrington and Andrew M. Sum, "College Survival and Economic Prosperity: Is There a Connection?" *Thrust: The Journal for Employment and Training Professionals* 8 (1987): 1–30; Paul E. Harrington and Andrew M. Sum, "Whatever Happened to the College Enrollment Crisis?" *Academe* (September–October 1988): 17–22.

37. Alexander W. Astin, Kenneth C. Green, and William S. Korn, *The American Freshman: Twenty Year Trends* (Los Angeles: Cooperative Institutional Research Program, University of California, Los Angeles, 1987); Alexander W. Astin, Kenneth C. Green, William S. Korn, and Marilyn Schalit, *The American Freshman: National Norms for Fall 1987* (Los Angeles: Cooperative Institutional Research Program, University of California, Los Angeles, 1987).

38. Astin et al., *The American Freshman: Twenty Year Trends;* Astin et al., *The American Freshman: National Norms for Fall 1987;* U.S. Department of Education, *Digest of Educational Statistics, 1987* (Washington, D.C.: Center for Educational Statistics, U.S. Department of Education, 1987).

39. Astin et al., *The American Freshman: Twenty Year Trends;* Astin et al., *The*

American Freshman: National Norms for Fall 1987; Office of Technology Assessment, *Educating Scientists and Engineers: Grade School to Grad School* (Washington, D.C.: Office of Technology Assessment, 1988); Office of Technology Assessment, *Technology and the American Economic Transition* (Washington, D.C.: Office of Technology Assessment, 1988); Freeman, *Market for College-Trained Manpower;* Freeman, "Cobweb Model."

40. Edward B. Fiske, "M.I.T. Widens Engineering Training," *New York Times,* September 8, 1987, pp. 1, 8; Joseph S. Johnston, Jr., Susan Shaman, and Robert Zemsky, *Unfinished Design: The Humanities and Social Sciences in Undergraduate Engineering Education* (Washington, D.C.: Association of American Colleges, 1988).

41. Stephen S. Cohen and John Zysman, *Manufacturing Matters: The Myth of the Post-Industrial Economy* (New York: Basic Books, 1987).

42. Michael Dertouzos, Richard K. Lester, and Robert M. Solow, *Made in America: Regaining the Productive Edge* (Cambridge, Mass.: MIT Press, 1989).

43. Rosabeth Moss Kanter, *The Change Masters: Innovation for Productivity in the American Corporation* (New York: Simon & Schuster, 1983), p. 386; also see Larry Hirschhorn, *Beyond Mechanization: Work and Technology in a Postindustrial Age* (Cambridge, Mass.: MIT Press, 1984); and Brian S. Moskal, "Tomorrow's Best Managers," *Industry Week,* July 19, 1988, pp. 32–34.

44. Henry M. Levin and Russell W. Rumberger, "Education and Training Needs for Using Computers in Small Businesses," *Education Evaluation and Policy Analysis* 8 (Winter 1986): 423–434; Henry M. Levin and Russell W. Rumberger, "Educational Requirements for New Technologies: Visions, Possibilities, and Current Realities," *Educational Policy* 1 (1987): 333–354.

45. Michael Useem, *Liberal Education and the Corporation: The Hiring and Advancement of College Graduates* (Hawthorne, N.Y.: Aldine de Gruyter, 1989).

46. Ann Howard, "College Experiences and Managerial Performance," *Journal of Applied Psychology* 71 (1986): 530–552. Liberal arts graduates are defined here to include those with degrees in the humanities and social sciences but not the sciences or mathematics.

47. L.C. Solmon, "New Findings on the Links Between College Education and Work," *Higher Education* 10 (1981): 615–648; Ann Bisconti and J.G. Kessler, *College and Other Stepping Stones: A Study of the Learning Experiences That Contribute to Effective Performance in Early and Long-Run Jobs* (Bethlehem, Pa.: College Placement Council Foundation, 1980).

48. Meryl Louis, "The Gap in Management Education," in Jagdish Sheth (ed.), *Developing Managers for a Competitive Environment* (San Francisco: Jossey-Bass, 1990).

49. Frank C. Pierson, *The Education of American Businessmen: A Study of University-College Programs in Business Administration* (New York: McGraw-Hill, 1959); Robert Aaron Gordon and James Edwin Howell, *Higher Education for Business* (New York: Columbia University Press, 1959); Joseph S. Johnston, Jr., Stanley T. Burns, David W. Butler, Marcie Schorr Hirsch, Thomas B. Jones, Alan M. Kantrow, Kathryn Mohrman, Roger B. Smith, and Michael Useem, *Educating Managers: Executive Effectiveness Through Liberal Learning* (San Francisco: Jossey-Bass, 1986); Useem, *Liberal Education and the Corporation.*

50. Lyman W. Porter and Lawrence E. McKibbin, *Management Education and Development: Drift or Thrust into the 21st Century?* (New York: McGraw-Hill, 1988), pp. 106–109.

51. Mark S. Granovetter, *Getting a Job: A Study of Contacts and Careers* (Cambridge, Mass.: Harvard University Press, 1974); Kaufman, *Professionals in Search of Work,* pp. 151–193.

52. Kaufman, *Professionals in Search of Work,* pp. 261–269.

53. Kanter, "Variations in Managerial Career Structures."

9

Business Restructuring and Strategic Human Resource Development

In its simplest terms, being *strategic* in the human resource area means (1) setting long- and intermediate-term people-management objectives that support organizational goals and (2) deciding on comprehensive programs that will achieve those objectives. In an organization with surplus people in manufacturing and a shortage in sales, for example, a strategic approach would be to set a specific objective for sales performance or market share and then develop a human resource program to get an effective sales force. One promising strategic method for creating this sales staff would be to transfer excess manufacturing employees to the sales department.

Unfortunately, human resource development is rarely used in this strategic way. In most organizations, "development" is interpreted as giving people knowledge and skills necessary for effective performance in their *current* job and is seldom seen as a strategic alternative to external recruitment for critical positions. For example, an organization will frequently go outside to hire a vice-president because, in the opinion of the president, no one inside the organization is qualified, even though there are several high potential (but undeveloped) candidates at the next lower level.

This focus on the short term has been accentuated by the massive restructuring that has taken place in U.S. businesses over the last five years and that is likely to continue into the next century.[1] The purpose of this chapter is to examine recent restructuring in U.S. business organizations from several perspectives. First, the highlights of what changes have occurred will be surveyed. The extent to which the changes were made in a short-term, crisis-oriented manner will then be examined. Next, the question of what human resource policies were used in relation to employment security, redeployment, and internal relocation will be answered. The chapter will conclude with an alternative approach to these rapid changes—strategic human resource development.

Absence of Strategic Change in Restructuring

A 1971 study of how defense contractors responded to federal reductions in military expenditures at the end of the Vietnam War identified a negative, self-reinforcing cycle.[2] The initial response was for top management to close ranks and deny the crisis. ("The pie may be shrinking, but we'll be able to get a larger share of it.") Then, as revenues and profits fell, top management began secretly planning organizational changes while rumors flew among the employees. Employees, recognizing the company was in trouble, had many useful ideas for coping with the problems and tried to engage top management in dialogue. But top management saw the problem as their responsibility and so would not involve employees in the search for solutions.

As a result, major restructuring was planned and imposed unilaterally in a top-down manner. Changes included workforce reductions and cutbacks in less profitable business areas, steps that had greater impact on lower-level employees than on top management. Thus, employees became more alienated and more critical of top management and less interested in helping the company cope. The less involved employees became, the more top management attempted to tighten controls and increase performance pressures, which only added to the employees' alienation. Thus, a downward, self-reinforcing cycle of decline set in.

A study of a number of bankrupt firms found a similar downward spiral as a business heads toward failure: early weaknesses in financial condition and performance, extreme and vacillating strategic actions, and abrupt environmental decline.[3] Most of these failed firms had substantial warning before they failed: often as long as ten years.

In the first stage of the decline, ten years before the failure, lagging levels of profit could be detected. The second stage was six to ten years before bankruptcy, when the firms deteriorated to a "marginal" financial condition. The third stage, three to six years before failure, was a period of weak, break-even performance, when the firm engaged in extreme strategic behavior—inaction or hyperaction. The final stage was the death struggle, years two and one before bankruptcy, when the firm's competitive position declined abruptly, firm performance deteriorated sharply, and death occurred.

The bad news here is that organizational inertia seems to play a major role in known management's responses; the good news is that "turnaround managers may generally have more time to conduct their task than is often thought."[4] If an organization suddenly finds itself in crisis, it may not have been adequately monitoring and responding to its environment.

An entire issue of *Human Resource Management* (Winter 1983) was devoted to organizational decline. The case studies represented in these articles demonstrate that top management's initial reactions to external crisis tend to be reactive, to put stress on technology and capital equipment rather than on using and developing people, and to be fragmented and not coupled to long-term business objectives.[5] A similar conclusion was reached in a 1988 study of corporate restructuring practices.[6] A survey of 19 Fortune 500 firms and one outplacement firm showed that all but one were reactive and not proactive in their downsizing decisions; that is, the changes originated from economic crisis rather than from a desire to increase organizational efficiency and effectiveness. Typically, the decision to downsize was made by the chief executive officer, who put together a task force to devise and implement a plan, with a very short time frame. It was not unusual for the plan to be created over a weekend. Most of the cuts were made at the middle-management levels, since, as one executive put it, "You'll save many more bucks that way."[7]

What are the forces driving firms to be so shortsighted? Probably the major single factor for publicly held companies is the evaluation of the firm in the financial markets. A lagging price per share can leave a firm vulnerable to takeover attempts, frustrate capital investment plans, devalue executive stock options, and lead to shareholder and director dissatisfaction (and, ultimately, to the ouster of management).

Strikingly, executive incentives are linked to short-term performance, which in turn works against such longer-term investments as employee development and research.[8] On the other hand, firms that reward executives over a longer time period (e.g., five years) engage in strategic development, and the stock market appears to look at a company's long-term activities, not just short-term performance. For many firms as much as 80% of the stock price is due to long-term prospects, as indicated by the difference between stock price and the present value of expected dividends over the next five years.[9]

Corporate Attitudes Toward New Skill Development

In examining corporate attitudes toward personnel development, McCune, Beatty, and Montagno focused on thirty-eight manufacturing companies in the midwest, half of which were unionized. Such firms have been particularly at risk from turbulence over the last ten or 15 years.[10] Sixteen hundred firms in the midwest had closed or had large layoffs in 1982 and 1983, displacing 227,000 workers, the highest number of any region in the United States.[11]

When asked, "Who is responsible for preparing displaced workers for new jobs?" the overwhelming answer of the human resource managers who responded was "the worker." To a lesser extent, respondents felt that the new employer and the educational system shared responsibility as well. *The organizations who laid off the workers felt little responsibility for helping them develop new skills.*

There is hope, however, from organizations such as Digital Equipment Corporation and Hewlett-Packard, that have redefined the concept of guaranteed employment. Instead of guaranteeing the employee a job for life (which was implied in the old "psychological contract"), these companies will attempt to provide *employability security*. That is, the firm accepts the responsibility to keep employees developed, armed with current skills, so that the employees would be able to compete successfully for jobs in other organizations should separation from their current employer ever occur.

Some 58% of all the firms surveyed had downsized over the last five years, and 74% said they have a downsizing policy. Unionized firms were much more likely to have downsized (73%) than were nonunion companies (25%). The authors explain that this result might be due to the union contracts' not being flexible enough to allow alternatives to layoffs. For instance, union firms were significantly less likely (37%) to use reduced hours than were nonunion companies (69%).

Seniority was by far the most common criterion for workforce reduction (used by 92% of firms studied), with no significant differences between union (95%) and nonunion firms (88%). Performance, however, was much less likely to be a criterion in union firms (55%) than in nonunion companies (75%). "Skills necessary to perform other jobs" was used significantly more by nonunion firms (69%) than by unionized companies (59%). Again, work rule flexibility was cited as a factor here.

Small firms (fewer than 500 employees) were neither more nor less likely to have downsized or to have a downsizing policy than were larger firms (more than 500 employees). The use of seniority and performance as layoff criteria was about the same in larger and smaller companies.

The main effect of firm size appeared to be that smaller firms were more concerned with transferability of skills (77% for small firms versus 44% for larger firms). Small firms were also more likely to consider transfers and retraining (41% versus 19%). Thus, small firms may be more concerned with employee skill breadth and flexibility than are larger firms.

Not only academics report discouraging conclusions about the willingness of businesses to invest in the development of people. A special issue of *Business Week* titled "Human Capital: The Decline of America's Work Force" stated:

> America, in short, has been scrimping on human capital. After trying to solve its serious competitiveness problems by pouring hundreds of billions of dollars into capital equipment, the country is discovering that it has been blindsided when it comes to its workers. Corporate restructuring and a sharply cheapened dollar may have arrested the economic decline, but investing in people is turning out to be the only way to reverse it.[12]

Determinants of Strategic Versus Tactical Workforce Management

How do organizations approach the problem of workforce reduction during periods of decline? One review of the literature on this topic, concludes that most organizations use layoffs.[13] However, some organizations do use such complex methods as early retirement inducements, shortened work weeks, and redeployment (see Table 9.1).

Table 9.1. **Strategies and Tactics for Work Force Reduction:
The Range of Options for Declining Organizations.**

Strategy	Sample Tactics
Redeployment Strategies	
Natural attrition	Selective hiring freeze Selective transfer-in freeze Total hiring freeze Total transfer-in freeze
Induced redeployment	Transfer-out incentive Early retirement incentive Severance pay incentive Curtailing of advancement opportunities Compensation freeze or reduction Optional part-time or short-week schedules, work sharing, or leave-without-pay
Involuntary redeployment	Involuntary transfer-out within plant Involuntary transfer-out within firm Demotion/downgrading Involuntary part-time or short-week schedules, work sharing, or leave-without-pay
Layoff Strategies	
Layoff with outplacement assistance	Layoff with: Retraining Job search counseling Severance pay Continuation of benefits Advance notice of layoff
Layoff without outplacement assistance	With recall rights Without recall rights

(Left vertical axis label: Increasing Protection of Employee Well-Being)

From Leonard Greenhalgh, Anne T. Lawrence, and Robert I. Sutton, "Determinants of Work Force Reduction Strategies in Declining Organizations," *Academy of Management Review* 13 (1988), p. 243.

This study also identifies factors such as labor force characteristics, organizational structural characteristics, and environmental characteristics that are likely to be related to management's choice of workforce reduction method. For example, layoffs are predicted to be less likely in internally diversified firms (with more options for redeployment), in firms where the threat is seen as short term, in firms with previous experience with decline, in firms with employee-oriented values, in publicly held firms, in countries or states with plant-closing legislation, and in firms whose employees are older, are more senior, and possess organization-specific skills.

When the concept of using strategic human resource development to lessen the impact of turbulence is presented to managers facing competitive pressures, their response is often, "Those are nice ideas, and we would certainly prefer to be more strategic in the way we manage people, but we're fighting for survival here, and we've got to deal with the crisis at hand."

There are two responses to this comment. First, if those managers had been more proactive and strategic earlier, when there was not a crisis, they might not be facing such a severe situation now. Or they might have prepared more flexible human resources to cope with the crisis.

Second, some organizations *do* engage in strategic adaptability. Even in a crisis it is possible to deal with business problems in terms of integrated actions, making use of long-term business objectives as a guide for planning changes regarding human resources. In fact, one could argue that the chances of success increase to the extent that the organization does respond in a manner consistent with long-term objectives.

Support for this idea is found in an innovative study of companies in three industries that have been hit hard by competitive and other environmental forces: airlines, energy, and banking.[14] The study focused on firms that had dealt successfully with these challenges and those that had not. It also measured the extent to which the firms were strategic in their approach to human resources (i.e., took the long term view in decision making, linked human resource actions with business objectives and plans, and chose actions that were part of an integrated plan of attack). The study found that *the firms that adapted most successfully to the environmental changes were those that tended to adopt more strategic human resource management* with regard to three structural issues: changed roles for the human resources department, exit practices, and strategic planning.

Specifically, regarding the role of the human resources department, the more adaptive firms were more likely than their less successful counterparts to change current training and development to meet strategic needs, to use selective freezes on hiring but continue hiring for strategically critical positions, to redesign jobs to add responsibility, to fine-tune performance appraisal systems, and to change compensation to attract the best people.

In the area of exit practices, the more effective firms were more likely to employ such practices as advance planning and retraining. And concerning strategy, the higher-performing companies tended to have planned and integrated strategies in which human resources were critical and linked to strategic planning. Less effective firms were more likely to see human resources as disposable assets and to use shotgun, crisis management techniques—layoffs, plant closings, and across-the-board cuts in programs and hiring.

Thus, it seems clear that U.S. business will have to be more competitive in facilitating development of the workforce. But this will mean more than just spending more money on public education and on corporate training and development. It will require new attitudes on the part of management and new structures in the organization. To develop a more flexible, adaptive workforce, we will need more adaptive organizations with developmental cultures—firms that promote human learning at all levels. The problem of the new technology is not a technical one; it is an intellectual one.[15]

Strategic Human Resource Development

An alternative for dealing with adaptability in the workforce, is the concept of strategic human resource development (SHRD), defined as *the identification and growth of wanted employee skills, experience, and motivation for the intermediate and long-range support of explicit corporate strategies.*

The critical element of SHRD most often missing is the linkage of development needs and activities to an explicit organizational mission and strategy. Many organizations invest considerable resources to train and develop employees, but they never really examine how this training and development can effectively promote organizational objectives, or how development activities should be altered in light of business plans. Even rarer is a recognition that business plans should be altered in relation to expected future employee capabilities. For example, a large commercial bank that intended to open a subsidiary in South Africa changed its mind when top management realized that there was no one in the organization who was qualified and available to head up the new enterprise.

Another hindrance to SHRD in many organizations is that the time span for development is often too short. The focus is frequently on skill requirements in new or present assignments rather than on requirements for positions five or ten years into the future.

Finally, inadequate energy is devoted to identification of future skill needs. To be strategic about development means to analyze future business opportunities and plans and to think deductively about the future employee skills necessary to implement these plans.

New View of Preparedness

One of the problems facing U.S. industry in its concern for workforce preparedness is that the problem has been defined too narrowly. Preparedness is usually defined in terms of *skills:* the ability of the workforce to acquire the new skills required for tomorrow's technologies, products, and services. In reality, however, preparedness is a process of enhancing an individual's present and future career effectiveness, where by career is meant the individually perceived sequence of attitudes and behaviors associated with work-related experiences over the span of a person's life. Thus, career development entails changing both *attitudes and behaviors*, as well as skills.

Attitudes toward the self are learned and changed as a result of work experiences. Because work-relevant self-attitudes result from critical experiences of psychological success and are thus generally at the core of a person's identity,[16] they are typically highly resistant to change. This resistance can be a major factor motivating a person to block organizational changes. Thus, altered self-attitudes can be a major factor facilitating enhanced personal and organizational adaptability.

A study by the U.S. Department of Labor and the American Society for Training and Development reached a similar conclusion. In a list of seven skill groups that are necessary for current performance and future adaptability, they include one "personal management" cluster defined as "self-esteem, goal setting/motivation, and personal and career development."[17] These personal qualities are seen as crucial for self-empowerment and self-directed lifelong learning.

To accomplish this, a person must become "unstuck" from routine career and task activities, become aware of an opportunity to choose new behaviors, explore these opportunities, and then try to choose new behaviors.[18] For these new behaviors to be internalized, the person's work-related identity and attitudes toward the self must be correspondingly altered.

The following "identity tasks" must be accomplished: fully leaving the old routine, learning the new activities, developing one's self-esteem in relation to these activities, and fully mastering them. Next, the person must become established in the eyes of superiors and peers as a performer on these new activities.

When the person has fully mastered the tasks and has achieved recognition for this mastery, two other self-attitudes are likely to develop: a sense of increased adaptability and a heightened sense of self as agent (being in control) vis à vis the work environment. *Therefore, to be truly prepared to learn new work skills in the future, a person must possess positive self-attitudes (identity and adaptability) as well as positive attitudes toward work.*

The literature on organization, job, and career changes has tended to overlook the role of self-attitudes in stabilizing and diffusing change. Theory and research can be a guide to identifying the conditions under which self-attitudes are and are not altered when career routines are modified.

Task Versus Personal Learning

The methods suited for personal learning can be described along four dimensions of career effectiveness: performance, attitudes, adaptability, and identity.[19] These four types of learning can be analyzed in terms of (1) the *time span* they represent (short term versus long term) and (2) the *focus* of the learning (task versus self), shown in Table 9.2. *All four types of learning are required for high levels of worker flexibility and preparedness.*

Two points can be made in relation to the learning types in Table 9.2:

- Most learning in formal organizational training and development has a short-term focus.
- Most learning in formal organizational training and development is aimed at *task* learning rather than personal learning. The concern is usually with the work-related knowledge, skills, and abilities the participant will need in the present or next job.

Table 9.2. **Task and Personal Learning Dimensions**

	Task Learning	Personal Learning
Short term	Improved performance-related knowledge, skills, and abilities	Resolving issues regarding attitudes toward career and personal life
Long term	Improving adaptability	Developing and extending identity

Source: Douglas T. Hall, "Dilemmas in Linking Succession Planning to Individual Executive Learning," *Human Resource Management* 25 (2) (1986): 235–265.

Obviously then, most development activity is aimed at current perform-ance. There is little concern for future adaptability on the task side and even less concern for self-related outcomes such as attitudes. It is becoming clear, however, that adaptability is at least as important as current performance. A joint study by the U.S. Departments of Labor, Education, and Commerce found that employers say they need employees "with positive attitudes and the ability to: learn, be flexible, and respond to change quickly."[20] In a similar vein, the joint U.S. Department of Labor/American Society of Training Directors study of needed future skills identified "learning how to learn" and "adaptability (creative thinking and problem-solving)" as two of seven needed skill groups.[21]

In the overall learning gap, however, the least amount of attention is usually devoted to personal learning. In the typical training program, either within a company or in a university, the cases, simulations, and even more recent action learning projects all are aimed at skills and knowledge that will aid perform-ance primarily, with some adaptability tossed in for good measure. There is little emphasis on the self or the skill of personal learning.

Why Is There So Little Personal Learning?

Why is there so little personal learning in today's organizational settings, particularly at the executive level? There seem to be several culprits:

- *Performance is so important.* One reason for the absence of concern for self-learning is the sheer criticality of improving performance in today's resource-constrained, competitive environment. It is difficult enough to keep people on the edge of new technology, new management concepts, and new business environments; there appears to be little time or energy left for the individual's learning about the self. (In fact, however, limited self-understanding can place constraints on task learning, through nega-tive attitudes, resistance, feelings of personal threat, and low self-esteem.)
- *Individuals, especially executives, tend to resist self-learning.* Because early success creates a self-reinforcing cycle (whereby success breeds success), the person becomes more and more involved in established ways. A strong routine is created. This routine becomes a barrier to new learning, especially learning related to one's identity. The person has a

high investment in the current identity, and so identity changes are threatening.

- *Organizations and colleagues protect the individual from change.* The more established a person becomes, and the higher the level reached in the organization, the less negative feedback the person receives, and negative feedback is required for growth and learning.[22] The senior person is usually in the position of the authority, the power figure, the expert. Rarely is the senior person in the position of learner.
- *Task learning is easier than personal learning.* More is known about how to facilitate task learning than personal learning. Studying cases and experiencing simulations can be powerfully effective. It is far easier to control the setting if learning takes place in a classroom, as opposed to on the job or in everyday relationships, and the classroom is far more conducive to task learning than to self-learning.[23]

Facilitating Strategic Human Resource Development

What can firms do to promote employee learning? *The most critical influences on employee learning lie in the basic organization design and human resource policies of the firm.* The critical facilitating conditions must start at the top.[24] No one set of specific techniques or practices for training or development can be effective if the underlying corporate philosophy regarding the management and use of people is not consistent with a long-term approach to the growth of human talent.

A summary model of the factors to be discussed in this section is shown in Figure 9.1.

Human Resource Policies

At the strategic level, the most important influence on human resource development is the basic policies of the organization. Human resource policies are based largely on deeply held values in the organizational culture regarding the appropriate ways to treat employees. Unfortunately, many organizations do not have explicit human resource policies.

Some of the human resource policies that affect the development of people are the following:

- *Promotion from within.* This policy reflects a clear corporate commitment to the development of internal candidates for job openings (Sears, AT&T).
- *Employment security.* This policy provides continuing employment for employees who have been with the organization for a specified period of time. Such a policy forces line managers to "think development" in the ways they manage people: more careful hiring; better performance feedback; lifelong learning; cross-functional, cross-business mobility; re-

HUMAN RESOURCE
POLICIES

- Promotion
  from within
- Employment
  security
- Internal
  mobility
- Max/min
  incumbency
  times
- Linking
  promotion
  to subordinate
  development

ORGANIZATION
DESIGN

- Developmental
  culture
- Focused strategy
- Management of
  socialization
- Use of
  structure for
  development
- Extended time
  span
- Power of
  human resource
  function
- Developmental
  structures

MANAGERIAL PRACTICES

- Performance appaisal
- Succession/human resource
  planning
- Internal placement
- Career planning
- Career feedback

OPERATIONAL DEVELOPMENT
ACTIVITIES

- Cognitive
- Behavioral
- Environmental

STRATEGIC
LEVEL

MANAGERIAL
LEVEL

OPERATIONAL
LEVEL

DESIRED OUTCOME: THE PREPARED, FLEXIBLE WORK FORCE

- Strong current performance skills
- Strong adaptability experience and skills
- Self-learning experience and skills
- Positive work attitudes

Figure 9.1   **Organizational Factors Facilitating Strategic Human Resource
Development**

wards for managers who are good people developers; creative, voluntary
approaches to downsizing; and so on. Many companies that have traditionally had employment security policies are now finding it more difficult to maintain them (IBM, DEC, Hewlett-Packard, Johnson's Wax).

- *Internal mobility.* This is a growing trend in many organizations to give
  employees cross-functional and cross-business transfers, and this is one
  of the best methods of promoting learning from experience. A new job in
  a new area simply forces the employee to develop new skills, attitudes,
  and identities.[25] Repeated experiences with such mobility engenders
  higher levels of employee adaptability. *The more this internal mobility occurs, when there is no organizational crisis, the more flexible and prepared
  employees will be to adapt under environmental threat* (AT&T, GE).
- *Maximum and minimum incumbency times.* When employees plateau in
  their careers, they tend to be left in one position for a long time. A simple
  way to promote ongoing learning is to have a policy that no employee
  should stay in the same job longer than a certain number of years. Or

there could be a mandated review after that time period to determine if a job change would be useful and possible. A minimum incumbency period is desirable to ensure that the person really masters the job before being moved. A minimum is especially important for younger and upwardly mobile employees who are impatient to advance, but who need to establish mastery.

- *Linking promotion to subordinate development.* A manager should not be considered a candidate for promotion unless that manager has developed one or more subordinates for promotion. Managers often are reluctant to invest energy in developing their people because they have little incentive to do so. The manager's own promotion represents a good incentive (IBM, Hewlett-Packard, Eli Lilly).

Organizational Design

Several organizational features also affect the extent to which energy is devoted to employee development.

- *Developmental culture.* In some organizations, the value of developing the employee is built into the fabric of the culture. Often, this developmental culture flows from the types of people policies listed in the previous section. Also, companies that are clans, as opposed to hierarchies or markets,[26] have denser human relationships and networks and place more value on the individual and individual development.
- *Focused business strategy.* The clearer and more focused the business strategy of the organization, the easier it is to link strategy with the development of human resources.
- *Management of socialization.* The more the organization actively manages the socialization of employees (often achieved through interunit mobility), the more stress there is on individual development because it is serving a critical function for the organization. The dense interpersonal networks created by rotation of officers in the military, priests in the Catholic Church, or managers at IBM or Eli Lilly represent not only development for those individuals but also a strong source of integration for the organization.[27]
- *Use of structure for development.* The structure of the organization represents the array of future job opportunities available to the employee. Because most employee learning takes place on the job, those job opportunities represent learning opportunities. The more management uses staffing in a strategic way to grow people as well as to fill jobs, the more development and adaptability become associated with simply running the business.

  An example of this would be the way that Sears was able to construct rational progressions of jobs, using Hay-point profiles (a job evaluation method), which would gradually advance a person to a store manager's job from a trainee's job, with no change being a jump of more than 15%

in Hay points. Using computer modeling, a number of paths were identified, some of which would get a person to the store manager's job in six or seven years. Most of those paths had never actually been used before but were quite feasible. And, in fact, by using logical, nontraditional job progressions, Sears was able to grow store managers in well under ten years.[28]

- *Extended time span.* The shorter the time span of top management's concerns, the lower the concern for human resource development because such development does not produce immediate "bottom line" results.

- *Power and orientation of the human resource function.* If the human resource function has a strategic orientation and has high power vis à vis line management, there will be a strong concern for employee development. The weaker the human resource function, the more concerned it will be with short-term, visible activities (which employee development is usually not). Furthermore, if the human resource function does not see itself in a strategic manner (i.e., if it has a control or administrative orientation), it will not be able to be proactive.

- *Developmental structures.* Certain structural arrangements companies employ to meet business needs also have the side benefit of developing people. Examples are dual ladders (managerial and professional advancement paths, with equal rewards), task forces, mentoring assignments, project teams, and liaison roles. These structures develop people while the people develop the organization.

Managerial Practices

Many activities that represent good management have the related benefit of developing people. Some of the most powerful, shown on the managerial level of the pyramid of Figure 9.1, are the following.

- *Performance appraisal.* When employees receive clear feedback on their performance, when rewards are tied to performance, and when performance expectations are stated in clear behavioral or goal-related terms, the employee's first question after asking, "How did I perform?" will be "How can I perform better?" Thus, one of the best ways for an organization to stimulate development is to start with performance feedback.

- *Use of succession planning and human resource planning.* Succession planning is another human resource activity that requires planned, long-term, corporate-wide development. Most senior managers see a clear payoff from executive succession planning; nothing is more important to them than where the next generation of leadership will come from. Succession planning and human resource planning use as their starting point business needs, which provide a strong incentive for employee development.

- *Internal placement.* Employee mobility is greatly facilitated if there is a specific human resource function responsible for facilitating employee job moves. Too often this function is left to such cumbersome systems as job posting, with little opportunity for good communication with employees and managers.
- *Career planning.* The more the organization provides resources to help employees with realistic self-assessment and career exploration, the more employees will be able to engage in self-development. The most important career development need for many employees is improved information about career opportunities in other parts of the organization.
- *Improved career feedback.* Increased feedback about the employee's career is needed. Feedback could be part of a career counseling discussion with the immediate supervisor and would provide frank, realistic information about the person's career prospects, strengths, weaknesses, and steps needed to increase career mobility.

Operational Activities

Wexley and Latham have proposed three basic categories of developmental strategies: *cognitive,* altering thoughts and ideas; *behavioral,* changing behavior directly; and *environmental,* altering the work environment.[29] Which strategies promote which types of learning? If the four types of learning (performance, attitudes, adaptability, and identity) are combined with these three development strategies, the result is the matrix shown in Table 9.3. This list of activities aimed at different types of learning is meant to be illustrative, not exhaustive, and some cells may represent difficult combinations (i.e., cognitive approaches to developing interpersonal skills). Also, several activities show up in several cells, as a given activity can produce multiple outcomes.

In the past, excessive reliance was placed on the cognitive strategies, especially formal, in-class methods. This approach may be useful for aiding performance (especially technical and conceptual), but it does little for adaptability, attitudes, and identity. For the latter types of learning, behavioral and environmental methods are more potent. For example, there is nothing quite so "stretching" for a person as a new job assignment in a new functional area.

Unfortunately, environmental changes are the most difficult to create and cognitive activities the easiest, which is why so much "development" takes place in classroom settings.

Individual Empowerment

A consistent theme running through all these ways of linking strategic business planning with planning for the development of individual employees is that top management needs to do more to manage SHRD. However, SHRD must be done through policy and organization design rather than through direct top management control of development programs and systems. It is simply not

Table 9.3. Developmental Methods to Attain Different Learning Outcomes

Development Strategy	Types of Learning					
	Performance (Technical)	Performance (Interpersonal)	Performance (Conceptual)	Attitudes	Adaptability	Identity
Cognitive	Basic knowledge in specialty (entry)	Self-improvement reading Films Inspirational lectures and speeches	University seminar in basic discipline University functional courses Sabbatical industry boards	Orientation training Retraining programs Company career information Sabbatical	University training programs Career planning seminars Company career information Sabbatical	Self-assessment Seminars for personal interests University training programs
Behavioral	On-the-job training Apprenticeship	Role-playing Apprenticeship Behavioral modeling Assessment centers	Role-playing	Socialization Phased retirement Flex-time Flex-place	Outplacement Career counseling Early retirement Flex-time Flex-place	Assessment centers Outplacement Career counseling Phased retirement
Environmental	Job challenge Job feedback Job autonomy Technical ladder Peer interaction Skill-based compensation	Team building Organization development Matrix management Project teams Task forces	Matrix management Project teams Task forces Employee exchange	Matrix management Project teams Job challenge Job feedback Job autonomy Technical ladder Internal consulting Outside consulting Employee exchange Recognition for career specialists Downward moves	Job rotation Temporary assignments Job variety Downward moves Employee exchange Full employment policies	Job challenge Job autonomy Technical ladder Internal consulting Downward moves Outside consulting Recognition for career specialists

From Douglas T. Hall and James G. Goodale, *Human Resource Management: Strategy, Design and Implementation* (Glenview, IL: Scott, Foresman, 1986).

possible for senior management or senior human resource planners to anticipate accurately future business needs with enough lead time to design formal
programs to develop employees in all the appropriate directions through top
down actions.

Hayes advocates a focus on resources, such as people (which he calls
means), as a starting point in strategy, rather than on ultimate objectives
(ends).[30] He argues that the excessively rational/logical planning approach of
working from ends to ways to means is out of touch with the real world of
everyday management and that we should turn the ends-ways-means paradigm
on its head: means-ways-ends.

This means that the company should invest in a wide range of developmental activities (means). It should train workers and managers in many different
jobs, educate them about the competitive environment, and teach them how to
identify problems, develop solutions, and sell those solutions to others. Management should experiment with new technologies and let workers and managers experience them and become comfortable with them. Managers should
be given cross-functional assignments to learn about the full range of the
company's business. These and other activities would grow a pool of skills in
the workforce that could be deployed in a variety of ways and on short notice.
Then these resources would be available to serve the changing needs of the
organization (ends) in a very flexible, adaptive manner.

At the managerial level, there would be a shift from a control orientation to
one of facilitating employee learning and empowerment.[31] With this new
orientation, the manager's focus is not on enforcing standards but on removing
constraints, assisting development, and unleashing the employee's energy,
information, and creativity. And these are precisely the competitive resources
demanded by new technologies and global markets.

Corporate Examples of "Strategic Adaptation"

Examples of the strategic adaptation approach to development can be found in
several corporations. At IBM and Hewlett-Packard there is now a focus on
employee self-learning. This means that the individual employee is given the
responsibility and the means to identify needs for acquiring new skills. Thus,
rather than learning and training needs being identified by a specialized human
resource planning function, they are spotted immediately as they occur, at the
point of performance. At Hewlett-Packard, this is referred to as *just-in-time
training,* according to the personnel operations manager, Jean Halloran.

This self-learning would amount to nothing, however, if it were not supported by top management policies and training systems. Perhaps most critical
at the strategic level is top management's commitment to employment continuity. This policy drives a long-term commitment to the relationship between
the organization and the employee and more specifically to ongoing development as a way of keeping the employee competitive. This does not mean that
the corporation can make a firm commitment to lifetime employment, but by

fostering lifelong learning and development, the company can help the employee remain adaptable and employable.

In terms of systems and programs, effective self-learning means the firm provides a variety of resources to assist employees in their self-development activities. These might be formal classroom training activities (i.e., cognitive and behavioral approaches, as shown in Table 9.3) or such environmental methods as on-the-job training and temporary assignments for development. Self-learning also implies that training and coaching have become important components of the supervisor's job, replacing the more traditional monitoring and controlling functions as the workforce becomes more autonomous.

An example of how this move toward strategic adaptation and self-learning has been translated into operational terms is the statement of Xerox training principles shown in Table 9.4.

An illustration of the difficulty—and the importance— of committing to a corporate policy of employment security through comprehensive human resource redeployment and development can be seen in a recent study by Kochan, MacDuffie, and Osterman, summarized in Box 9.1.[32] Using Digital Equipment Corporation (DEC) as a case example, the study addressed the thorny issue of how a company can maintain a commitment to employment security in the turbulance of contemporary market and technological environments. Employment in the five plants studied by Kochan, MacDuffie, and Osterman went from 4,975 people in 1984 to 3,430 in 1986.[33] Most of the people who completed transition (1,157) were in the program for six months or

Table 9.4. **Xerox Training Principles**

1. Xerox is committed to providing our customers training opportunities and product documentation required to ensure their satisfaction and self-sufficiency.

2. Xerox is committed to having a work force prepared to meet current and future business objectives by providing its employees, at all levels, appropriate education and training opportunities.

3. Xerox is committed to clearly defining minimum training requirements which are related to the job incumbent's role, responsibilities, and needs, including customer satisfaction and Leadership Through Quality.

4. All new Xerox employees will be oriented in Xerox' philosophy, ethics, values, principles, and business priorities, including Leadership Through Quality, in their first 90 days of employment.

5. Xerox employees will interact with customers only after having successfully completed specified training.

6. Xerox dealers/agents will interact with customers only after having successfully completed specified training.

7. All newly hired and/or first-time Xerox managers will successfully complete specified supervisory training within 120 days of appointment.

8. Xerox managers will successfully complete functional knowledge and skills training to properly coach, inspect, and reinforce the work of their employees.

Source: Xerox Corporation Corporate Training Department.

BOX 9.1

EMPLOYMENT SECURITY AT DEC

Employment security at Digital Equipment Corporation was supported by a combination of "DEC values," rapid growth accompanied by various avenues for staff redeployment, and an internal labor market supported by large training resources, permeable job boundaries, and rewards for individual initiative.

After years of steady growth in the 1970s and early 1980s, however, several factors combined to produce an overstaffing crisis: technological change, outsourcing, elimination of inventory buffers, and an October 1983 stock price crisis that followed four bad quarters.

DEC's response to this overstaffing crisis was a plan called the Transition Process. In keeping with the idea of linking employee development with business strategy, the main responsibility for managing transition was given to key line managers; it was not a human resource activity. Initial steps were a hiring freeze and elimination of all contract and temporary employees, so that layoffs could be avoided.

Next, a cross-functional transition task force was created. The task force developed the primary strategy—that transition would be a decentralized, plant-level process guided by centralized, human resource policies. This approach fit with the DEC culture of local autonomy. Each plant was given the choice of participating in transition or not, and each was given flexibility in shaping the plan to fit its needs.

Corporate resources were used to assist plant managers, and financial incentives were given to corporate departments to encourage their participation, so that the burden did not fall totally on the plants.

There were three stages in the transition. First, *selection* required that each plant assess staffing levels. Within each work group, selection of excess workers was based on most recent performance ratings, with seniority used in case of ties.

The second stage was *training and counseling*. A two-week program was developed to help the excess employees deal with the shock of being selected and to teach practical development skills. The managers of these employees were given a mandatory one-week training program, covering their responsibility in supporting the employees' job search activities. Also, a limited retraining program was offered for employees who had applied and been accepted for a new job inside DEC that required new skills. However, a surprising result was that very few excess employees (600, or 23%) were willing to take the risk of training for a new occupation.

Stage three was *exit from transition*, either placement outside DEC or reassignment within DEC. A computerized job-skill matching system was used, but this was often bypassed in favor of the informal network of contacts among managers.

less (63.2%), and virtually all were finished within 12 months (92.1%). About one third left DEC voluntarily. Only 14.7% of those who stayed at DEC moved to new plants. As a result of the restructuring, the plants studied had relatively higher percentages of managers, professionals, and technicians and relatively fewer operatives.

What was the main effect of transition at DEC? Kochan, MacDuffie, and Osterman conclude:

> What occurred at DEC was, in the broadest sense, a transition from one set of policies supporting employment security to another set, necessitated by a more competitive and uncertain environment. Sustaining the credibility of the employment security policy, during its most severe challenge, was perhaps the most important goal of transition planners. To succeed meant, first and foremost, preserving DEC values. This explains the strong emphasis of the Transition Task Force on those aspects of the process concerning individual dignity and choice.[34]

It seems that the *process* by which transition was managed was at least as important as the specific activities that were employed. It was guided by basic *DEC values,* it was planned *participatively* by a *cross-functional task force* that formulated corporate-wide *policies* to direct specific human resource plans made at the *plant-level.* The combination of centralized policies and plant-level responsibility is noteworthy.

Does the DEC example truly represent SHRD? If DEC had been effectively practicing SHRD earlier, the overstaffing crisis might have been averted. Perhaps it is more accurate to call this an example of strategic adaptability.

Public Policy Implications

The public sector can facilitate networks of companies to promote employee redeployment, and it can disseminate information about DEC-type policies and strategies for dealing with employee adaptability. Also, states like Arizona have found creative ways of using funds that otherwise would have been used for unemployment insurance to subsidize in-company training. Public information systems, such as jobs and skills banks, could be vastly improved, perhaps through public-private partnerships.

Thus, the public sector can provide a supportive and informational role. It can draw public and corporate attention to the issue of preparedness. It can encourage companies to take innovative action and can publicize and recognize private sector accomplishments.

The public sector can also develop linkages between publicly funded business and the development of new skills. For example, New York City requires that companies doing business with the city hire a certain number of welfare trainees.

Another possible role for the public sector would be regulation to require a business to set aside a certain amount of its budget for employee renewal. One could develop an analogy between the need for continuing employee development and the need for environmental protection. Just as an organization might exploit the environment if it were not forced to include the costs of prevention or clean-up in its current business expenses, it is now possible for most businesses to exploit employees' current skills without taking responsibility for renewing them. And as we stated earlier, the employer who displaces a worker currently feels no responsibility to pay for any needed training. It may take some sort of pressure (regulation, linkage, payroll tax) to help an employer see that responsibility.

It is also possible for unions to exert pressure in the same ways. A model here would be the GM-UAW agreement establishing a retraining fund or the ATT/CWA Alliance (see Chapter 6).

Another critical area for contributions by the public sector is basic education at the elementary and high-school levels. In addition in vocational education, it should be possible for the schools to work more on adaptability skills. Instead of focusing solely on specific occupations, which is the current practice in vocational education, the schools could encourage students to examine how they deal with change and how they can be more proactive learners (the way they will have to be after they finish school). The schools could teach career "survival skills," such as how to develop a personal network to identify good job opportunities, information about future business directions, and career coaching; how to present oneself well in an interview; and how to "read" the cultural and political environment of an organization. They could also teach adaptability through work experience projects, internships, or work-study jobs in quite different industries. Other experimental attempts to help young people grow up feeling comfortable with change should be encouraged.

The role of the private sector in lifelong development should be tied to its core function of producing goods and services. Business seems best suited to providing learning through job experience and through training that is closely job-related. Thus, we would argue for specific, rather than general, training and that it be done by the private sector. The public sector can contribute by channeling people and funds into these activities. But it should be left to the private sector to identify the proper combination of on-the-job learning, classroom training, and learning through relationships and coaching.

And, as stated earlier, one way current training might be conducted with an eye to the future would be to rotate and train employees more widely than is the current practice. By developing broad pools of talent, the chances are increased that the particular mix of skills needed at some future date will be available.

Notes

This chapter is primarily the responsibility of Douglas T. Hall.

1. William B. Johnston and Arnold E. Packer, *Workforce 2000: Work and Workers for the Twenty-first Century* (Indianapolis: Hudson Institute, 1987).

2. Douglas T. Hall and Roger Mansfield, "Organizational and Individual Response to External Stress," *Administrative Science Quarterly* 16, no. 4 (December 1971): 533–547.

3. Donald C. Hambrick and Richard A. D'Aveni, "Large Corporate Failures as Downward Spirals," *Administrative Science Quarterly* 33, no. 1 (March 1988): 1–33.

4. Hambrick and D'Aveni, "Large Corporate Failures," p. 20.

5. Leonard Greenhalgh, "Managing the Job Insecurity Crisis." *Human Resource Management* 22, no. 4 (Winter 1983): 431–444; Thomas Gilmore and Larry Hirschhorn, "Management Challenges Under Conditions of Retrenchment," *Human Resource Management* 22, no. 4 (Winter 1983): 341–358; Todd D. Jick, "As the Ax Falls; Budget Cuts and the Experience of Stress in Organizations," in Terry A. Beehr and Rabi S. Bhagat (eds.), *Human Stress and Cognition in Organizations: An Integrated Perspective* (New York: Wiley, 1985), pp. 83–113.

6. Laurie Michael Roth, "Downsizing and Restructuring Practices in Corporate America: An Interview Study," *Career Center Bulletin* 6 (1986): 8–13.

7. Roth, "Downsizing and Restructuring Practices."

8. Alfred Rapoport, "Executive Incentives vs. Corporate Growth," *Harvard Business Review* 56 (July–August 1978): 81–88; Alfred Rapoport, *Creating Shareholder Value: The New Standard for Business Performance* (New York: Free Press, 1986).

9. Gary Hector, "Yes, You Can Manage Long Term," *Fortune* 118 (July–September 1988): 64–76.

10. Joseph T. McCune, Richard W. Beatty, and Raymond V. Montagno, "Downsizing: Practices in Manufacturing Firms," *Human Resource Management* 27, no. 2 (Summer 1988): 145–161.

11. General Accounting Office, *Dislocated Workers: Extent of Business Closures, Layoffs, and the Public and Private Response* (Gaithersburg, Md.: General Accounting Office, 1986).

12. *Business Week,* September 19, 1988, pp. 101–102.

13. Leonard Greenhalgh, Anne T. Lawrence, and Robert I. Sutton, "Determinants of Work Force Reduction Strategies in Declining Organizations," *Academy of Management Review* 13, no. 2 (April 1988): 241–254.

14. Deborah Smith Cook and Gerald R. Ferris, "Strategic Human Resource Management and Firm Effectiveness in Industries Experiencing Decline," *Human Resource Management* 25, no. 3 (Fall 1986): 441–457.

15. Robert H. Hayes and Ramchandram Jaikumar, "Manufacturing's Crisis: New Technologies, Obsolete Organizations," *Harvard Business Review 63* (November–December 1985): 111–119.

16. Douglas T. Hall, "A Theoretical Model of Career Subidentity Development in Organizational Settings," *Organizational Behavior and Human Performance* 6, no. 1 (January 1971): 50–76.

17. Anthony P. Carnevale, Leila J. Gainer, and Ann S. Meltzer, *Workplace Basics: The Skills Employers Want* (Alexandria, Va.: American Society for Training and Development and the U.S. Department of Labor, 1988).

18. Douglas T. Hall, "Dilemmas in Linking Succession Planning to Individual Executive Learning," *Human Resource Management* 25, no. 2 (Summer 1986): 235–265.

19. Hall, "Dilemmas in Linking Succession Planning."

20. U.S. Department of Labor, U.S. Department of Education, and U.S. Department of Commerce, *Building a Quality Workforce* (Washington, D.C.: U.S. Departments of Labor, Education, and Commerce, 1988), p. 18.

21. Carnevale, Gainer, and Meltzer, *Workplace Basics*.

22. Robert E. Kaplan, William H. Drath, and Joan Kofodimos, *High Hurdles: The Challenge of Executive Self-Development* (Greensboro, N.C.: Center for Creative Leadership, Technical Report No. 25, April 1985).

23. Hall, "Dilemmas in Linking Succession Planning."

24. Charles Fombrun, Noel M. Tichy, and Mary Ann Devanna (eds.), *Strategic Human Resource Management* (New York: Wiley, 1984).

25. Douglas T. Hall, "Breaking Career Routines: Midcareer Choice and Identity Development," in Douglas T. Hall and Associates, *Career Development in Organizations* (San Francisco: Jossey-Bass, 1986), pp. 120–159.

26. Oliver E. Williamson, *Markets and Hierarchies: Analysis and Antitrust Implications* (New York: Free Press, 1975).

27. Douglas T. Hall and Benjamin Schneider, *Organizational Climates and Careers: The Work Lives of Priests* (New York: Academic Press, 1973).

28. Harry L. Wellbank, Douglas T. Hall, Marilyn A. Morgan, and W. Clay Hamner, "Planning Job Progression for Effective Career Development and Human Resources Management," *Personnel* 55 (January 1978): 54–64.

29. Kenneth N. Wexley and Gary P. Latham, *Developing and Training Human Resources in Organizations* (Glenview, Ill.: Scott, Foresman, 1981).

30. Robert H. Hayes, "Strategic Planning—Forward or Reverse?" *Harvard Business Review* 63 (November–December 1985): 111–119.

31. Hayes and Jaikumar, "Manufacturing's Crisis"; Lloyd S. Baird, "Value Based Management," working paper, School of Management, Boston University, 1988.

32. Thomas A. Kochan, John P. MacDuffie, and Paul Osterman, "Employment Security at DEC: Sustaining Values Amid Environmental Change," *Human Resource Management* 27, no. 2 (Summer 1988): 121–143.

33. Kochan, MacDuffie, and Osterman, "Employment Security at DEC."

34. Kochan, MacDuffie, and Osterman, "Employment Security at DEC," pp. 138–139.

III

PUBLIC AND PRIVATE POLICIES

10

Preparing the Future Workforce:
A Labor-Management Consensus

The previous chapters have documented how workers and workplaces in the United States have been hard hit by economic shocks since the mid-1970s. More intense global competition, business deregulation, and corporate mergers and acquisitions have caused major shifts in the sectoral composition of employment. Technological change has altered skill needs, and demographic change has affected labor supply in ways that particularly impact on the job prospects of youth, older workers, and minorities. Throughout the labor market, work careers have become much less certain as fewer jobs are stable, as promotion opportunities are diminishing, and as compensation increases are becoming less routine.

For example, plant closings and corporate downsizing have displaced about 2 million workers a year since the late 1970s, resulting in long-term unemployment, repeated spells of joblessness, and substantial earnings losses for many of those who become displaced. The largest group of displaced workers are those in blue-collar occupations, but 20% come from the retail trade and services sector, and 40% are white collar, including middle- and upper-level managers.

This labor market turbulence is felt in different ways by different demographic groups. Career establishment has slowed for many younger workers because relatively high-wage entry jobs in manufacturing are being replaced by lower-wage entry jobs in the retail sales and service sectors. As a result, more and more younger workers hold jobs that provide little or no training. The career jobs of older workers are ending early, and many are turning to alternative work that has substantially lower pay and status. The effects of turbulence are most acute for minorities and those with educational disadvantages.

Much of this turbulence reflects a renewed drive for competitiveness in U.S. industry that has helped the economy to outperform those of many other industrialized countries in the 1980s.[1] For workers in growth occupations and industries, change has been beneficial, but many of those affected by change (especially youth and displaced workers in economically depressed industries and communities) have only minimal shelters against long-term job and income inadequacy.

Turbulence is a problem for business as well. Increased competition and falling profits have led to business restructuring and widespread employment cutbacks. These employment contractions are raising the costs of workforce redeployment and severance. On top of these costs, however, many companies fear that the potential savings from downsizing will be undermined by falling employee commitment and reduced labor productivity resulting from the uncertain job climate. There are also concerns that the political reaction to turbulence may lead to further government regulation of layoffs and plant closings, and higher mandated adjustment costs for employers.

If present trends continue, almost all workers will be at risk from turbulence at some time in their working lives. This growth in employment risk underscores the need for public and private policies to ensure that every segment of the workforce has the opportunity to be more productive and that all those who are now at risk can share in future economic progress.

Limits of Public Policy

Current government programs are not adequate to address today's high levels of labor market turbulence. The deficiencies of public schools in making students job-ready have been well documented.[2] Equally serious are the short-comings of public programs for helping those who are out of school and in the labor market. Two thirds of the workforce for the year 2000 has already left school and, for these workers, current programs are increasingly problematic.

Although employment gains have been strong in the U.S. economy of the 1980s, many of the underlying problems of job loss and slow growth in earnings seem highly resistant to both macroeconomic policy and traditional labor market adjustment programs. For example, federal government training programs have been only minimally effective,[3] and the share of GNP devoted to these programs fell by almost half between 1978 and 1988.[4] Not only are the consequences of workplace turbulence accumlating, but there is the danger that many of the short-term responses to turbulence—the early retirement of experienced workers, the increased reliance on contingent labor, inadequate re-training programs, and the delayed transition from school to work—may ultimately inhibit productivity gains and the restoration of national competitiveness.

Numerous reports have called for a rethinking of conventional solutions to workplace turbulence as a means of renewing American competitiveness.[5] These studies, however, have largely focused on ways to improve *public* policies and have emphasized solutions involving *public* programs of education, training, and job placement. What has been neglected is the important direct role that the private sector plays in preparing the workforce for change, and how this private sector human resources capacity needs to be adapted in response to the more turbulent economic environment.

Private Sector Contributions

Most skills training occurs at the workplace, and a substantial amount of labor market turbulence is absorbed within firms through retraining and redeploying workers. Human resources development and adjustment policies at the workplace are the first-line defense against labor market turbulence.[6]

Previous chapters have shown that if adjustments to change can be contained within the workplace, labor market turbulence results in far fewer adverse effects than when it has to be accommodated outside the firm. When displacement cannot be contained within the firm, adjustment programs designed and operated by companies or unions often appear to be more effective than counterpart programs undertaken solely by government.

There remains, however, a need for improving the human resources development capacity of the private sector. For example, business must become better at anticipating workforce change and at preparing employees for a broader range of jobs than is the common practice. Companies also need to integrate their human resources planning more effectively with overall corporate strategies, and new human resources networks *among* firms need to be devised.

Where trade unions are present at the workplace, they need to participate fully in designing and implementing adjustment programs. There is also room for unions to play a more ambitious role in improving the human resources capability in the small and medium-size enterprise sector. Together, business and unions can take the lead in mobilizing resources for workforce preparedness, both at the workplace and in the wider community.

Improving Public and Private Policies

Redirecting public and private policy to meet the workforce preparedness needs of today's economy requires both an understanding of the problems caused by labor market turbulence and an appreciation of what solutions make sense in terms of economic needs of workers and the operating concerns of employers. The preceding chapters have analyzed the problems: the balance of this chapter addresses the question of what should be done.

Because issues of educational reform, basic skills needs, and family policy have been widely addressed by other organizations[7], the focus here is on policies that affect the vast majority of the working age population that is already out of school and in the workforce. Unlike much policy research that is directed at government action, these proposals aim at both public *and private* approaches.

The potential effectiveness of the policies have been evaluated from the perspective of business and labor. After extensive deliberations involving academic specialists and corporate and trade union representatives, the recommendations have been endorsed by the *Committee on New American Realities (NAR)* of the National Planning Association (see Appendix for NAR membership).

The recommendations therefore reflect a broad labor-management consensus over the direction that public and private policies should take to better prepare the workforce of the future. Although some of these proposals echo the common wisdom regarding the need for better management of public human resources programs and for better coordination between public and private efforts, many represent new directions for policy.

One recurrent theme is the need to make human resources development a *lifelong* process in which workplace training is a central force. A second is the importance of enlarging the career prospects of employees beyond the confines of a single occupation, functional area, or employer. A third is the payoff to be had from encouraging the adoption throughout the economy of "best practice" human resources planning and development programs.

Specific proposals are made for improving four elements of the human resources system—training, job security, income security, and policy planning—that are essential for addressing the most immediate preparedness needs of today's and tomorrow's workforce. In each of these areas, there is a recognition of the need for across-the-board increases in the resources devoted to preparing the workforce and a commitment to ensuring that improvements in productivity and competitiveness are linked to improvements in the well-being of workers. There is also an emphasis on the importance of private sector leadership and on stronger partnerships with government to effect policy change.

Training for a Turbulent Environment

The current system of education and training was designed for an economy that is very different from that which business and labor face today. The formal part of the system—schools, vocational and technical training programs, community colleges, and universities—is largely intended to provide once-in-a-lifetime preparation for the labor market. Despite recent attention to vocational skills and to the training needs of adults, the formal system still concentrates primarily on young persons and on the provision of common denominator skills that can be applied to many entry jobs in the economy.

Thereafter, public programs offer only patchwork coverage of training and preparedness needs for workers who are out of school. The principal pieces of training legislation—the Perkins Vocational Education Act, the Job Training Partnership Act (JTPA), and the Trade Adjustment Assistance Act—provide uneven levels of training and are often uncoordinated with one another. Eligibility for programs is defined around distinct categories of workers—youth, older workers, and displaced workers—and often depends on restrictive criteria based on prior income and employment experience. Program accountability also leaves much to be desired.[9]

Poor program coordination and inconsistent eligibility criteria have resulted in a segmented approach to workforce preparedness that is badly matched to the concept of lifelong human resources development. Lifelong preparation of the workforce has also been hampered by policies that have focused narrowly on the remedy of particular labor market difficulties rather than on integrated solutions to the longer-term needs of industry, workers, and the community.

Employers and unions, therefore, continue to carry the burden of workforce preparedness. Skills training is largely provided on the job, but it too tends to be narrow, building as best it can upon the general foundations provided by schools and training programs. With a few notable exceptions, such as apprenticeship training or cooperative education, a sharp boundary is drawn between schools and work.

A high priority of business and labor is to make workforce preparedness a lifelong process that is central to enhancing labor productivity and competitiveness, rather than being a crisis-driven and largely episodic activity. The goal is to create a public-private system of human resources development that has the capacity *(1) to provide all workers with appropriate skills; (2) to encourage greater labor productivity; (3) to foster positive approaches to change among workers and their employers; and (4) to allow for greater economic mobility without economic loss.* Accomplishing this goal will require a significant diffusion of changes now underway in private sector human resources policies, as well as substantial adjustments in public sector policies.

PROPOSALS FOR IMPROVING TRAINING AND PRODUCTIVITY

- Reverse the thrust of current public human resources policy from the provision of training and placement assistance only for particular segments of the labor force to the provision of assistance for a broader cross-section of workers who are at risk from turbulence.

  As a first step, this will mean easing substantially the income restrictions on program eligibility and reducing the emphasis on targeting resources on specific demographic groups.

- Improve resources and financial incentives for individual employees and organizations to invest in continuous lifelong development.

  These incentives include federal trust funds for training (similar to those for unemployment insurance) that would support industry-based training activities; private sector human resources development; accounts for employees to draw on for education and training related to current or potential future employment; and training and tuition programs for individuals.

- Foster workplace training programs such as apprenticeship training, cooperative education, and other on-the-job learning opportunities that effectively combine formal training with experiential learning.

  These programs will encourage more substantial training investments and will help build meaningful linkages between public sector education and training programs and private sector human resources development.

- Support greater internal mobility of employees and encourage employees to accumulate skills in advance of permanent job reassignments.

  These goals can be accomplished in many ways—by establishing internal "apprenticeship" programs that prepare workers to be deployed more widely within the company; by redefining job and career "ladders" to be more adaptable to change; by providing programs that facilitate movement across broad occupational groups, traditional functional divisions, and business unit boundaries; and by strengthening managerial and professional development programs. Particularly for managers and professionals, experience with internal mobility should be provided as part of early and mid-career development to build a more effective capability for managing change at the workplace.

- Encourage broad employee representation at all levels in designing preparedness programs. In unionized settings, such programs should be jointly designed and administered by unions and employers.

- Improve the efficiency and accountability of public training and employment service programs by requiring that they achieve long-term improvements in income and employment security.

  Steps in this direction include devising improved performance criteria and long-term performance monitoring systems; expanding arrangements (such as voucher systems) that allow workers and employers to select effective programs and to become stakeholders in the training process; and requiring that starting jobs for trainees pay wages commensurate with those of other jobs requiring comparable skills and proficiencies.

Broadening Job Security

Employment security practices in U.S. industry have changed dramatically in recent years. Companies that have provided strong employment guarantees are finding such guarantees harder and harder to sustain, whereas companies that have used layoffs as an adjustment strategy are now finding it necessary to increase job security as a condition for gaining improved workplace performance. Regardless of whether particular employees have more or less job security, work in general is becoming less stable and more contingent.

One solution to this rising instability is greater employment flexibility and increased training; a second is advance notification and outplacement assistance that permit a more orderly transition from one job to another. Smoothing the impact of layoffs and plant closing through advance notice, however, will not enhance overall employment security. New job-to-job networks among employers are also needed to improve reemployment prospects.

Job transitions within a firm are usually accomplished with less disruption than involuntary job changes from one company to another. A major reason why changing firms is more haphazard is that the organizational and information links that facilitate redeployment within a firm are absent. This argues for forming employee transfer linkages among larger employers and for developing multiemployer referral and adjustment programs (along the lines of union referral and joint labor-management training systems in the construction industry) for smaller firms.

PROPOSALS FOR IMPROVING JOB SECURITY

- Extend the concept of employee redeployment to include linkages among firms.

    This will involve actions such as establishing area-wide "company-to-company" employment networks that can be combined with training where appropriate. Special opportunities may exist for unions and governments to help build networks between large companies and their vendors and among small and medium-size firms in specific business sectors.
- Devise mechanisms that will facilitate the "portability" of certain employee benefits, such as health insurance, for workers required to move from one employer to another.
- Provide employees with reasonable advance notification of layoffs and other major employment disruptions.
- Offer employment "preparedness" and relocation assistance to spouses as well as employees.
- Adopt "best practice" workforce preparedness guidelines.

    These guidelines should cover issues such as strategic human resources planning and development, advance notification of employment disruptions, transfer and severance policies, and continuation of employee benefits.

Extending the Income Safety Net

As job changing has increased, there has been a corresponding rise in the incidence of unemployment. The federal-state unemployment insurance system is the major source of income to fill this earnings gap.

Over time, this system has developed numerous inconsistencies in payment levels and eligibility criteria. Moreover, as the economy has become more turbulent, the percentage of unemployed workers eligible for unemployment insurance benefits has diminished and earnings replacement rates have fallen.

As a result, unemployment insurance has become less and less adequate in meeting the economic needs of workers who are between jobs.

In recent years, much less than half of all unemployed workers have received unemployment insurance payments—largely because they have not met eligibility requirements or have been unemployed for so long that they have exhausted their benefits. Job-taking incentives also change abruptly when benefits are exhausted and there are inadequate incentives for training and for gaining potentially useful work experience.

PROPOSALS FOR IMPROVING THE INCOME SAFETY NET

- Increase the scope of the unemployment insurance system by making it more equitable.

    This will mean establishing minimum replacement earnings standards (adjusted for regional differences in the cost of living) and making eligibility criteria more uniform across states; allowing interstate transfers of benefits; and making unemployment insurance payments available on a pro-rata basis to workers who demonstrate substantial attachment to the labor force, but who may be disqualified from receiving unemployment insurance benefits because of low earnings.
- Extend the duration of unemployment insurance in recognition that increased turbulence can result in long-duration, or repeated periods of, unemployment that raise the probability of benefit exhaustion.
- Ensure that unemployment insurance benefits are available to otherwise eligible workers who are in training programs that meet suitable performance standards.
- Improve the effectiveness of job search and job placement assistance by implementing new approaches that have proved successful in pilot projects and demonstration programs.

    These approaches include intensive employee counseling, job "clubs," relocation benefits, and various forms of employer incentives.

Public-Private Partnerships

A number of these policy reforms will require close collaboration between public and private human resources programs. Public-private education and training partnerships—local educational compacts, "adopted" schools, vocational school advisory committees, and the Private Industry Councils under JTPA—are often thought to be a vehicle for such collaboration, but these partnerships have produced too few tangible successes.[10] One reason for this lack of success is that many public-private partnerships have been formed to meet a political, rather than a business, need.

In contrast, the most effective examples of public-private human resources collaboration are found where there is a business necessity for such programs and where the private sector has been involved in the program design and implementation. Examples include joint labor-management apprenticeship programs, land grant agricultural schools, university-based technical and engineering programs, business-education compacts, and cooperative education programs.

Business and labor can foster such collaboration by providing leadership in linking human resources development to jobs. The private sector can also help to improve public sector human resources planning. It can provide experienced staff resources and assistance in gathering data, analyzing local trends in the supply and demand for skills, and coordinating public programs with private sector human resources development.

At a minimum, such a planning capacity would fill a major gap in the information now available to the numerous public education and training advisory committees. Ideally, such a capacity would also provide a foundation for addressing the human resources needs of specific industries and occupations at the state or local level. Although the current system of JTPA advisory committees nominally has this capacity, greater resources and stronger participation by business and labor are needed to bring the quality of such planning up to the standards of strategic human resources planning within the most progressive private sector firms.

PROPOSALS FOR IMPROVING PLANNING PARTNERSHIPS

- Assist in developing and staffing state and local labor market planning boards that bring together labor, management, and government to create a public planning counterpart to private sector strategic human resources planning.

   These boards should have the capacity to analyze local labor market and employment data, provide an early warning of emerging human resources development problems, and recommend strategic responses to be adopted by public sector programs, employers, and unions.
- Provide more information to schools, training organizations, and unions on the changing realities and needs of the world of work.

   Students and inexperienced workers need to be given a more realistic assessment of what to expect at the workplace, and schools need to be made more aware of the importance of communication and leadership skills as well as the educational basics necessary for today's work environment.
- Create direct linkages between schools and employers to facilitate the timely transfer of workplace skill development programs to schools as soon as new skills resulting from technological change become broadly demanded within a community.

   Changes in skills and occupational requirements due to technological change cannot be accurately forecast. Employers need to monitor their changing needs and be responsible for conveying these trends to the schools in a timely way.
- Increase the awareness among schools, unions, and community organizations of the broad changes confronting firms and workers—underscoring

the impacts of technological change and workplace reorganization as potential sources of economic progress, and recognizing that such changes must be coupled with adequate programs of workforce preparedness and adequate protection against income loss.

Dealing with these issues will require an expanded public dialogue with equal participation from labor and management.

Workforce Preparedness and Community Preparedness

Workforce preparedness, by itself, is too narrow a concept to deal with current economic changes. A much broader approach is needed—that of community economic preparedness—whereby communities, companies, and workers become better prepared for change.

For example, in some southern states, utility companies are playing a leading role in coordinating industrial development to diversify the economic base of local communities; in the case of plant closings, some companies have continued to make contributions to impacted communities in lieu of taxes while others have participated in programs to help promote recovery in local communities adversely impacted by change;[11] and business and union participation in special programs to upgrade basic education and to improve the job prospects of the hard to employ is growing in central city areas.[12]

Promoting the concept of community economic preparedness will help to create the capacity in states and localities to respond to the problems posed by continuing turbulence in the U.S. economy. To accomplish this goal will require special business and labor leadership in working with government to promote economic development, to encourage economic diversification, and to restore the economic vitality of communities that have already been hard hit by economic turbulence.

Community institutions with strong business and labor involvement, such as the regional labor market planning boards described previously, are as central to the task of building stronger local economies as they are to fostering better workforce preparedness.

Workforce Preparedness and the Future Economy

The proposals outlined provide both an ambitious and a workable package of policies around which governmental and private sector resources can be mobilized. They address the most visible problems of workplace turbulence— displaced workers, delayed career establishment of youth, and the employment of older workers in transition to retirement. The data show that these are serious problems, but of manageable proportions.

A better prepared workforce, a better prepared private sector, and better prepared communities hold promise for restoring U.S. competitiveness and reversing the decline in well-being that has affected many segments of U.S.

society. What remains to be seen, however, is whether the country's human resources development capacity will be sufficient to this task.

The rise of employment-at-will practices, the increases projected in the disadvantaged labor force, the growth of contingent employment, and the uncertain contribution of small and medium-size enterprises to human resources development are making the job of preparing the future workforce more and more difficult. Unless these long-term problems can be addressed, the role of the workplace in human resources development will be diminished and the full productivity potential of the workforce will not be realized.

In addition, the effectiveness of human resources policy depends on the wider economic environment as well as on the specific efforts of business, government, and labor. Realizing an ambitious workforce preparedness agenda also requires a commitment—again from business, government, and labor—to promote faster growth and to reduce economic uncertainty, both domestically and globally.

Notes

This chapter is primarily the responsibility of Peter B. Doeringer.

1. U.S. President, Council of Economic Advisers, *Economic Report of the President* (Washington, D.C.: Government Printing Office, 1989).

2. American Society for Training and Development and U.S. Department of Labor, *Workplace Basics* (Alexandria, Va.: American Society for Training and Development, 1989); National Alliance of Business, *The Fourth R* (Washington, D.C.: National Alliance of Business, 1987).

3. Robert A. Taggart, *A Fisherman's Guide: An Assessment of Training and Remediation Strategies* (Kalamazoo: Mich.: Upjohn Institute for Employment Research, 1981); Howard Bloom, "Estimating the Effect of Job Training Programs Using Longitudinal Data: Ashenfelter's Findings Reconsidered," *Journal of Human Resources* 14, no. 4 (Fall 1984): 545–555; JTPA Advisory Committee, *Working Capital* (Washington, D.C.: Government Printing Office, 1989).

4. U.S. Department of Labor, Commission on Workforce Quality and Labor Market Efficiency, *Investing in People* (Washington, D.C.: Government Printing Office, 1989).

5. Ford Foundation, *The Common Good* (New York: Ford Foundation, 1989); William B. Johnston and Arnold H. Packer, *Workforce 2000: Work and Workers for the 21st Century* (Indianapolis: Hudson Institute, 1987); JTPA Advisory Committee, *Working Capital*; Business–Higher Education Forum, *American Potential* (Washington, D.C.: American Council on Training and Development and U.S. Department of Labor, *Workplace Basics*; Michael L. Dertouzos, Richard K. Lester, and Robert M. Solow, *Made in America* (Cambridge, Mass.: MIT Press, 1989); Commission on Workforce Quality and Labor Market Efficiency, *Investing in People*.

6. American Society for Training and Development and U.S. Department of Labor, *Workplace Basics*; Ernest Stromsdorfer, "Training in Industry," Peter B. Doeringer (ed.), *Workplalce Perspectives on Education and Training* (Hingham, Mass.: Martinus Nijhoff Publishing, 1981).

7. U.S. Department of Labor, American Society for Training and Development and U.S. Department of Labor, *Workplace Basics*; Dertouzos, Lester, and Solow, *Made in America*; Commission on Workforce Quality and Labor Market Efficiency, *Investing in People*; Ford Foundation, *Common Good*.

8. National Planning Association, *Preparing for Change*, National Planning Association Report No. 245 (Washington, D.C.: National Planning Association, 1990).

9. JTPA Advisory Committee, *Working Capital*.

10. National Alliance of Business, *The Fourth R*.

11. Ross Gittell, *A Critical Analysis of Local Initiatives in Economic Revitalization*, unpublished Ph.D. thesis, Harvard University, 1989; Winthrop Knowlton, "One's Own Place: Reflections on Community Revitalization in America," *21st Congress of the World Management Council* (mimeo), September 21–23, 1989.

12. John T. Dunlop, "Management Challenges in the 1990's," *21st Congress of the World Management Council* (mimeo), September 21–23, 1989.

APPENDIX

NATIONAL PLANNING ASSOCIATION

Committee on New American Realities

ROGER ACKERMAN
Group President
Specialty Glass & Ceramics
Corning Glassworks

PAUL A. ALLAIRE
President and Chief Executive Officer
Xerox Corporation

ELIZABETH E. BAILEY
Dean, Carnegie Mellon University
Graduate School of Industrial
   Administration

WALLACE B. BEHNKE
Kiawa Island, South Carolina

JAMES B. BOOE
Secretary-Treasurer
Communications Workers of America

DENIS BOVIN
Managing Director
Salomon Brothers

HAROLD W. BURLINGAME
Senior Vice President, Human
   Resources
AT&T

MICHAEL A. CALLEN
Director and Sector Executive
Citibank, N.A.

JOHN B. CARON
President, Caron International

JOHN DeCONCINI
President
Bakery, Confectionery & Tobacco
   Workers International Union

JOHN T. DUNLOP
Lamont University Professor
Harvard University

DONALD F. EPHLIN
Senior Fellow
National Planning Association

MURRAY H. FINLEY
President Emeritus
Amalgamated Clothing and Textile
   Workers' Union; and
Chairman of the Advisory Committee
Amalgamated Bank of New York

THEODORE GEIGER
Distinguished Research Professor of
   Intersocietal Relations
School of Foreign Service
Georgetown University

ROBERT A. GEORGINE
President
Building & Construction Trades
   Department
AFL-CIO

215

JACK GOLODNER
President
Department for Professional Employees
AFL-CIO

JACK M. GREENBERG
Senior Executive Vice President and
  Chief Financial Officer
McDonald's Corporation

GERALD GRINSTEIN
President & Chief Executive Officer
Burlington Northern, Inc.

DALE E. HATHAWAY
Principal Consultant
Consultants International Group, Inc.

R. J. HILDRETH
Managing Director
Farm Foundation

ROY B. HOWARD
Senior Vice President
Corporate Human Resources
Bell South Corporation

CHARLES S. JOHNSON
Senior Vice President and Treasurer
Pioneer Hi-Bred International, Inc.

EDWARD G. JORDAN
Carmel, California

EUGENE J. KEILIN
Senior Partner
Keilin & Bloom

RICHARD J. KRUIZENGA
Vice President, Corporate Planning
Exxon Corporation

CHARLES R. LEE
President and Chief Operating Officer
GTE Corporation

LEON LYNCH
International Vice President, Human
  Affairs
United Steelworkers of America

EDWARD E. MASTERS
President and Chief Executive Officer
National Planning Association

JAMES N. McGEEHAN
International Treasurer
United Steelworkers of America

B. JACK MILLER
Vice President and Controller
Philip Morris Companies, Inc.

JOHN MILLER
Chocorua, New Hampshire

LENORE MILLER
President
Retail, Wholesale and Department Store
  Union

DAVID MORGENTHALER
Managing Partner
Morgenthaler Ventures

EDWARD A. O'NEAL, JR.
Group Executive
Consumer Banking Group
Chemical Bank

RUDOLPH A. OSWALD
Director
Department of Economic Research
AFL-CIO

JAMES R. PAINTER
Executive Vice President
AMCENA Corporation

DEAN P. PHYPERS
New Canaan, Connecticut

GEORGE J. POULIN
General Vice President
International Association of Machinists
  & Aerospace Workers

JOHN S. REED
Chairman, Citicorp

JOHN W. ROSENBLUM
Dean, Darden Graduate School of
    Business Administration
University of Virginia

ROBERT L. SHAFER
Vice President, Public Affairs and
    Government Relations
Pfizer Inc.

JACK SHEINKMAN
President
Amalgamated Clothing & Textile
    Workers' Union

ROBERT C. STEMPEL
Chief Executive Officer and Chairman
General Motors Corporation

MILAN STONE
International President
United Rubber, Cork, Linoleum and
    Plastic Workers of America

PATRICK A. TOOLE
Senior Vice President and
General Manager, Operations
IBM Corporation

RICHARD L. TRUMKA
International President
United Mine Workers of America

BRIAN TURNER
Executive Assistant to the President
Industrial Union Department
AFL-CIO

J. C. TURNER
General President Emeritus
International Union of Operating
    Engineers

RALPH S. YOHE
Mt. Horeb, Wisconsin

STAFF

JAMES A. AUERBACH
Director and Vice President
National Planning Association

REFERENCES

Aaron, Henry J., Barry B. Bosworth, and Gary Burtless, *Can America Afford to Grow Old? Paying for Social Security* (Washington, D.C.: Brookings Institution, 1989).

Abernathy, William J., and James M. Utterback, "A General Model," in William J. Abernathy, *The Productivity Dilemma* (Baltimore, Md.: Johns Hopkins University Press, 1978), pp. 68–84.

Adams, Terry K., and Greg J. Duncan, *The Persistence of Urban Poverty and Its Demographic and Behavioral Correlates* (Ann Arbor, Mich.: Survey Research Center, University of Michigan, 1988).

Addison, John T., and Pedro Portugal, "The Effect of Advance Notification of Plant Closings on Unemployment," *Industrial and Labor Relations Review* 41, no. 1 (October 1987): 3–16.

American Management Association, *Responsible Reductions in Force* (New York: American Management Association, 1988).

American Society for Training and Development and U.S. Department of Labor, *Workplace Basics* (Alexandria, Va.: American Society for Training and Development, 1989).

Apgar, William C., and James H. Brown, *State of the Nation's Housing 1988* (Cambridge, Mass.: Joint Center for Housing Studies of Harvard University, 1988).

Argyris, Chris, *Integrating the Individual and the Organization* (New York: Wiley, 1964).

Argyris, Chris, *Personality and the Organization* (New York: Harper & Row, 1957).

Argyris, Chris, *Reasoning, Learning, and Action* (San Francisco: Jossey-Bass, 1982).

Asinof, Lynn, "Rent-An-Exec Firm," in Labor Letter, *Wall Street Journal*, August 4, 1988.

Astin, Alexander W., Kenneth C. Green, and William S. Korn, *The American Freshman: Twenty Year Trends* (Los Angeles: Cooperative Institutional Research Program, University of California, Los Angeles, 1987).

Astin, Alexander W., Kenneth C. Green, William S. Korn, and Marilyn Schalit, *The American Freshman: National Norms for Fall 1987* (Los Angeles: Cooperative Institutional Research Program, University of California, Los Angeles, 1987).

Attewell, Paul, and James Rule, "Computing and Organizations: What We Know and What We Don't Know," *Communications of the ACM* 27, no. 12 (December 1984): 1184–1192.

Axel, Helen (ed.), *Employing Older Americans: Opportunities and Constraints*, Research Bulletin No. 916 (New York: The Conference Board, 1988).

Axel, Helen, *Job Banks for Older Workers*, Research Bulletin No. 929 (New York: The Conference Board, 1989).

Baird, Lloyd S., "Value Based Management," Working Paper, School of Management, Boston University, 1988.

Bardwick, Judith M., *The Plateauing Trap* (New York: Bantam, 1988).

Barnow, Burt S., "The Impact of CETA Programs on Earnings," *Journal of Human Resources* 22, no. 2 (Spring 1987): 157–193.

Barocci, Thomas A., and Paul Cournoyer, "Make or Buy: Computer Professionals in a Demand-Driven Environment," Working Paper 1342, Sloan School of Management, MIT, September 1982.

Barocci, Thomas A., and Kirsten R. Wever, "Information Systems Careers and Human Resource Management," Working Paper 1482, Sloan School of Management, MIT, September 1983.

Baron, James N., Alison Davis-Blake, and William T. Bielby, "The Structure of Opportunity: How Promotion Ladders Vary Within and Among Organizations," *Administrative Science Quarterly* 31 (1986): 248–273.

Barton, Paul E., and Bryna Shore Frazer, *Between Two Worlds—Youth Transition from School to Work* (Washington, D.C.: U.S. Government Printing Office, 1976).

Beer, Michael, Bert Spector, Paul R. Lawrence, D. Quinn Mills, and Richard E. Walton, *Managing Human Assets: The Groundbreaking Harvard Business School Program* (New York: Free Press, 1984).

Bell, Donald, and William Marclay, "Trends in Retirement Eligibility and Pension Benefits, 1974–83," *Monthly Labor Review*, April 1987, pp. 18–25.

Bell, Linda A., and Richard B. Freeman, "The Facts About Rising Industrial Wage Dispersion in the U.S.," *Industrial Relations Research Association, 39th Annual Proceedings* (Madison, Wisc.: Industrial Relations Research Association, 1987), pp. 331–337.

Belous, Richard S., *The Contingent Economy: The Growth of the Temporary, Part-time and Subcontracted Workforce*, NPA Report #239 (Washington, D.C.: National Planning Association, 1989).

Bendix, R., *Work and Authority in Industry* (New York: Wiley, 1956).

Bennis, Warren G., "Organizations of the Future," in Robert A. Sutermeister (ed.), *People and Productivity*, 3rd ed. (New York: McGraw-Hill, 1976).

Bennis, Warren G., and Bert Nanus, *Leaders: Strategies for Taking Charge* (New York: Harper & Row, 1985).

Berenbeim, Ronald E., *Company Programs to Ease the Impact of Shutdowns* (New York: The Conference Board, 1986).

Berger, Mark C., "Predicted Future Earnings and Choice of College Major," *Industrial and Labor Relations Review* 41 (1988): 418–429.

Bergman, Edward M., and Harvey A. Goldstein, "Dynamics, Structural Change and Economic Development Paths," in Edward M. Bergman (ed.), *Local Economies in Transition* (Durham, N.C.: Duke University Press, 1986), pp. 84–110.

Berlin, Gordon, and Andrew M. Sum, *Toward a More Perfect Union: Basic Skills, Poor Families, and Our Economic Future* (New York: Ford Foundation Project on Social Welfare and the American Future, Occasional Paper No. 3, 1988).

Birch, David, "The Hidden Economy," *Wall Street Journal*, June 10, 1988.

Bisconti, Ann S., and J. G. Kessler, *College and Other Stepping Stones: A Study of the Learning Experiences That Contribute to Effective Performance in Early and Long-Run Jobs* (Bethlehem, Pa.: College Placement Council Foundation, 1980).

Bishop, John H., *The Social Payoff from Occupationally Specific Training: The Employer's Point of View* (Columbus, Ohio: National Center for Research in Vocational Education, Ohio State University, 1983).

Bloom, Howard, "Estimating the Effect of Job Training Programs Using Longitudinal Data: Ashenfelter's Findings Reconsidered," *Journal of Human Resources* 14, no. 4 (Fall 1984): 545–555.

Bluestone, Barry, and Bennett Harrison, *The Deindustrialization of America* (New York: Basic Books, 1982).

Borus, Michael, "A Description of Employed and Unemployed Youth in 1981," in *Youth and the Labor Market: Analyses of the National Longitudinal Surveys* (Kalamazoo, Mich.: Upjohn Institute for Employment Research, 1984), pp. 13–56.

Boskin, Michael J., and Michael D. Hurd, "The Effect of Social Security on Retirement in the Early 1970's," *Quarterly Journal of Economics* 99, no. 4 (1984): 767–790.

Boston Private Industry Council, *The Class of 1987: A Follow-Up Survey* (Boston: Boston Private Industry Council, January 1988).

Bould, Sally, "Unemployment as a Factor in Early Retirement Decisions," *American Journal of Economics and Sociology* 39 (1980): 124–136.

Braverman, Harry, *Labor and Monopoly Capital: The Degradation of Work in the Twentieth Century* (New York: Monthly Review, 1974).

Bright, James, R., *Automation and Management* (Boston: Harvard University Graduate School of Business Administration, 1958).

Bright, James R., "Does Automation Raise Skill Requirements?" *Harvard Business Review* 36 (1958): 84–98.

Brockner, Joel, Stephen Grover, Thomas Reed, Rocki DeWitt, and Michael O'Malley, "Survivors' Reactions to Layoffs: We Get By with a Little Help from Our Friends," *Administrative Science Quarterly* 32 (December 1987): 526–541.

Brussell, Shirley, "Prepared Statement of Shirley Brussell, Executive Director, Operation ABLE, Inc.," in *Retirement: The Broken Promise* (Washington, D.C.: Government Printing Office, 1981), pp 76–81.

Bulow, Jeremy J., and Lawrence H. Summers, "A Theory of Dual Labor Markets with Application to Industrial Policy, Discrimination, and Keynesian Unemployment," *Journal of Labor Economics* 4, no. 3, Part 1 (1986): 376–414.

Buono, Anthony F., and James L. Bowditch, *The Human Side of Mergers and Acquisitions: Managing Collisions Between People, Cultures, and Organizations* (San Francisco: Jossey-Bass, 1989).

Bureau of National Affairs, *The Changing Workplace: New Directions in Staffing and Scheduling*, A BNA Report (Washington, D.C.: Bureau of National Affairs, 1986).

Burtless, Gary, "Why Is the Insured Unemployment Rate So Low?" *Brookings Papers on Economic Activity*, no. 1, 1983, pp. 225–249.

Burtless, Gary, and Robert Moffitt, "The Effects of Social Security Benefits on the Labor Supply of the Aged," in Henry Aaron and Gary Burtless (eds.), *Retirement and Economic Behavior* (Washington, D.C.: Brookings Institution, 1984).

Burtless, Gary, and Larry Orr, "Are Classical Experiments Needed for Manpower Policy?" *Journal of Human Resources* 21, no. 4 (Fall 1986): 606–639.

Business-Higher Education Forum, *American Potential* (Washington, D.C.: American Council on Education, Business-Higher Education Forum, 1988).

Business Week, "The Forgotten Americans: Minority Joblessness Is Stubbornly High—But There Are Ways to Help," September 5, 1985, pp. 50–55.

Byrne, John, "Caught in the Middle—Six Managers Speak Out on Corporate Life," *Business Week*, September 12, 1988, pp. 80–88.

Cameron, Kim, and Raymond Zammuto, "Matching Managerial Strategies to Conditions of Decline," *Human Resource Management* 22 (1983): 359–375.

Cameron, Kim, Myung Kim, and David Whetten, "Organizational Effects of Decline and Turbulence," *Administrative Science Quarterly* 32 (June 1987): 222–240.

Cappelli, Peter, "Union Gains Under Concession Bargaining," unpublished manuscript, 1983.

Carey, John, "The Changing Face of a Restless Nation," *Business Week*, September 25, 1989, pp. 92–106.

Carnevale, Anthony P., Leila J. Gainer, and Ann S. Meltzer, *Workplace Basics: The Skills Employers Want* (Alexandria, Va.: American Society for Training and Development and U.S. Department of Labor, 1988).

Casner-Lotto, Jill, and Associates, *Successful Training Strategies* (San Francisco: Jossey-Bass, 1988).

Chinitz, Benjamin, "Contrasts in Agglomeration: New York and Pittsburgh," *American Economics Association, Papers and Proceedings* 50, no. 3 (1961): 279–289.

Christensen, Kathleen, *Flexible Staffing and Scheduling in U.S. Corporations*, Research Bulletin No. 240 (New York: The Conference Board, 1989).

Christensen, Kathleen, "Flexible Work Arrangements and Older Workers: Older Workers' Experiences with Part-Time, Temporary, Off-the-Books Jobs, and Self-Employment," paper prepared for the Commonwealth Fund Commission on Elderly People Living Alone, New York, 1988.

Christensen, Kathleen, "Rising Use of Part-time and Temporary Workers: Who Benefits and Who Loses?" Testimony Before the Committee on Government Operations, U.S. House of Representatives (Washington, D.C.: Government Printing Office, 1988): 82–83.

Christensen, Kathleen, and Mary Murphree, "Introduction," in *Flexible Workstyles: A Look at Contingent Labor* (Washington, D.C.: U.S. Department of Labor, Women's Bureau, 1988).

Cohany, Sharon R., "What Happened to the High School Class of 1985?" *Monthly Labor Review*, October 1986, pp. 28–30.

Cohen, Stephen S., and John Zysman, *Manufacturing Matters: The Myth of the Post-Industrial Economy* (New York: Basic Books, 1987).

Commission on Workforce Quality and Labor Market Efficiency, *Investing in People* (Washington, D.C.: Government Printing Office, 1989).

Commonwealth Fund Commission on Elderly People Living Alone and ICF Incorporated, *Old, Alone, and Poor* (New York: Commonwealth Fund, 1987).

Conference Board, "Managing Restructuring" (New York: The Conference Board, 1987).

Cook, Deborah Smith, and Gerald R. Ferris, "Strategic Human Resource Management and Firm Effectiveness in Industries Experiencing Decline," *Human Resource Management* 25, no. 3 (Fall 1986): 441–457.

Cooper, Martha R., "Changing Employee Attitudes: Fast Growth vs. Slow Growth Organizations," Hay Management Consultants, n.d..

Cooper, M. R., B. S. Morgan, P. M. Foley, and L. B. Kaplan, "Changing Employee Values: Deepening Discontent?" *Harvard Business Review* 57 (January–February 1979): 117–125.

Crowley, Joan E., "Longitudinal Effects of Retirement on Men's Psychological and Physical Well-Being," in Herbert S. Parnes, Joan E. Crowley, R. Jean Haurin, Lawrence J. Less, William R. Morgan, Frank L. Mott, and Gilbert Nestel, *Retirement Among American Men* (Lexington, Mass.: Heath, 1985), 147–173.

Crystal, Stephen, *America's Old Age Crisis: Public Policy and the Two Worlds of Aging* (New York: Basic Books, 1982).

Cyert, Richard M., and David C. Mowery (eds.), *The Impact of Technological Change on Employment and Economic Growth* (New York: Ballinger, 1988).

Cyert, Richard M., and David C. Mowery (eds.), *Technology and Employment* (Washington, D.C.: National Academy Press, 1987).

Daniel Yankelovich Group, *The Climate for Giving: The Outlook of Current and Future CEOs* (New York: Council on Foundations, 1988).

Daymont, Thomas, and Russell Rumberger, "The Impact of High School Curriculum on the Earnings and Employability of Youth," in Robert E. Taylor, Howard Rosen, and Frank C. Pratzner (eds.), *Job Training for Youth* (Columbus, Ohio: National Center for Research in Vocational Education, Ohio State University, 1982), pp. 297–305.

Dean, Joel, *Capital Budgeting* (New York: Columbia University Press, 1951).

Denison, Edward F., *Trends in American Economic Growth, 1929–82* (Washington, D.C.: Brook ˙ ıgs Institution, 1985).

Dertouzos, Michael L., Richard K. Lester, and Robert M. Solow, *Made in America* (Cambridge, Mass.: MIT Press, 1989).

Devens, Richard M., "Displaced Workers: One Year Later," *Monthly Labor Review*, January 1986, pp. 40–43.

Diamond, Peter, and Jerry Hausman, "The Retirement and Unemployment Behavior of Older Men," in Henry Aaron and Gary Burtless (eds.), *Retirement and Economic Behavior* (Washington, D.C.: Brookings Institution, 1984).

Doeringer, Peter B. (ed.), *Bridges to Retirement: Older Workers in a Changing Labor Market* (Ithaca, N.Y.: ILR Press, Cornell University, 1990).

Doeringer, Peter B., "Internal Labor Markets and Paternalism in Rural Labor Markets," in Paul Osterman (ed.), *Internal Labor Markets* (Cambridge, Mass.: MIT Press, 1984).

Doeringer, Peter B., and Patricia F. Pannell, "Manpower Strategies for Growth and Diversity in New England's High Technology Sector," in John C. Hoy and Melvin H. Bernstein (eds.), *New England's Vital Resource: The Labor Force* (Washington, D.C.: American Council on Education, 1982), pp. 11–35.

Doeringer, Peter B., Philip I. Moss, and David G. Terkla, "Capitalism and Kinship: Do Institutions Matter in the Labor Market?" *Industrial and Labor Relations Review* 40, no. 1 (October 1986): 48–60.

Doeringer, Peter B., and Michael J. Piore, *Internal Labor Markets and Manpower Analysis*, 1st ed. (Lexington, Mass.: Heath, 1971).

Doeringer, Peter B., and Michael J. Piore, *Internal Labor Markets and Manpower Analysis*, 2nd ed. with a new introduction (Armonk, N.Y.: M.E. Sharpe, 1985).

Doeringer, Peter B., and Andrew M. Sum, *Job Markets and Human Resource*

Programs for Older Workers in New England, paper prepared for the New England Board of Higher Education, Boston, 1984.

Doeringer, Peter B., and David G. Terkla, "Jobs for Older Workers: Is the Non-Bureaucratic Firm the Answer?" *Proceedings of the Forty-First Annual Meeting of the Industrial Relations Research Association* (Madison, Wisc.: Industrial Relations Research Association, 1989).

Doeringer, Peter B., Gregory C. Topakian, and David G. Terkla, *Invisible Factors in Local Economic Development* (New York: Oxford University Press, 1987).

Drucker, Peter F. "The Coming of the New Organization," *Harvard Business Review* 66 (January–February 1988): 45–53.

Dunlop, John T., "Management Challenges in the 1990's," *21st Congress of the World Management Council*, mimeo, September 21–23, 1989.

Dunne, Timothy, Mark Roberts, and Lawrence Samuelson, "Plant Turnover and Gross Employment Flows in the U.S. Manufacturing Sector 1963–82," *Journal of Labor Economics* 7 (1987): pp. 48–71.

Edsall, Thomas B., "Extending a Helping Hand to the Working Poor," *Washington Post, National Weekly Edition*, vol. 6, no. 43, August 28 to September 3, 1989, p. 12.

Ehrenberg, Ronald G., and George H. Jakubson, *Advance Notice Provisions in Plant Closing Legislation* (Kalamazoo, Mich.: Upjohn Institute for Employment Research, 1988).

Ehrlich, Elizabeth, and Susan B. Garland, "For American Business: A New World of Workers," *Business Week*, September 19, 1988, pp. 112–120.

Eisdorfer, Carl, and Donna Cohen, "Health and Retirement: Retirement and Health," in *Policy Issues in Work and Retirement* (Kalamazoo, Mich.: Upjohn Institute for Employment Research, 1983), pp. 57–73.

Ellwood, David, *Divide and Conquer: Responsible Security for America's Poor* (New York: Ford Foundation Project on Social Welfare and the American Future, Occasional Paper No. 2, 1987).

Ellwood, David, *Poor Support: Poverty in the American Family* (New York: Basic Books, 1988).

Fedrau, Ruth H., and Kevin P. Balfe, "A Case Study Monograph on Labor-Management Worker Adjustment Programs" (Washington, D.C.: Bureau of Labor-Management Relations and Cooperative Programs, U.S. Department of Labor, 1987).

Feinstein, Selwyn, "More Small Firms Get Help from Rent-A-Boss Service," *Wall Street Journal*, January 5, 1989.

Finegan, T. Aldrich, *The Measurement, Behavior, and Classification of Discouraged Workers* (Washington, D.C.: National Commission on Employment and Unemployment Statistics, 1979).

Fields, Gary S., and Olivia S. Mitchell, "Economic Determinants of the Optimal Retirement Age: An Empirical Investigation," *Journal of Human Resources* 19, no. 2 (1984): 245–262.

Fields, Gary S., and Olivia S. Mitchell, "Restructuring Social Security: How Will Retirement Ages Respond?" in Steven H. Sandell (ed.), *The Problem Isn't Age: Work and Older Americans* (New York: Praeger, 1987), pp. 192–205.

Fiske, Edward B., "M.I.T. Widens Engineering Training," *New York Times*, September 8, 1987, pp. 1, 8.

Flaim, Paul O., and Ellen Sehgal, "Displaced Workers of 1979–83: How Well Have They Fared?" *Monthly Labor Review* 108, no. 6 (June 1985): 3–16.

Flaim, Paul O., and Ellen Sehgal, "Reemployment and Earnings," in Paul D.

Staudohar and Holly E. Brown (eds.), *Deindustrialization and Plant Closure* (Lexington, Mass.: Lexington Books, 1987), pp. 101–130.

Flamm, Kenneth, "The Changing Patterns of Industrial Robot Use," in Richard M. Cyert and David C. Mowery (eds.), *The Impact of Technological Change on Employment and Economic Growth* (New York: Ballinger, 1988), pp. 267–328.

Flynn, Patricia M., *Facilitating Technological Change: The Human Resource Challenge* (New York: Ballinger, 1988).

Flynn, Patricia M., "Introducing New Technology into the Workplace: The Dynamics of Technological and Organizational Change," *Investing in People: A Strategy to Address America's Workforce Crisis, Background Papers* (Washington, D.C.: Commission on Workforce Quality and Labor Market Efficiency, U.S. Department of Labor, 1989), pp. 411–456.

Flynn, Patricia M.,"Production Life Cycles and Their Implications for Education and Training," Report Prepared for National Institute of Education, Washington, D.C., February, 1984.

Fombrum, Charles, Noel M. Tichy, and Mary Ann Devanna (eds.), *Strategic Human Resource Management* (New York: Wiley, 1984).

Ford, David, and Chris Ryan, "Taking Technology to Market," *Harvard Business Review* 59 (March/April 1981): 117–126.

Ford Foundation, *The Common Good* (New York: Ford Foundation, 1989).

Ford Motor Company, *Asset Is the Answer*, n.d..

Form, William, "On the Degradation of Skills," *Annual Review of Sociology* 13 (1987): 29–47.

Form, William, Robert L. Kaufman, Toby L. Parcel, and Michael Wallace, "The Impact of Technology on Work Organization and Work Outcomes," in George Farkas and Paula England (eds.), *Industries, Firms, and Jobs: Sociological and Economic Approaches* (New York: Plenum, 1988).

Foster, Richard N., "A Call for Vision in Managing Technology," *Business Week*, May 24, 1982, pp. 24, 26, 28, & 33.

Foulkes, Fred K., *Personnel Policies in Large Nonunion Companies* (Englewood Cliffs, N.J.: Prentice Hall, 1980).

Fraker, Thomas, and Rebecca Maynard, "The Adequacy of Group Designs for Evaluations of Employer Related Programs," *Journal of Human Resources* 22, no. 2 (Spring 1987): 194–227.

Francis, Arthur, *New Technology at Work* (New York: Oxford University Press, 1986).

Freedman, Audrey, *The New Look in Wage Policy and Employee Relations*, Report No. 865 (New York: The Conference Board, 1985).

Freedman, Audrey, "Rising Use of Part-time and Temporary Workers: Who Benefits and Who Loses?" Testimony Before the Committee on Government Operations, U.S. House of Representatives (Washington, D.C.: Government Printing Office, 1988), p. 35.

Freedman, Marcia, "The Youth Labor Market," in Paul E. Barton and Bryna Shore Frazer, *Between Two Worlds—Youth Transition from School to Work* (Washington, D.C.: U.S. Government Printing Office, 1976).

Freeman, Richard B., "A Cobweb Model of the Supply and Starting Salary of New Engineers," *Industrial and Labor Relations Review* 30 (1976): 236–248.

Freeman, Richard B., *The Market for College-Trained Manpower* (Cambridge, Mass.: Harvard University Press, 1971).

Freeman, Richard B., *The Overeducated American* (New York: Academic Press, 1976).

Freeman, Richard B., and John A. Hansen, "Forecasting the Changing Market for College-Trained Workers," in Robert E. Taylor, Howard Rosen, and Frank C. Pratzner (eds.), *Responsiveness of Training Institutions to Changing Labor Market Demands* (Columbus, Ohio: National Center for Research in Vocational Education, Ohio State University, 1983), pp. 79–99.

Freeman, Richard B., and James L. Medoff, "The Two Faces of Unionism," *The Public Interest* number 57 (Fall 1979): 69–93.

Freeman, Richard B., and James L. Medoff, *What Do Unions Do?* (New York: Basic Books, 1984).

Fromstein, Mitchell, personal communication, 1988.

Fullerton, Howard N., "Labor Force Projections: 1986 to 2000," in *Projections 2000*, BLS Bulletin 2302 (Washington, D.C.: Government Printing Office, 1988), pp. 17–27.

Garfinkle, Stuart H., "The Outcome of a Spell of Unemployment," *Monthly Labor Review*, January 1977, pp. 54–57.

Gilmore, Thomas, and Larry Hirschhorn, "Management Challenges Under Conditions of Retrenchment," *Human Resource Management* 22, no. 4 (Winter 1983): 341–358.

Ginzberg, Eli, "The Job Problem," *Scientific American* 237, no. 5 (November 1977): 43–51.

Ginzberg, Eli, "Life Without Work: Does It Make Sense?" in Herbert S. Parnes (ed.), *Policy Issues in Work and Retirement* (Kalamazoo, Mich.: Upjohn Institute for Employment Research, 1983), pp. 29–37.

Gittell, Ross, *A Critical Analysis of Local Initiatives in Economic Revitalization*, unpublished Ph.D. thesis, Harvard University, 1989.

Glover, Robert, "American Apprenticeship and Disadvantaged Youth," in Robert E. Taylor, Howard Rosen, and Frank C. Pratzner (eds.), *Job Training for Youth* (Columbus, Ohio: National Center for Research in Vocational Education, Ohio State University, 1982), pp. 165–201.

Goldstein, Harold, "The Accuracy and Utilization of Occupational Forecasts," in Robert E. Taylor, Howard Rosen, and Frank C. Pratzner (eds.), *Responsiveness of Training Institutions to Changing Labor Market Demands* (Columbus, Ohio: National Center for Research in Vocational Education, Ohio State University, 1983), pp. 39–70.

Goldstein, Harold, and Bryna Shore Fraser, "Training for Work in the Computer Age: How Workers Who Use Computers Get Their Training" (Washington, D.C.: National Commission for Employment Policy, Research Report RR-85-09, 1985).

Gollub, James O., "Increasing Employment Opportunities for Older Workers: Emerging State and Local Initiatives," in Steven H. Sandell (ed.), *The Problem Isn't Age: Work and Older Americans* (New York: Praeger, 1987), pp. 143–164.

Gordon, David M., Richard Edwards, and Michael Reich, *Segmented Work, Divided Workers: The Historical Transformation of Labor in the United States* (New York: Cambridge University Press, 1982).

Gordon, Robert Aaron, and James Edwin Howell, *Higher Education for Business* (New York: Columbia University Press, 1959).

Gordus, Jeanne Prial, Paul Jarley, and Louis A. Ferman, *Plant Closings and Economic Dislocation* (Kalamazoo, Mich.: Upjohn Institute for Employment Research, 1981).

Granovetter, Mark S., *Getting a Job: A Study of Contacts and Careers* (Cambridge, Mass.: Harvard University Press, 1974).

Green, Ernest, "Apprenticeship: A Potential Weapon Against Minority Youth Unemployment," in Eli Ginzberg (ed.), *From School to Work: Improving the Transition* (Washington, D.C.: Government Printing Office, 1977), pp. 201–226.

Greenbaum, Joan, *In the Name of Efficiency: A Study of Change in Data Processing Work* (Philadelphia: Temple University Press, 1979).

Greenhalgh, Leonard, "Managing the Job Insecurity Crisis," *Human Resource Management* 22, no. 4 (Winter 1983): 431–444.

Greenhalgh, Leonard, Anne T. Lawrence, and Robert I. Sutton, "Determinants of Work Force Reduction Strategies in Declining Organizations," *Academy of Management Review* 13, no. 2 (April 1988): 241–254.

Grubb, Norton W., "The Bandwagon Once More: Vocational Preparation for High Technology Occupations," *Harvard Educational Review* 54, no. 4 (November 1984): 429–451.

Guth, William D., "Productivity and Corporate Strategy," in Arthur P. Brief (ed.), *Productivity Research in the Behavioral and Social Sciences* (New York: Praeger, 1984).

Hackman, J. Richard, Edward Lawler III, and Lyman W. Porter, *Perspectives on Organizational Behavior* (New York: McGraw-Hill, 1983).

Hahn, Andrew, and Robert Lerman, *What Works in Youth Employment Policy?* (Washington, D.C.: Committee on New American Realities, National Planning Association, 1985).

Hall, Douglas T., "Breaking Career Routines: Midcareer Choice and Identity Development," in Douglas T. Hall and Associates, *Career Development in Organizations* (San Francisco: Jossey-Bass, 1986), pp. 120–159.

Hall, Douglas T., *Careers in Organizations* (Glenview, Ill.: Scott, Foresman, 1976).

Hall, Douglas T., "Dilemmas in Linking Succession Planning to Individual Executive Learning," *Human Resource Management* 25, no. 2 (Summer 1986): 235–265.

Hall, Douglas T., "Human Resource Development and Organizational Effectiveness," in Charles Fombrun, Noel M. Tichy, and Mary Ann Devanna (eds.), *Strategic Human Resource Management* (New York: Wiley, 1984).

Hall, Douglas T., "A Theoretical Model of Career Subidentity Development in Organizational Settings," *Organizational Behavior and Human Performance* 6, no. 1 (January 1971): 50–56.

Hall, Douglas T., and James G. Goodale, *Human Resource Management: Strategy, Design, and Implementation* (Glenview, Ill.: Scott, Foresman, 1986).

Hall, Douglas T., and Roger Mansfield, "Organizational and Individual Response to External Stress," *Administrative Science Quarterly* 16, no. 4 (December 1971): 533–547.

Hall, Douglas T., and Benjamin Schneider, *Organizational Climates and Careers: The Work Lives of Priests* (New York: Academic Press, 1973).

Hambrick, Donald C., and Richard A. D'Aveni, "Large Corporate Failures as Downward Spirals," *Administrative Science Quarterly* 33, no. 1 (March 1988): 1–33.

Hamermesh, Daniel S., "What Do We Know About Worker Displacement in the U.S.?" *Industrial Relations* 28, no. 1 (Winter 1989): 51–59.

Hamilton, Stephen F., *Adolescent Problem Behavior in the United States and the Federal Republic of Germany: Implications for Prevention* (Washington, D.C.: Grant Foundation Project on Youth and the Future, 1987).

Hamilton, Stephen F., "Work and Maturity: Occupational Socialization of Non-College Youth in the United States and West Germany," *Research in the Sociology of Education and Socialization* 7 (1987): 283–312.

Hanami, Tadashi A., "Japan," in Edward Yemin (ed.), *Workforce Reductions and Undertakings* (Geneva: International Labor Office, 1982), pp. 174–185.

Harrington, Paul E., Marilyn Boyle, and Andrew M. Sum, *High Technology Careers in Massachusetts* (Boston: Massachusetts Division of Employment Security, 1987).

Harrington, Paul E., and Andrew M. Sum, "College Survival and Economic Prosperity: Is There a Connection?" *Thrust: The Journal for Employment and Training Professionals* 8, no. 1–2 (1987): 1–30.

Harrington, Paul E., and Andrew M. Sum, "Whatever Happened to the College Enrollment Crisis?" *Academe* 74, no. 5, (September–October 1988): 17–22.

Harris, Louis, *Inside America* (New York: Vintage, 1987).

Harrison, Bennett, and Barry Bluestone, *The Great U-Turn: Corporate Restructuring and the Polarizing of America* (New York: Basic Books, 1988).

Harrison, Bennett, Chris Tilly, and Barry Bluestone, "Wage Inequality Takes a Great U-Turn," *Challenge* 29, no. 1 (March–April 1986): 26–32.

Hartman, Paul T., *Collective Bargaining and Productivity* (Berkeley: University of California Press, 1973).

Hay Group, *Achieving Competitive Advantage Through the Effective Management of People, 1986–87* (Wellesley, Mass.: Center for Management Research, Hay Group, 1987).

Hayes, Robert H., "Strategic Planning—Forward or Reverse?" *Harvard Business Review* 63 (November–December 1985): 111–119.

Hayes, Robert H., and William J. Abernathy, "Managing Our Way to Decline," *Harvard Business Review* (July–August 1980): 67–77.

Hayes, Robert H., and Ramchandran Jaikumar, "Manufacturing's Crisis: New Technologies, Old Organizations," *Harvard Business Review* 66 (September–October 1988): 77–85.

Hayes, Robert H., and Steven C. Wheelwright, "The Dynamics of Process-Product Life Cycles," *Harvard Business Review* 57 (March/April, 1979): 127–136.

Hayes, Robert H., and Steven C. Wheelwright, "Link Manufacturing Process and Product Life Cycles," *Harvard Business Review* 57 (January/February, 1979): 133–140.

Hecksher, Charles, *The New Unionism* (New York: Basic Books, 1988).

Hector, Gary, "Yes, You Can Manage Long Term," *Fortune* 118 (July–Sept. 1988): 64–76.

Herz, Diane E., "Employment Characteristics of Older Women, 1987," *Monthly Labor Review*, September 1988, pp. 3–12.

Herz, Diane E., "Employment in Perspective: Women in the Labor Force," Bureau of Labor Statistics, Report 758, Washington, D.C., 1988.

Hills, Stephen M., "How Craftsmen Learn Their Skills: A Longitudinal Analysis," in Robert E. Taylor, Howard Rosen, and Frank C. Pratzner (eds.), *Job Training for Youth* (Columbus, Ohio: National Center for Research in Vocational Education, Ohio State University, 1982), pp. 201–239.

Hirsch, Paul, *Pack Your Own Parachute: How to Survive Mergers, Takeovers, and Other Corporate Disasters* (Reading, Mass.: Addison-Wesley, 1987).

Hirsch, Seev, "The United States Electronics Industry in International Trade," in Louis T. Wells, Jr. (ed.), *The Product Life Cycle and International Trade* (Cambridge, Mass.: Harvard University Press, 1972).

Hirschhorn, Larry, *Beyond Mechanization: Work and Technology in a Post-industrial Age* (Cambridge, Mass.: MIT Press, 1984).

Hooks, Gregory, "The Policy Response to Factory Closings: A Comparison of the

United States, Sweden, and France," *Annuals of the American Academy of Political and Social Science*, no. 475, 1984, pp. 110–124.

Hogarth, Jeanne M., "Accepting an Early Retirement Bonus," *Journal of Human Resources* 23, no. 1 (Winter 1988): 21–33.

Holland, Daniel M., and Stewart C. Myers, "Profitability and Capital Costs for Manufacturing Corporations and All Nonfinancial Corporations," *American Economic Review* 70 (1980): 320–325.

Hollenbeck, Kevin, Frank C. Pratzner, and Howard Rosen (eds.), *Displaced Workers: Implications for Educational and Training Institutions* (Columbus, Ohio: National Center for Research in Vocational Education, Ohio State University, 1984).

Horvath, Francis W., "The Pulse of Economic Change: Displaced Workers of 1981–85," *Monthly Labor Review* 110 (June 1987): 3–12.

Howard, Ann, "College Experiences and Managerial Performance," *Journal of Applied Psychology* 71 (1986): 530–552.

Howard, Ann, and Douglas W. Bray, *Managerial Lives in Transition: Advancing Age and Changing Times* (New York: Guilford, 1988).

Howland, Marie, and George E. Peterson, "Labor Market Conditions and the Reemployment of Displaced Workers," *Industrial and Labor Relations Review* 42 (1988): 109–122.

Iacobelli, John L., and S. Ray Schultz, "Earnings Impact of Employment and Training Programs for Young Men," *Growth and Change* 10, no. 4 (1979): 32–37.

Iams, Howard M., "Employment of Retired-Worker Women," *Social Security Bulletin* 49, no. 3 (March 1986): 5–13.

Ingrassia, Lawrence, "Recession Haunts City That Believed It Was Saved by High-Tech," *Wall Street Journal*, January 25, 1990, pp. 1, A-8.

Jacoby, Sanford M., *Employing Bureaucracy: Managers, Unions, and the Transformation of Work in American Industry* (New York: Columbia University Press, 1985).

Jaikumar, Ramchandran, "Postindustrial Manufacturing," *Harvard Business Review* 64, no. 6 (November–December 1986): 69–76.

Jick, Todd D., "As the Ax Falls: Budget Cuts and the Experience of Stress in Organizations," in Terry A. Beehr and Rabi S. Bhagat (eds.), *Human Stress and Cognition in Organizations: An Integrated Perspective* (New York: Wiley, 1985), pp. 83–113.

Job, Barbara Cottman, "How Likely Are Individuals to Enter the Labor Force?" *Monthly Labor Review*, September 1979, pp. 28–34.

Johnson, Clifford, and Andrew M. Sum, *Declining Earnings of Young Men: Their Relation to Poverty, Teen Pregnancy, and Family Formation* (Washington, D.C.: Children's Defense Fund, 1987).

Johnson, Clifford, Andrew M. Sum, and James Weill, *Vanishing Dreams: The Growing Economic Plight of America's Young Families* (Washington, D.C.: Children's Defense Fund, 1988).

Johnson, Leonard, and Alan Frohman, "Identifying and Closing the Gap in the Middle of Organizations," *Academy of Management Executive* 3 (May 1989).

Johnson, Terry R., Katherine P. Dickinson, and Richard W. West, "Older Workers, Job Displacement, and the Employment Service," in Steven H. Sandell (ed.), *The Problem Isn't Age: Work and Older Americans* (New York: Praeger, 1987), pp. 100–119.

Johnston, Joseph S., Jr., Stanley T. Burns, David M. Butler, Marcie Schorr Hirsch, Thomas B. Jones, Alan M. Kantrow, Kathryn Mohrman, Roger B. Smith, and Michael

Useem, *Educating Managers: Executive Effectiveness Through Liberal Learning* (San Francisco: Jossey-Bass, 1986).

Johnston, Joseph S., Jr., Susan Shaman, and Robert Zemsky, *Unfinished Design: The Humanities and Social Sciences in Undergraduate Engineering Education* (Washington, D.C.: Association of American Colleges, 1988).

Johnston, William B., and Arnold E. Packer, *Workforce 2000: Work and Workers for the 21st Century* (Indianapolis: Hudson Institute, 1987).

Jondrow, Jim, Frank Brechling, and Alan Marcus, "Older Workers in the Market for Part-Time Employment," in Steven H. Sandell (ed.), *The Problem Isn't Age: Work and Older Americans* (New York: Praeger, 1987).

Jones, Calvin C., Susan Campbell, and Penny A. Sebring, *Four Years After High School: A Capsule Description of 1980 Seniors*, Report Prepared for the Center for Statistics (Washington, D.C.: U.S. Department of Education, Government Printing Office, 1986).

JTPA Advisory Committee, *Working Capital* (Washington, D.C.: Government Printing Office, 1989).

Kalleberg, Arne L., and Ivar Berg, *Work and Industry: Structures, Markets, and Processes* (New York: Plenum, 1987).

Kanter, Donald L., and Philip H. Mirvis, *Cynicism at Work* (San Francisco: Jossey-Bass, 1989).

Kanter, Rosabeth Moss, *The Change Masters: Innovation for Productivity in the American Corporation* (New York: Simon & Schuster, 1983).

Kanter, Rosabeth Moss, "Variations in Managerial Career Structures in High Technology Firms: The Impact of Organizational Characteristics on Internal Labor Market Patterns," in Paul Osterman (ed.), *Internal Labor Markets* (Cambridge, Mass.: MIT Press, 1984), pp. 109–131.

Kaplan, Robert E., William H. Drath, and Joan Kofodimos, *High Hurdles: The Challenge of Executive Self-Development* (Greensboro, N.C.: Center for Creative Leadership, Technical Report No. 25, April 1985).

Kasarda, John, "Contemporary U.S. Migration and Urban Demographic-Job Opportunity Mismatches," Paper Presented to the Joint Economic Committee, Subcommittee on Economic Resources, Competitiveness, and Security Economics, September 1986.

Kasarda, John, "Urban Change and Minority Opportunities," in Paul Peterson (ed.), *The New Urban Reality* (Washington, D.C.: Brookings Institution, 1985).

Kassalow, Everett M., "Employee Training and Development: A Joint Union-Management Response to Structural and Technological Change," *Proceedings of the Industrial Relations Research Association* (Madison, Wisc.: Industrial Relations Research Association, December 1987), pp. 107–117.

Katz, Harry, *Shifting Gears* (Cambridge, Mass.: MIT Press, 1985).

Kaufman, H.G., *Professionals in Search of Work: Coping with the Stress of Job Loss and Underemployment* (New York: Wiley, 1982).

Kearns, David T., and Denis P. Doyle, *Winning the Brain Race: A Bold Plan to Make Our Schools Competitive* (San Francisco: Institute for Contemporary Studies, 1988).

Kelley, Maryellen R., "Programmable Automation and the Skill Question: A Reinterpretation of the Cross-National Evidence," *Human Systems Management* 6, no. 3 (1986): 223–241.

Kelley, Maryellen R., and Harvey Brooks, "The State of Computerized Automation in U.S. Manufacturing'' (Cambridge, Mass.: Harvard University, John F. Kennedy School of Government, 1988).

Kelley, Maryellen, and Bennett Harrison, "The Subcontracting Behavior of Single vs. Multi-Plant Enterprises in U.S. Manufacturing: Implications for Economic Development," *World Development* (forthcoming).

Kennedy, Kim, and Rachael Winkeller, *Major Findings and Recommendations Regarding the Feasibility of a Part-Time Employment Demonstration Program for AFDC Recipients and CETA-Eligible Older Workers* (Boston: Policy and Evaluation Division, Department of Manpower Development, November 1980).

Kimberly, John R., and Robert E. Quinn (eds.), *Managing Organizational Transitions* (Homewood, Ill.: Irwin, 1984).

Kingson, Eric R., "The Health of Very Early Retirees," *Social Security Bulletin* 45 (September 1982): 3–9.

Kirsch, Irwin S., and Ann Jungeblut, *Literacy: Profiles of America's Young Adults* (Princeton, N.J.: Educational Testing Service, National Assessment of Educational Progress, 1986).

Kletzer, Lori G., "Determinants of the Reemployment Probabilities of Displaced Workers: Do High Wage Workers Have Longer Durations of Unemployment?" mimeo, Williams College, 1987.

Knowlton, Winthrop, "One's Own Place: Reflections on Community Revitalization in America," *21st Congress of the World Management Council*, mimeo, September 1989, pp. 21–23.

Kochan, Thomas A., "Industrial Relations Research: An Agenda for the 1980s," *Monthly Labor Review*, September 1980, pp. 20–25.

Kochan, Thomas A., and Harry C. Katz, "Collective Bargaining, Work Organization and Worker Participation: The Return to Plant Level Bargaining," *Labor Law Journal* 34 (August 1983): 524–530.

Kochan, Thomas A., John P. MacDuffie, and Paul Osterman, "Employment Security at DEC: Sustaining Values Amid Environmental Change," *Human Resource Management* 27, no. 2 (Summer 1988): 121–143.

Kochan, Thomas A., Harry C. Katz, and Robert B. McKersie, *The Transformation of American Industrial Relations* (New York: Basic Books, 1986).

Kochan, Thomas A., Harry C. Katz, and Nancy Mower, *Worker Participation and American Unions: Threat or Opportunity?* (Kalamazoo, Mich.: Upjohn Institute for Employment Research, 1984).

Kolberg, William (ed.), *The Dislocated Worker: Preparing America's Workforce for New Jobs* (Cabin John, Md.: Seven Locks Press, 1984).

Kotlikoff, Laurence J., and Daniel E. Smith, *Pensions in the American Economy* (Chicago: University of Chicago Press, 1983).

Kraft, Philip, *Programmers and Managers: The Routinization of Programming in the United States* (New York: Springer-Verlag, 1977).

Krumme, Gunter, and Roger Hayter, "Implications of Corporate Strategies and Product Cycle Adjustments for Regional Employment Changes," in Lyndhurst Collins and David Walker (eds.), *Location Dynamics of Manufacturing Activities* (New York: Wiley, 1975), pp. 325–356.

Kruse, Douglas L., "International Trade and the Labor Market Experience of Displaced Workers," *Industrial and Labor Relations Review* 41, no. 3 (April 1988): 402–417.

Lalonde, Robert J., "Evaluating the Econometric Evaluations of Training Programs with Experimental Data," *American Economic Review* 76, no. 4 (September 1986): 604–20.

Lawler, Edward E., III, "Creating High-Involvement Work Organizations," in J. Richard Hackman, Edward E. Lawler, III, and Lyman W. Porter, *Perspectives on Organizational Behavior* (New York: McGraw-Hill, 1983).

Lawler, Edward E., III, *Pay and Organizational Effectiveness: A Psychological View* (New York: McGraw-Hill, 1971).

Lawrence, Paul R., "How to Deal with Resistance to Change," *Harvard Business Review* 32 (May–June 1954).

Lawrence, Robert Z., *Can America Compete?* (Washington, D.C.: Brookings Institution, 1984).

Lawrence, Robert Z., and Robert E. Litan, "Living with the Trade Deficit: Adjustment Strategies to Preserve Free Trade," *Brookings Review* 4 (1985): 10.

Lawrence, Robert Z., and Charles L. Schultze, *Barriers to European Growth* (Washington, D.C.: Brookings Institution, 1987).

Leonard, Jonathan S., "In the Right Place at the Wrong Time: The Extent of Frictional and Structural Unemployment," in Kevin Lang and Jonathan Leonard (eds.), *Unemployment and the Structure of Labor Markets* (New York: Basil Blackwell, 1987), pp. 141–163.

Levin, Henry M., and Russell W. Rumberger, "Education and Training Needs for Using Computers in Small Businesses," *Education Evaluation and Policy Analysis* 8 (Winter 1986): 423–434.

Levin, Henry M., and Russell W. Rumberger, "Educational Requirements for New Technologies: Visions, Possibilities, and Current Realities," *Educational Policy* 1 (1987): 333–354.

Levitan, Sar A., and Frank Gallo, *A Second Chance: Training for Jobs*, (Kalamazoo, Mich.: Upjohn Institute for Employment Research, 1988).

Levitan, Sar, Garth L. Mangum, and F. Ray Marshall, *Human Resources and Labor Markets*, 3rd ed. (New York: Harper & Row, 1982).

Levitan, Sar A., and Isaac Shapiro, *Working but Poor: America's Contradiction* (Baltimore: Johns Hopkins University Press, 1987).

Levitt, Theodore, "Exploit the Product Life Cycle," *Harvard Business Review* 43 (November–December 1965): 81–94.

Leventman, Paula Goldman, *Professionals Out of Work* (New York: Free Press, 1981).

Levy, Frank, *Dollars and Dreams* (New York: Norton, 1988).

Liker, Jeffrey, David B. Roitman, and Ethel Roskies, "Changing Everything at Once: Worklife and Technological Change," *Sloan Management Review* 28 (Summer 1987): 29–46.

Likert, Rensis, *The Human Organization* (New York: McGraw-Hill, 1967).

Lispet, Seymour Martin, and William Schneider, *The Confidence Gap: Business, Labor, and Government in the Public Mind* (New York: Free Press, 1983).

Louis, Meryl, "The Gap in Management Education," in Jagdish Sheth (ed.), *Developing Managers for a Competitive Environment* (San Francisco: Jossey-Bass, forthcoming).

Louis Harris and Associates, Inc., *Aging in the Eighties* (New York: National Council on Aging, 1981).

Louis Harris and Associates, Inc., *Problems Facing Elderly Americans Living Alone*, report prepared for the Commonwealth Fund Commission on Elderly People Living Alone, New York, 1986.

Loveman, Gary, Michael J. Piore, and Werner Sengenberger. "The Evolving Role of Small Business in Industrialized Economies and Some Implications for Employment and Training," in Katharine Abraham and Robert B. McKersie (eds.), *New Developments in the Labor Market* (Cambridge, Mass.: MIT Press, forthcoming).

Malecki, Edward J., "High Technology Sectors and Local Economic Development," in Edward M. Bergman (ed.), *Local Economies in Transition* (Durham, N.C.: Duke University Press, 1986), pp. 129–142.

Malecki, Edward J., "Technology and Regional Development: A Survey," *International Regional Science Review* 8, no. 2 (1983): 89–125.

Mangum Steven L., and Arvil V. Adams, "The Labor Market Impacts of Post-School Occupational Training for Young Men," in *Growth and Change* 18, no. 4 (Fall 1987): 57–73.

Mansfield, Edwin, *The Economics of Technological Change* (New York: Norton, 1968).

Markey, James P., "The Labor Market Problems of Today's High School Dropouts," *Monthly Labor Review*, June 1988, pp. 36–43.

Marshall, Ray, and Robert Glover, *Training and Entry into Union Construction* (Washington, D.C.: U.S. Department of Labor, R&D Monograph No. 34, Government Printing Office, 1975).

Martin, Philip, *Labor Displacement and Public Policy* (Lexington, Mass.: Lexington Books, 1983).

Massachusetts Department of Employment and Training, *Section 30 Training Participation and Outcomes*, Research Report, Boston, June 1989.

Maxfield, Linda Drazga, "Income of New Retired Workers by Age at First Benefit Receipt: Findings from the New Beneficiary Survey," *Social Security Bulletin* 48, no. 7 (July 1985): 7–26.

Mayo, Elton, *The Human Problems of Industrial Civilization* (New York: Macmillan, 1933).

McCune, Joseph T., Richard W. Beatty, and Raymond V. Montagno, "Downsizing: Practices in Manufacturing Firms," *Human Resource Management* 27, no. 2 (Summer 1988): 145–161.

McGregor, Douglas M., *The Human Side of Enterprise* (New York: McGraw-Hill, 1960).

McKenzie, Richard B., *Competing Visions: The Political Conflict Over America's Economic Future* (Washington, D.C.: Cato Institute, 1985).

Meier, Elizabeth L., "Managing an Older Work Force," in Michael E. Borus, Herbert S. Parnes, Steven H. Sandell, and Bert Seidman, (eds.), *The Older Worker* (Madison, Wisc.: Industrial Relations Research Association, 1988), pp. 167–189.

Mellor, Earl F., "Shift Work and Flextime: How Prevalent Are They?" *Monthly Labor Review*, November 1986, pp. 14–21.

Meyer, Robert, and David Wise, "High School Preparation and Early Labor Market Experience," in Richard B. Freeman and David A. Wise, (eds.), *The Youth Labor Market Problem: Its Nature, Causes, and Consequences* (Chicago: University of Chicago Press, 1982), pp. 277–347.

Milkman, Ruth, "Technological Change and Job Security: A Case Study from the Auto Industry," unpublished paper, Department of Sociology, CUNY Graduate Center, April 1988.

Mirkin, Barry Alan, "Early Retirement as a Labor Force Policy: An International Overview," *Monthly Labor Review*, March 1987, pp. 19–33.

Mitchell, Olivia S., "Pensions and Older Workers," in Michael E. Borus, Herbert

S. Parnes, Steven H. Sandell, and Bert Seidman (eds.), *The Older Worker* (Madison, Wisc.: Industrial Relations Research Association, 1988), pp. 151–166.

Mitchell, Olivia S., and Gary S. Fields, "The Effects of Pensions and Earnings on Retirement: A Review Essay," in *Research in Labor Economics*, vol 5 (Greenwich, Conn.: JAI Press, 1982), pp. 115–155.

Monroe, Sylvester, "Blacks in Britain: Grim Lives, Grimmer Prospects," *Newsweek*, January 4, 1988, p. 32.

Morrison, Malcolm H., "The Aging of the U.S. Population: Human Resource Implications," *Monthly Labor Review*, May 1983, pp. 13–19.

Moskal, Brian S., "Tomorrow's Best Managers," *Industry Week*, July 19, 1988, pp. 32–34.

Mowery, David C., "The Diffusion of New Manufacturing Technologies," in Richard M. Cyert and David C. Mowery (eds.), *The Impact of Technological Change on Employment and Economic Growth* (New York: Ballinger, 1988).

Muro, Mark, "Granny Is Soda Jerk of '80s as Firms Seek to Fill Jobs Void," *Boston Sunday Globe*, November 27, 1988, p. A23.

Murphy, Kevin, and Finis Welch, "Wage Premiums for College Graduates: Recent Growth and Possible Explanations," *Educational Researcher* (1989): 17–26.

Murray, Victor V., and Todd D. Jick, "Taking Stock of Organizational Decline Management: Some Issues and Illustrations from an Empirical Study," *Journal of Management* 11 (1985): 111–123.

Myers, Robert J., "Why Do People Retire from Work Early?" *Social Security Bulletin* 45, no. 9 (September 1982): 10–14.

National Alliance of Business, *The Fourth R* (Washington D.C.: National Alliance of Business, 1987).

National Commission for Employment Policy, *The Job Training Partnership Act* (Washington, D.C.: Government Printing Office, September 1987).

National Commission for Employment Policy, *Labor Market Problems of Older Workers* (Washington, D.C.: Government Printing Office, January 1987).

National Commission for Employment Policy, *Older Worker Employment Comes of Age: Practice and Potential* (Washington, D.C.: Government Printing Office, 1984).

National Commission on Employment and Unemployment Statistics, *Counting the Labor Force* (Washington, D.C.: Government Printing Office, 1979).

National Commission on Technology, Automation and Economic Progress, *Technology and the American Economy* (Washington, D.C.: National Commission on Technology, Automation and Economic Progress, 1966).

National Planning Association, *Preparing for Change: Workforce Excellence in a Turbulent Economy*, National Planning Association Report No. 245 (Washington, D.C.: National Planning Association, 1990).

National Research Council, Center for the Effective Implementation of Advanced Manufacturing Technology, Manufacturing Studies Board, and the Commission on Engineering and Technical Systems, *Human Resource Practices for Implementing Advanced Manufacturing Technology* (Washington, D.C.: National Academy Press, 1986).

Nelson, Richard R., and Victor D. Norman, "Technological Change and Factor Mix over the Product Cycle," *Journal of Development Economics* 4 (1977): 3–24.

Nelson, Richard R., and Sidney G. Winter, *An Evolutionary Theory of Economic Change* (Cambridge, Mass.: Harvard University Press, 1982),

Newman, Katherine S., *Falling from Grace: The Experience of Downward Mobility in the American Middle Class* (New York: Vintage, 1988).

Nulty, Peter, "Pushed Out at 45—Now What?" *Fortune* 115, no. 5 (1987): 26–30.

Operation ABLE of Greater Boston, *1987 Annual Report*, Boston, 1988.

Opinion Research Corporation, *Changing Employee Values in America: Strategic Planning for Human Resources* (Princeton, N.J.: Opinion Research Corporation, Employee Relations Groups Professional Staff, 1981).

Osterman, Paul, *Employment Futures: Reorganization, Dislocation and Public Policy* (New York: Oxford University Press, 1988).

Osterman, Paul, "The Impact of Computers on the Employment of Clerks and Managers," *Industrial and Labor Relations Review* 39 (1986): 175–186.

Osterman, Paul, "White Collar Internal Labor Markets," in Paul Osterman (ed.), *Internal Labor Markets* (Cambridge, Mass.: MIT Press, 1984), pp. 163–189.

Ouchi, William G., and Raymond L. Price, "Hierarchies, Clans, and Theory z: A New Perspective on Organizational Development," in J. Richard Hackman, Edward Lawler III, and Lyman W. Porter (eds.), *Perspectives on Organizational Behavior* (New York: McGraw-Hill, 1983).

Pannell, Patricia F., "Occupational Education and Training: Goals and Performance," in Peter B. Doeringer and Bruce Vermeulen (eds.), *Jobs and Training: Vocational Policy and the Labor Market* (Boston: Martinus Nijhoff Publishing, 1981), pp. 50–71.

Parnell, Dale, *The Neglected Majority* (Washington, D.C.: Community College Press, 1985).

Parnes, Herbert S., Joan E. Crowley, R. Jean Haurin, Lawrence J. Less, William R. Morgan, Frank L. Mott, and Gilbert Nestel, *Retirement Among American Men* (Lexington, Mass.: Heath, 1985).

Parnes, Herbert S. (ed.), "Introduction and Overview," in *Policy Issues in Work and Retirement* (Kalamazoo, Mich.: Upjohn Institute for Employment Research, 1983).

Parnes, Herbert S., "The Retirement Decision," in Michael E. Borus, Herbert S. Parnes, Steven H. Sandell, Bert Seidman (eds.), *The Older Worker* (Madison, Wisc.: Industrial Relations Research Association, 1988) pp. 115–150.

Parnes, Herbert S., Mary G. Gagen, and Randall H. King, "Job Loss Among Long Service Workers," in Herbert S. Parnes, *Work and Retirement: A Longitudinal Study of Men* (Cambridge, Mass.: MIT Press, 1981).

Parnes, Herbert S., and Randall H. King, "Middle Aged Job Losers," *Industrial Gerontology* 4, no. 2 (Spring 1977): 77–95.

Parnes, Herbert S., and Lawrence J. Less, "Economic Well-Being in Retirement," in Herbert S. Parnes, Joan E. Crowley, R. Jean Haurin, Lawrence J. Less, William R. Morgan, Frank L. Mott, and Gilbert Nestel, *Retirement Among American Men* (Lexington, Mass.: Heath, 1985), pp. 91–118.

Parnes, Herbert S., and Gilbert Nestel, "Middle-Aged Job Changers," in *The Pre-Retirement Years*, vol. 4, U.S. Department of Labor, R&D Monograph 15 (Washington, D.C.: Government Printing Office, 1975).

Paul, Carolyn, "Work Alternatives for Older Americans: A Management Perspective," in Steven H. Sandell (ed.), *The Problem Isn't Age: Work and Older Americans* (New York: Praeger, 1987), pp. 165–176.

Personick, Valerie A., "Industry Output and Employment Through the End of the Century," *Monthly Labor Review* 110, no. 9 (September 1987): 30–45.

Personick, Valerie A., "Industry Output and Employment Through the End of the Century," in *Projections 2000*, BLS Bulletin 2302 (Washington, D.C.: Government Printing Office, 1988), pp. 28–43.

Peters Thomas J., and Robert H. Waterman Jr., *In Search of Excellence* (New York: Harper & Row, 1982).

Pierson, Frank C., *The Education of American Businessmen: A Study of*

University-College Programs in Business Administration (New York: McGraw-Hill, 1959).

Piore, Michael J., and Charles Sabel, *The Second Industrial Divide* (New York: Basic Books, 1984).

Podgursky, Michael, and Paul Swaim, "Duration of Joblessness Following Job Displacement," *Industrial Relations* 26 (1987): 213–226.

Podgursky, Michael, and Paul Swaim, "Job Displacement and Earnings Loss: Evidence from the Displaced Worker Survey," *Industrial and Labor Relations Review* 41, no. 1 (October 1987): 17–29.

Polivka, Anne, and Thomas Nardone, "On the Definition of Contingent Work," *Monthly Labor Review* 112, no. 12 (December 1989): 9–16.

Porter, Lyman W., and Lawrence E. McKibbin, *Management Education and Development: Drift or Thrust into the 21st Century* (New York: McGraw-Hill, 1988).

Portes, Alejandro, and Saskia Sassen-Koob, "Making It Underground: comparative Material on the Informal Sector in Western Market Economies," *American Journal of Sociology* 93, no. 53 (1987).

Pursell, Donald E., and William D. Torrence, "Age and the Job-Hunting Methods of the Unemployed," *Monthly Labor Review*, January 1979, pp. 68–69.

Quinn, Joseph F., "Job Characteristics and Early Retirement," *Industrial Relations* 17 (October 1978): 315–323.

Quinn, Joseph F., "Labor Force Participation Patterns of Older Self-Employed Workers," *Social Security Bulletin* 43, no. 3 (April 1980): 17–28.

Rapoport, Alfred, *Creating Shareholder Value: The New Standard for Business Performance* (New York: Free Press, 1986).

Rapoport, Alfred, "Executive Incentives vs. Corporate Growth," *Harvard Business Review* 56 (July–August 1978): 81–88.

Rees, Albert, "An Essay on Youth Joblessness," *Journal of Economic Literature* 24, no. 2 (June 1986): 613–628.

Reubens, Beatrice G., *Apprenticeship in Foreign Countries* (Washington, D.C.: U.S. Department of Labor R&D Monograph No. 77, Government Printing Office, 1980).

Rhine, Shirley H., *Managing Older Workers: Company Policies and Attitudes*, Report No. 860 (New York: The Conference Board, 1984).

Rich, Spencer, "The End of Upward Mobility," *Washington Post National Weekly Edition*, June 13–19, 1988, pp. 6–7.

Riche, Richard W., Daniel E. Hecker, and John V. Burgan, "High Technology Today and Tomorrow: A Small Slice of the Employment Pie," *Monthly Labor Review*, November 1983, pp. 50–58.

Roberts, Markley, "A Labor Perspective on Technological Change," in Eileen Collins and Lucretia Tanner (eds.), *American Jobs and the Changing Industrial Base* (Cambridge, Mass.: Ballinger, 1984), pp. 183–205.

Rones, Philip L., "Employment, Earnings, and Unemployment Characteristics of Older Workers," in Michael E. Borus, Herbert S. Parnes, Steven H. Sandell, and Bert Seidman (eds.), *The Older Worker* (Madison, Wisc.: Industrial Relations Research Association, 1988), pp. 21–53.

Rones, Philip L., "The Labor Market Problems of Older Workers," *Monthly Labor Review*, May 1983, pp. 3–12.

Rones, Philip L., "Older Men—The Choice Between Work and Retirement," *Monthly Labor Review*, November 1978, pp. 3–10.

Rones, Philip L., "Using the CPS to Track Retirement Trends Among Older Men," *Monthly Labor Review*, February 1985, pp. 46–49.

Roomkin, Myron J., "United States," in Myron J. Roomkin (ed.), *Managers as Employees: An International Comparison of the Changing Character of Managerial Employment* (New York: Oxford University Press, 1989).

Rosenbaum, James E., *Career Mobility in a Corporate Hierarchy* (New York: Academic Press, 1984).

Rosenbaum, James E., "Organizational Career Mobility: Promotion Chances in a Corporation During Periods of Growth and Contraction," *American Journal of Sociology* 85 (1979): 21–48.

Rosenberg, Nathan, "Factors Affecting the Diffusion of Technology," in Nathan Rosenberg, *Explorations in Economic History* (New York: Academic Press, 1972).

Rosenberg, Nathan, *Inside the Black Box: Technology and Economics* (Cambridge, England: Cambridge University Press, 1982).

Roth, Laurie Michael, "Downsizing and Restructuring Practices in Corporate America: An Interview Study," *Career Development Bulletin* 6 (New York: School of Business, Columbia University, 1986): 8–13.

Ruhm, Christopher J., "Advance Notice and Postdisplacement Joblessness," mimeo, Boston University, 1989.

Ruhm, Christopher, "Career Jobs, Bridge Employment, and Retirement," in Peter B. Doeringer (ed.), *Bridges to Retirement: Older Workers in a Changing Labor Market* (Ithaca, N.Y.: ILR Press, Cornell University, 1990).

Ruhm, Christopher J., "Do Long Tenure Workers Have Special Problems Following Job Displacement?" *Economic Development Quarterly* 3, no. 4 (1989): 320–326.

Ruhm, Christopher J., "The Economic Consequences of Labor Mobility," *Industrial and Labor Relations Review* 41, no. 1 (1987): 30–42.

Ruhm, Christopher J., "The Extent and Persistence of Unemployment Following Permanent Quits and Layoffs," mimeo, Boston University, 1987.

Ruhm, Christopher J., "The Impact of Formal and Informal Advance Notice on Postdisplacement Wages," mimeo, Boston University, 1990.

Ruhm, Christopher J., "Why Older Americans Stop Working," *The Gerontologist* 29, no. 3 (1989): 294–299.

Ruhm, Christopher J., "Career Employment and Job Stopping," *Industrial Relations* (forthcoming).

Ruhm, Christopher J., "Are Workers Permanently Scarred by Job Displacements?" *American Economic Review* (forthcoming).

Rupp, Kalman, Edward Bryant, Richard Mantovani, and Michael Rhoads, "Government Employment and Training Programs and Older Americans," in Steven H. Sandell (ed.), *The Problem Isn't Age: Work and Older Americans* (New York: Praeger, 1987), pp. 121–142.

Sabel, Charles J., Gary Herrigel, Richard Kazis, and Richard Deeg, "How To Keep Mature Industries Innovative," *Technology Review* 90, no. 3 (April 1987): 26–35.

Sandell, Steven H. (ed.), *The Problem Isn't Age: Work and Older Americans* (New York: Praeger, 1987).

Sandell, Steven H., "Public Policies and Programs Affecting Older Workers," in Michael E. Borus, Herbert S. Parnes, Steven H. Sandell, and Bert Seidman (eds.), *The Older Worker* (Madison, Wisc.: Industrial Relations Research Association, 1988), pp. 207–228.

Sandell, Steven H., and Kalman Rupp, "Who Is Served in JTPA Programs?: Patterns of Participation and Intergroup Equity" (Washington, D.C.: National Commission for Employment Policy, 1988).

Sanderson, Susan R., and Lawrence Schein, "Sizing Up the Down-Sizing Era," *Across the Board* , 23 (November 1986): 15-23.

Saporito, Bill, "Cutting Costs Without Cutting People," *Fortune*, May 25, 1987, pp. 27-32.

Sares, Ted, "Downsizing/Redeployment at a Full Employment Company," Presentation to Boston University Human Resources Policy Institute, Digital Equipment Company, Maynard, Mass, October 20, 1988.

Schiemann, William A., and Brian S. Morgan, "Managing Human Resources: Employee Discontent and Declining Productivity" (Princeton, N.J.: Opinion Research Corporation, 1982).

Schmidt, William E., "Community Colleges Emerge as Centers for Job Training," *New York Times*, June 20, 1988, pp. 1, B8.

Schumpeter, Joseph, *The Theory of Economic Development* (Cambridge, Mass.: Harvard University Press, 1934).

Shanklin, William L., and John K. Ryans, Jr., *Marketing High Technology* (Lexington, Mass.: Lexington Books, 1984).

Shapiro, David, and Steven H. Sandell, "Economic Conditions, Job Loss, and Induced Retirement," Proceedings of the 37th Annual Meeting, Industrial Relations Research Association (Madison, Wisc.: Industrial Relations Research Association, 1985).

Shapiro, David, and Steven H. Sandell, "The Reduced Pay of Older Job Losers: Age Discrimination and Other Explanations," in Steven H. Sandell (ed.), *The Problem Isn't Age: Work and Older Americans* (New York: Praeger, 1987).

Shaw, Lois B., "Retirement Plans of Middle-Aged Married Women," *The Gerontologist*, 24, no. 2 (1984): 154-159.

Shaw, Lois B., "Special Problems of Older Women Workers," in Michael E. Borus, Herbert S. Parnes, Steven H. Sandell, and Bert Seidman (eds.), *The Older Worker* (Madison, Wisc.: Industrial Relations Research Association, 1988), pp. 55-86.

Shultz, George P., and Arnold Weber, *Strategies for the Displaced Worker* (New York: Harper & Row, 1966).

Shultz, George P., and Thomas L. Whisler (eds.), *Management, Organization and the Computer* (Glencoe, Ill.: Free Press, 1960).

Silvestri, George T., and John M. Lukasiewicz, "A Look at Occupational Employment Trends to the Year 2000," in *Projections 2000*, BLS Bulletin 2302 (Washington, D.C.: Government Printing Office, 1988), pp. 44-61.

Skrzycki, Cindy, "Downsizing Isn't Just for Downturns," *Washington Post National Weekly Edition*, August 28-September 3, 1989, pp. 20-21.

Slichter, Sumner H., "The American System of Industrial Relations: Some Contrasts with Foreign Systems," *Arbitration Today, Proceedings of the Eighth Annual Meeting, National Academy of Arbitrators* (Washington D.C.: BNA, 1955).

Smith, Victoria A., *Managing in the Corporate Interest: Control and Resistance in an American Bank* (Berkeley: University of California Press, 1990).

Smith, Victoria A., "Restructuring Management and Restructuring: The Role of Managers in Corporate Change," in Joyce Rothchild and Michael Wallace (eds.), *Research in Politics and Society* (Greenwich, Conn.: JAI Press, forthcoming).

Snyder, Donald C., "Pension Status of Recently Retired Workers on Their Longest Job: Findings from the New Beneficiary Survey," *Social Security Bulletin* 49, no. 8 (August 1986): 5-21.

Solmon, L.C., "New Findings on the Links Between College Education and Work," *Higher Education* 10 (1981): 615-648.

Spenner, Kenneth I., "Deciphering Prometheus: Temporal Change in the Skill Level of Work," *American Sociological Review* 48, (December 1983): 824–837.

Spenner, Kenneth I., "Technological Change, Skill Requirements and Education: The Case for Uncertainty," in Richard M. Cyert and David C. Mowery (eds.), *The Impact of Technological Change on Employment and Economic Growth* (New York: Ballinger, 1988).

Spring, William J., "Youth Unemployment and the Transition from School to Work," *New England Economic Review* (March–April 1987): pp. 3–16.

Stevens, David W., *Employment Projections for Planning Vocational Technical Education Curricula: Mission Impossible?* (Columbia, Mo.: University of Missouri, Human Resources Research Program, 1976).

Stromsdorfer, Ernest, "Training in Industry," in Peter B. Doeringer and Bruce Vermeulen (eds.), *Workplace Perspectives on Education and Training* (Hingham, Mass.: Martinus Nijhoff Publishing, 1981).

Sum, Andrew, "Estimating Potential Labor Force Participants Among the Older Population: Findings of Previous Research and Their Implications for the Design of Future Surveys," Paper prepared for the Commonwealth Fund Commission on Elderly People Living Alone, Boston, 1988.

Sum, Andrew M., "The Labor Market Impacts of Vocational Education Programs in the United States," in Gustav Schachter (ed.), *Brazil: Vocational Education, Aspects of Economic Policy and Planning* (Boston: Center for International Higher Education Documentation, Northeastern University, 1985).

Sum, Andrew M., "Poverty/Near Poverty Problems and Literacy Proficiencies of Young Adults," unpublished working paper (Boston: Center for Labor Market Studies, Northeastern University, August 1986).

Sum, Andrew, Lorraine Amico, and Paul E. Harrington, *Cracking the Labor Market for Human Resource Planning* (Washington, D.C.: National Governor's Association, 1985).

Sum, Andrew, and Neal Fogg, "Labor Market and Poverty Problems of Older Workers and Their Families," in Peter B. Doeringer (ed.), *Bridges to Retirement: Older Workers in a Changing Labor Market* (Ithaca, N.Y.: ILR Press, Cornell University, 1990), pp. 64–91.

Sum, Andrew M., and Neal Fogg, "Profile of the Labor Market for Older Workers," in Peter B. Doeringer (ed.), *Bridges to Retirement: Older Workers in a Changing Labor Market* (Ithaca, N.Y.: ILR Press, Cornell University, 1990), pp. 33-63.

Sum, Andrew M., and Neal Fogg, *Trends in the Real Annual Earnings of Young Adult Women, 1967–1986*, Research paper submitted to the Ford Foundation (Boston: Center for Labor Market Studies, Northeastern University, 1988).

Sum, Andrew M., Neal Fogg, and William Goedicke, *The Economic and Social Consequences of Poor Basic Skills Among Teens and Young Adults in the U.S.*, Paper presented to the CCP Second Annual Conference, San Antonio (Boston: Center for Labor Market Studies, Northeastern University, October 1987).

Sum, Andrew M., Neal Fogg, and Robert Taggart, *Withered Dreams: The Decline in the Economic Fortunes of Young Non-College Educated Male Adults and Their Families*, Report prepared for the Grant Foundation Commission on Work, Family, and Citizenship (Boston: Center for Labor Market Studies, Northeastern University, April 1988).

Sum, Andrew M., Paul E. Harrington, and William Goedicke, *Basic Skills of America's Teens and Young Adults: Findings of the 1980 National ASVAB Testing and*

Their Implications for Education, Employment, and Training Policies and Programs (Boston: Center for Labor Market Studies, Northeastern University, 1986).

Sum, Andrew M., Paul E. Harrington, and William Goedicke, "One-fifth of the Nation's Teenagers: Employment Problems of Poor Youth in America, 1981–1985," *Youth and Society* 18, no. 3 (March 1987): 195–237.

Sum, Andrew M., Paul E. Harrington, and Gustav Schachter, "High Technology Industries in Massachusetts: An Analysis of Worker Earnings Levels and Their Distribution," Paper prepared for the New England Business and Economic Development Conference, Lowell, Mass., 1986).

Svahn, John A., and Mary Ross, "Social Security Amendments of 1983: Legislative History and Summary of Provisions," *Social Security Bulletin* 46, no. 7 (July 1983): 3–48.

Swaim, Paul, and Michael Podgursky, "Do More-Educated Workers Fare Better Following Job Loss?" *Monthly Labor Review*, August 1989, pp. 43–45.

Swoboda, Frank, and Albert B. Crenshaw, "Assessing the Liabilities of Retirement Benefits," *Washington Post National Weekly Edition*, February 20–26, 1989, p. 19.

Taggart, Robert A., *A Fisherman's Guide: An Assessment of Training and Remediation Strategies* (Kalamazoo, Mich.: Upjohn Institute for Employment Research, 1981).

Taylor, Robert E., Howard Rosen, and Frank Pratzner (eds.), *Job Training for Youth* (Columbus, Ohio: National Center for Research in Vocational Education, Ohio State University, 1982).

Taylor, Robert E., Howard Rosen, and Frank Pratzner (eds.), *Responsiveness of Training Institutions to Changing Labor Market Demands* (Columbus, Ohio: National Center for Research in Vocational Education, Ohio State University, 1983).

Thurow, Lester, *The Zero-Sum Solution: An Economic and Political Agenda for the 1980's* (New York: Simon and Schuster, 1985).

Tilly, Chris, Barry Bluestone, and Bennett Harrison, "What Is Making American Wages More Unequal?" in *Industrial Relations Research Association, 39th Annual Proceedings* (Madison, Wisc.: Industrial Relations Research Association, 1987), pp. 338–348.

Time, "Today's Native Sons," December 1, 1986, pp. 26–29.

Tomasko, Robert M., *Downsizing: Reshaping the Corporation for the Future* (New York: American Management Association, 1987).

U.S. Bureau of the Census, Current Population Reports, Series P-25, No. 1018, *Projections of the Population of the United States, by Age, Sex and Race: 1988 to 2080*, by Gregory Spencer (Washington, D.C.: Government Printing Office, 1989).

U.S. Bureau of the Census, Current Population Reports, Series P-70, No. 16-Rd-2, *Spells of Job Search and Layoff and Their Outcomes* (Washington, D.C.: Government Printing Office, 1989).

U.S. Bureau of the Census, *Money Income of Households, Families, and Persons in the United States: 1985*, Current Population Reports, Series P-60, No. 156 (Washington, D.C.: Government Printing Office, 1987).

U.S. Bureau of the Census, *Statistical Abstract of the United States, 1989* (Washington, D.C.: Government Printing Office, 1989).

U.S. Congress, Budget Office, *Trends in Family Income: 1970–1986* (Washington, D.C.: Government Printing Office, 1988).

U.S. Congress, Office of Technology Assessment, *Automation of America's Offices* (Washington, D.C.: Government Printing Office, 1985).

U.S. Congress, Office of Technology Assessment, *Educating Scientists and Engineers: Grade School to Grad School* (Washington, D.C.: Government Printing Office, 1988).

U.S. Congress, Office of Technology Assessment, *Plant Closing: Advance Notice and Rapid Response* (Washington, D.C.: Government Printing Office, 1986).

U.S. Congress, Office of Technology Assessment, *Structural Unemployment: Reemploying Displaced Adults* (Washington, D.C.: Government Printing Office, 1986).

U.S. Congress, Office of Technology Assessment, *Technology and the American Economic Transition* (Washington, D.C.: Government Printing Office, 1988).

U.S. Congress, *Public Law 97-300: The Job Training Partnership Act*, 1982.

U.S. Department of Education, *Digest of Educational Statistics, 1987* (Washington, D.C.: Government Printing Office, 1987).

U.S. Department of Labor, *Older Worker Task Force: Key Policy Issues for the Future* (Washington, D.C.: Government Printing Office, January 1989).

U.S. Department of Labor, Bureau of Apprenticeship and Training, *Apprenticeship 2000: The Public Speaks* (Washington, D.C.: Government Printing Office, 1988).

U.S. Department of Labor, Bureau of Labor Statistics, *BLS Reports on Worker Displacement* (Washington, D.C.: Government Printing Office, December 9, 1988).

U.S. Department of Labor, Bureau of Labor Statistics, *Employee Benefits in Medium and Large Firms*, Bulletin 2176 (Washington, D.C.: Government Printing Office, 1983).

U.S. Department of Labor, Bureau of Labor Statistics, *Employment and Earnings* (Washington, D.C.: Government Printing Office, January 1988).

U.S. Department of Labor, Bureau of Labor Statistics, *Employment and Earnings* (Washington, D.C.: Government Printing Office, July 1988).

U.S. Department of Labor, Bureau of Labor Statistics, *Employment and Earnings* (Washington, D.C.: Government Printing Office, January 1989).

U.S. Department of Labor, Bureau of Labor Statistics, *Labor Force Statistics Derived from the Current Population Survey, A Databook: Volume 1*, BLS Bulletin 2096 (Washington, D.C.: Government Printing Office, 1983).

U.S. Department of Labor, Bureau of Labor Statistics, *Projections 2000*, BLS Bulletin 2302 (Washington, D.C.: Government Printing Office, 1988).

U.S. Department of Labor, Bureau of Labor Statistics and U.S. Department of Commerce, Bureau of the Census, *Concepts and Methods Used in Labor Force Statistics Derived from the Current Population Survey*, BLS Report No. 463 (Washington, D.C.: Government Printing Office, 1976).

U.S. Department of Labor, Commission on Workforce Quality and Labor Market Efficiency, *Investing in People* (Washington, D.C.: Government Printing Office, 1989).

U.S. Department of Labor, Division of Performance Management and Evaluation, Office of Strategic Planning and Policy Development, *Job Training Quarterly Survey: JTPA Title IIA and III Enrollments and Terminations During the First Three Quarters of FY 1988* (Washington, D.C.: Government Printing Office, September 1989).

U.S. Department of Labor, Employment and Training Administration, *JTPA Quarterly Data Book, Program Year 1986: JTPA Data Through June 30, 1987* (Washington, D.C.: Government Printing Office, 1988).

U.S. Department of Labor, Employment and Training Administration, *Training and Employment Report of the Secretary of Labor* (Washington, D.C.: Government Printing Office, 1988).

U.S. Department of Labor, Task Force on Economic Adjustment and Worker

Dislocation, *Economic Adjustment and Worker Dislocation in a Competitive Society* (Washington, D.C.: Government Printing Office, 1986).

U.S. Department of Labor, U.S. Department of Education, and U.S. Department of Commerce, *Building a Quality Workforce* (Washington, D.C.: Government Printing Office, 1988).

U.S. Department of Labor and U.S. Department of Health, Education, and Welfare, *Employment and Training Report of the President, 1979* (Washington, D.C.: Government Printing Office, 1979).

U.S. Department of Labor and U.S. Department of Health and Human Services, *Employment and Training Report of the President* (Washington, D.C.: Government Printing Office, 1981).

U.S. General Accounting Office, *Dislocated Workers: Extent of Business Closures, Layoffs, and the Public and Private Response* (Washington, D.C.: Government Printing Office, 1986).

U.S. General Accounting Office, *Dislocated Workers: Labor-Management Committees Enhance Reemployment Assistance* (Washington, D.C.: Government Printing Office, November 1989).

U.S. General Accounting Office, *Local Programs and Outcomes Under the Job Training Partnership Act*, GAO/HRD-87-411 (Washington, D.C.: Government Printing Office, 1987).

U.S. General Accounting Office, *Plant Closings: Information on Advance Notice and Assistance to Dislocated Workers* (Washington, D.C.: Government Printing Office, 1987).

U.S. General Accounting Office, *Plant Closings: Limited Advance Notice and Assistance Provided Dislocated Workers* (Washington, D.C.: Government Printing Office, 1987).

U.S. House of Representatives, Ninety-Sixth Congress, Select Committee on Aging, *Retirement: The Broken Promise* (Washington, D.C.: Government Printing Office, 1981).

U.S. President, Council of Economic Advisers, *Economic Report of the President* (Washington, D.C.: Government Printing Office, 1989).

U.S. President, Report of the President, *The State of Small Business* (Washington, D.C.: Government Printing Office, 1986).

Useem, Michael, "Business Restructuring, Management Control, and Corporate Organization," *Theory and Society* (forthcoming).

Useem, Michael, *Liberal Education and the Corporation: The Hiring and Advancement of College Graduates* (Hawthorne, N.Y.: Aldine de Gruyter, 1989).

Utterback, James M., and William J. Abernathy, "A Dynamic Model of Process and Product Innovation," *Omega* 3, no. 6 (1975): 639–656.

Venezky, Richard L., Carl F. Kaestle, and Andrew M. Sum, *The Subtle Danger: Reflections on the Literacy Abilities of America's Young Adults* (Princeton, N.J.: Educational Testing Service, Center for the Assessment of Educational Progress, January 1987).

Vernon, Raymond, "The Product Life Cycle Hypothesis in a New International Environment," *Oxford Bulletin of Economics and Statistics* 41, no. 4 (1979): 255–267.

Washington Post, November 20, 1986.

Wasson, Chester R., *Dynamic Competitive Strategy and Product Life Cycles*, 3rd ed. (Austin, Texas: Austin Press, 1978).

Wellbank, Harry L., Douglas T. Hall, Marilyn A. Morgan, and W. Clay Hamner,

"Planning Job Progression for Effective Career Development and Human Resources Management," *Personnel* 55 (Jan–Feb 1978): 54–64.

Wexley, Kenneth N., and Gary P. Latham, *Developing and Training Human Resources in Organizations* (Glenview, Ill.: Scott, Foresman, 1981).

Whyte, William F. (ed.), *Money and Motivation* (New York: Harper & Row, 1955).

William T. Grant Foundation Commission on Work, Family and Citizenship, *The Forgotten Half: Non-College Youth in America* (Washington, D.C.: William T. Grant Foundation, 1988).

Williamson, Oliver E., *Markets and Hierarchies: Analysis and Antitrust Implications* (New York: Free Press, 1975).

Willis, Rod, "What's Happened to America's Middle Managers?" *Management Review* 76 (January 1987): pp 24–33.

Wilms, Wellford W., "The Nonsystem of Education and Training," in Peter B. Doeringer and Bruce Vermeulen (eds.), *Jobs and Training in the 1980s* (Hingham, Mass.: Martinus Nijhoff Publishing, 1981).

Wilson, William Julius, *The Truly Disadvantaged* (Chicago: University of Chicago Press, 1987).

Wilson, William Julius, and Kathryn M. Neckerman, "Poverty and Family Structure: The Widening Gap Between Evidence and Public Policy Issues," in Sheldon H. Danziger and Daniel Weinberg (eds.), *Fighting Poverty: What Works and What Doesn't* (Cambridge, Mass.: Harvard University Press, 1987).

Work in America Institute, *Training for New Technology*, Parts 1–5 (White Plains, N.Y.: Work in America, 1985–1987).

AUTHOR INDEX

SUBJECT INDEX

251

OCT 2 8 1991

DEC 3 0 1991

NOV 0 8 1992

NOV 0 8 1992

FEB 2 4 1993

MAR 2 5 1993

MAY 0 8 1993

OCT 2 8 1995

FEB 2 5 1997

JUL 1 1 1998

Printed
in USA